A note to the student ...

This book represents a brand new concept in revision guides, and allows you, the student to learn in a combination of different ways ...

'Big Picture' Concept Map 1

Before each section there is a 'Big Picture' page that connects the main ideas and information in the section. This means you can jump about from idea to idea within a topic. This is good for everyone but especially those people who like to know how everything fits together before they start to look at all the different bits.

Structured Sequence 2

The pages within the section present the information in appropriate steps and sequences using words, colours and pictures as 'memory pegs' to increase the amount that you remember.

Simple Summary Statements 3

Each section ends with a summary page which reviews and consolidates the work you have just covered by concentrating simply on the main ideas. This enables you to 'Hang Memories' from short, simple statements.
All the pages work together to give you a 'WHOLE BRAIN' LEARNING EXPERIENCE.

In short the information you need to help you succeed in your examination ...

... has been LINKED TOGETHER to give you an overall picture of each section ...

... has been CLEARLY SEQUENCED, to help you learn by reading ...

... can be TAPED ONTO A WALKMAN from the summary to help you learn by listening and ...

... can be WRITTEN OUT FROM THE SUMMARY and/or BIG PICTURE to help you to learn by doing.

This approach to learning gives your brain the VARIED DIET of experiences that it needs.

This HELPS YOUR MEMORY to retain the key information which will GET YOU THE GRADES YOU WANT.

ALSO, HAVE A LOOK AT THE WORKBOOK THAT SUPPORTS THIS GUIDE.
IT CONTAINS A PAGE OF QUESTIONS FOR EVERY PAGE OF THE GUIDE FOR ONLY £1.50!

CONTENTS

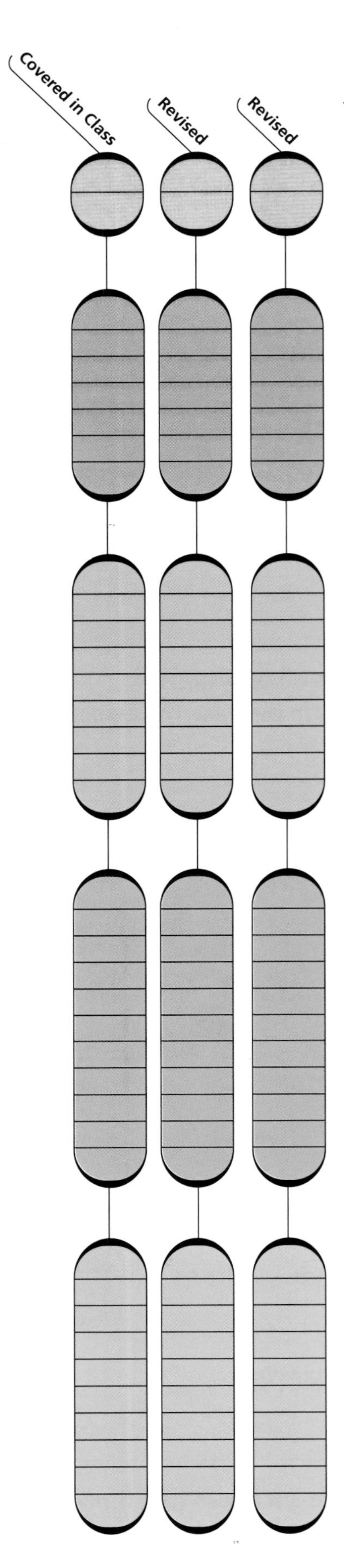

CONTENTS

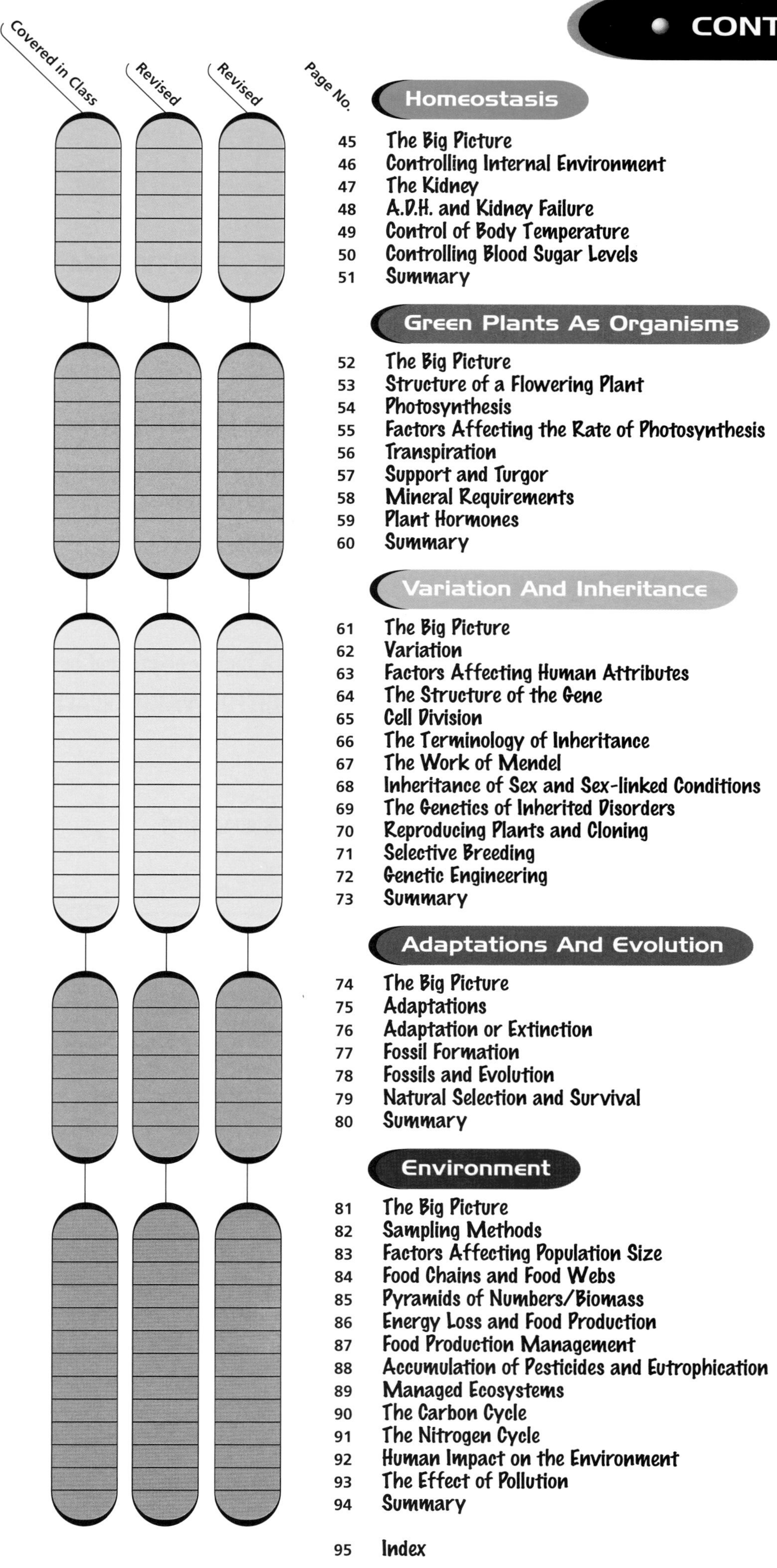

Homeostasis

Green Plants As Organisms

Variation And Inheritance

Adaptations And Evolution

Environment

HOW TO USE THIS REVISION GUIDE

- Don't just read! LEARN ACTIVELY!

- Constantly test yourself ... WITHOUT LOOKING AT THE BOOK.

- When you have revised a small sub-section or a diagram, PLACE A BOLD TICK AGAINST IT. Similarly, tick the "progress and revision" section of the contents when you have done a
- page. This is great for your self confidence.

- Jot down anything which will help YOU to remember - no matter how trivial it may seem.

- DON'T BE TEMPTED TO HIGHLIGHT SECTIONS WITH DIFFERENT COLOURS. TOO MUCH COLOUR REDUCES CLARITY AND CAUSES CONFUSION. YOUR EXAM WILL BE IN BLACK AND WHITE!

- These notes are highly refined. Everything you need is here, in a highly organised but user-friendly format. Many questions depend only on STRAIGHTFORWARD RECALL OF FACTS, so make sure you LEARN THEM.

- THIS IS YOUR BOOK! Use it throughout your course in the ways suggested and your revision will be both organised and successful.

HIGHER/SPECIAL TIER

Material, identified by the major syllabuses as being HIGHER/SPECIAL TIER is enclosed in a red box.

CONSULTANT EDITORS ...

- **Stephen Tierney** - Formerly Head of Science at De La Salle, St. Helens.
  Currently Deputy Head at Our Lady's Catholic High School, Lancaster.
- **Kerry Stevenson-Woods** - Biology teacher and Assessment Manager at St. Josephs R.C. High School, Horwich, Bolton.

NOTES

Your Science coursework will involve you doing an investigation.
We have chosen as our example a photosynthesis investigation using ELODEA (pondweed).

Carbon Dioxide + Water $\xrightarrow[\text{CHLOROPHYLL}]{\text{LIGHT}}$ Glucose + Oxygen

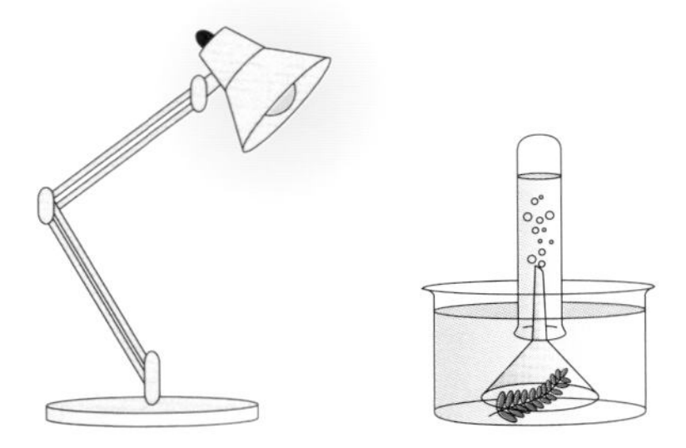

Stage 1(a): Planning

- Work out which factors affect the rate of Photosynthesis. Decide on **one** to investigate.
- Write down a clear **prediction** and then use **scientific ideas** to explain the prediction you have made. You can use the section on 'Photosynthesis' from this revision guide to help you.
- Too many students don't get top marks because they rush this first part - don't make this mistake!

Having worked out that the amount of light (light intensity) or the concentration of carbon dioxide in the water may affect the rate of reaction I have decided to investigate the affect of light intensity.

Prediction: I think that as I increase the light intensity then more bubbles of oxygen will be produced. (Now explain your prediction using your knowledge of photosynthesis).

Stage 1(b): More Planning

- Write down how you will carry out the experiment. Remember to include how you will make the **test fair and safe**.
- Plan to investigate **five values** for the variable you have chosen and to **repeat** your experiment (at least two sets of results are needed).
- Do some **preliminary work** to find out the best range of distances to put the light from the plant, and a suitable length of time to count bubbles for (If that's what you are going to do). Include your preliminary work in your final write-up, it will gain you extra marks.

Stage 2: Obtaining Evidence

- During your experimental work keep a careful note of all the measurements you make.
- Remember to **measure accurately** and to **repeat** your experiment.
- Your results should be presented in a table.

Distance of lamp from plant (cm)	Number of bubbles of Oxygen			
	Test 1	Test 2	Test 3	Average
10				
20				
30				
40				
50				

Five different values for distance

Make sure you put in the **units** at the top of the table in the column heading. Do **not** repeat units down the columns.

To work out the average (mean) results:

$$\text{Average} = \frac{\text{Test 1} + \text{Test 2} + \text{Test 3}}{\text{3 (Number of tests)}}$$

Stage 3: Analysing Evidence And Drawing Conclusions

- Decide on the best way to identify any trends in your results - use graphs.
- When drawing a line graph make sure you draw a line of **"best fit"** (this is a line with the points evenly balanced on each side) if this is appropriate.
- Spot any **anomalous results** (ones that do not fit the pattern - these are important later).
- Think of ways to analyse your results.
- In your conclusion write down clearly any **patterns** you have identified from your results. Say how these compare with your **original prediction** and explain the patterns using **scientific ideas** (if you have done your planning properly look back at what you wrote there!).

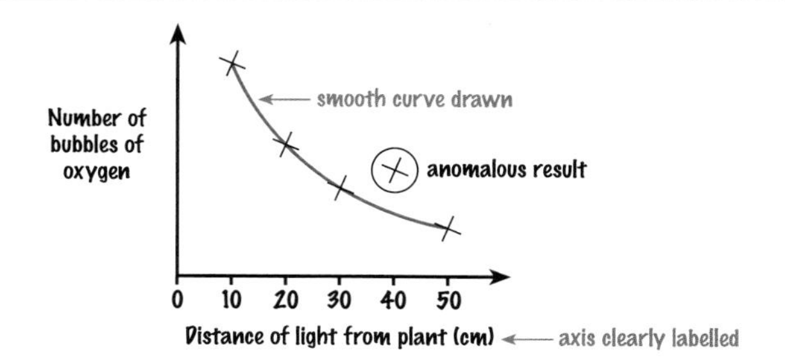

Stage 4: Evaluating Your Evidence

- This is the section that students find the most difficult, so lets take it step by step.
- First look back at your results. Comment on whether you got any **anomalous results** - look at both your test results and the averages.
- Try to give reasons why you got any anomalous results or even why you didn't.
- Go carefully through the method you used. Try to think of whether the apparatus and method you used were the most accurate, or whether they could have been improved.

From the graph, you can see that an anomalous result has been obtained for the 40cm distance (If you get something similar in your investigation try to give a reason why).

Some possible explanations

- You changed to a new piece of pondweed prior to obtaining this result.
- The result was obtained on a sunnier day compared to the other results.

Think about the method you used

- Were all the bubbles the same volume (size)? How could you measure the volume more accurately?
- Could you obtain more accurate readings for the light intensity? Maybe a light meter could have been used.

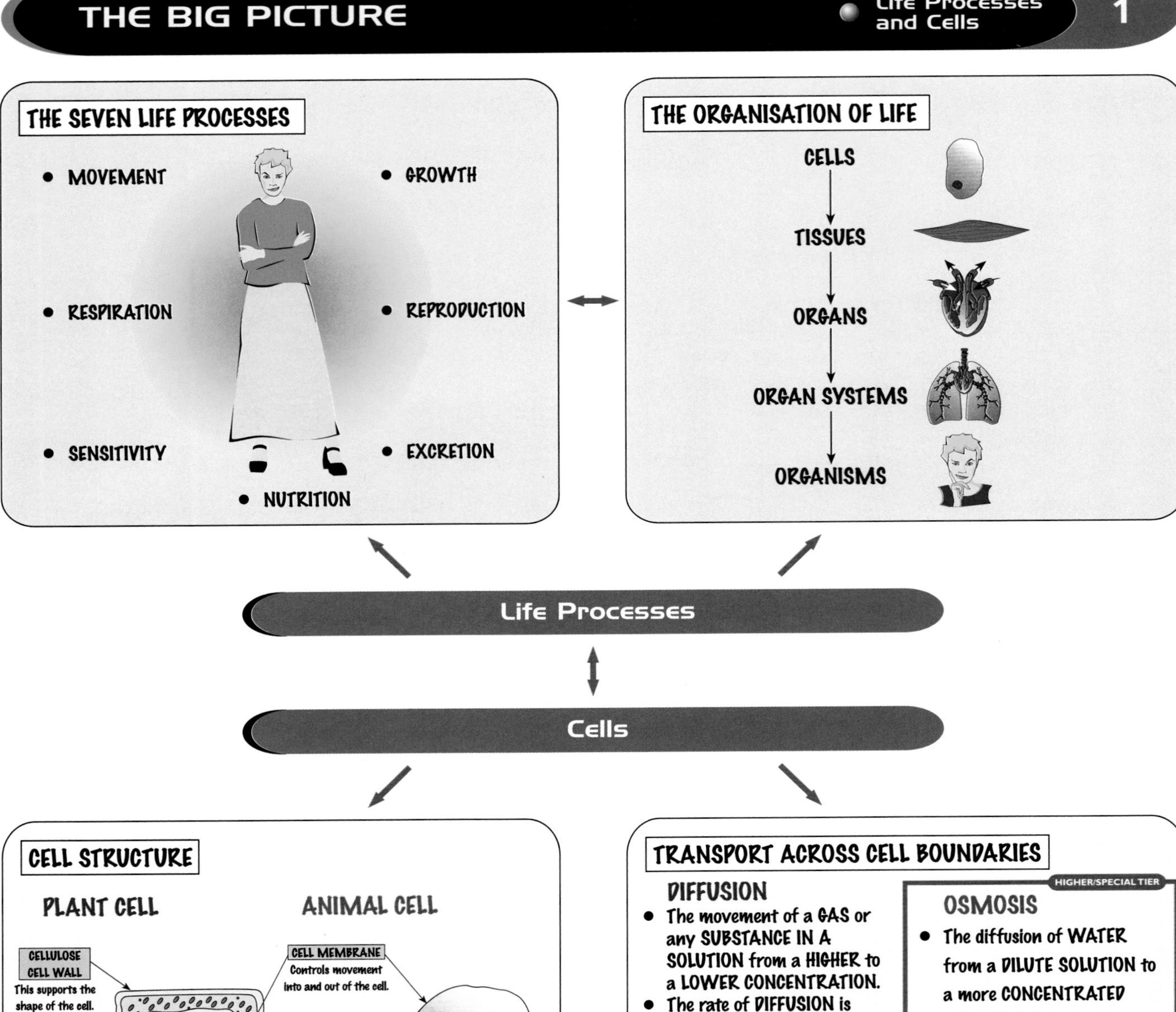

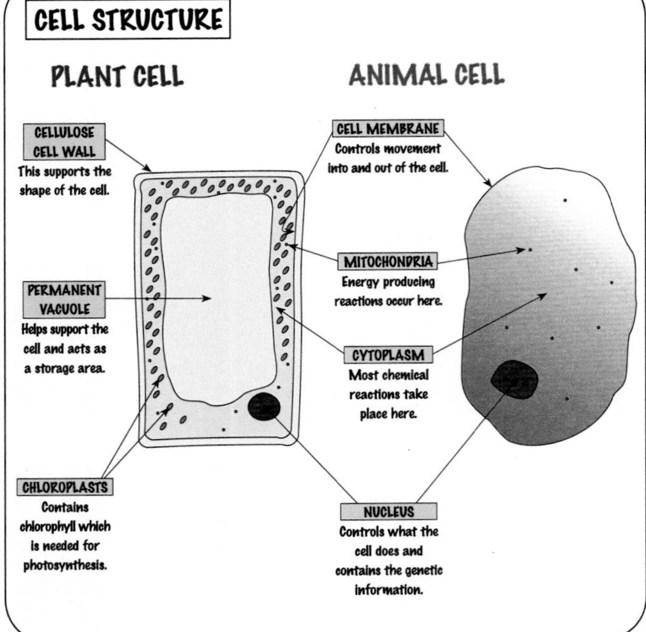

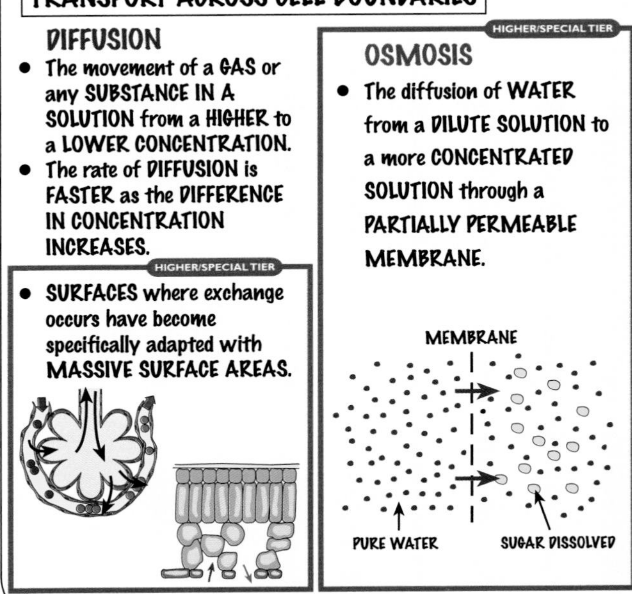

SPECIALISED CELLS

- Cells which are adapted to perform a particular task.

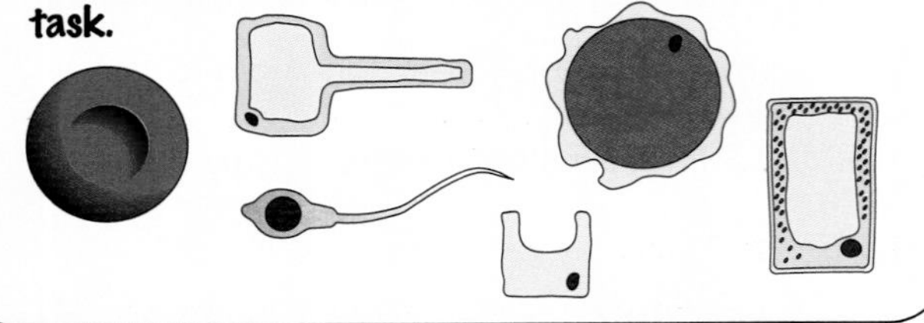

HIGHER/SPECIAL TIER

ACTIVE UPTAKE

- Substances can be absorbed AGAINST THE CONCENTRATION GRADIENT.
- ENERGY is REQUIRED for this to happen.
- Examples include uptake of nitrate ions in root hair cells and reabsorption of glucose in the kidneys.

All living things have SEVEN simple life processes in common.
The names of the SEVEN life processes are remembered by MRS GREN.

Movement

Movement
Respiration
Sensitivity

Growth
Reproduction
Excretion
Nutrition (feeding)

Growth

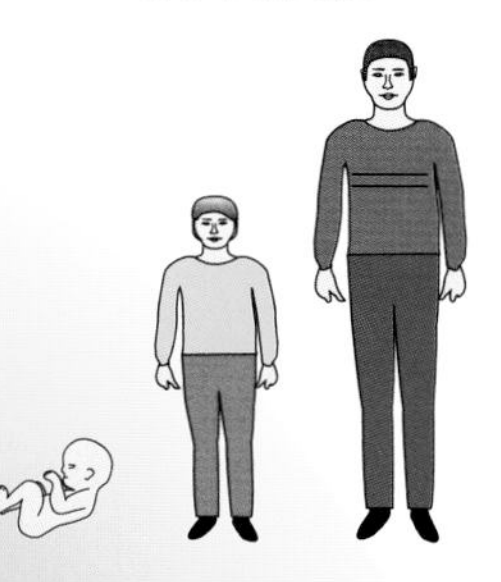

Reproduction

Respiration

Excretion

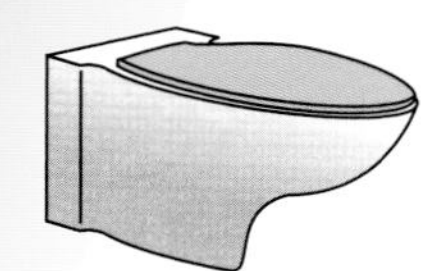

Sensitivity

Nutrition (feeding)

Life Process	Further Explanation
Movement	The ability to move parts of the body. In animals muscles can contract.
Respiration	The release of energy from food by combining it with oxygen in the cells of all living things.
Sensitivity	The ability to respond to changes in the surroundings. Plants can detect changes in light intensity and the light's direction. Humans can detect hot and cold etc.
Growth	All living things tend to grow to an adult size.
Reproduction	Producing offspring. Flowering plants have a process of pollination followed later by fertilisation and seed dispersal.
Excretion	Releasing waste products. Carbon Dioxide is a waste material removed from the human body by the lungs and urea is removed in urine.
Nutrition	Food is needed for growth and movement. Plants obtain food by photosynthesis.

Organisation Of Life

Large organisms, like humans and flowering plants, are organised in a particular way.

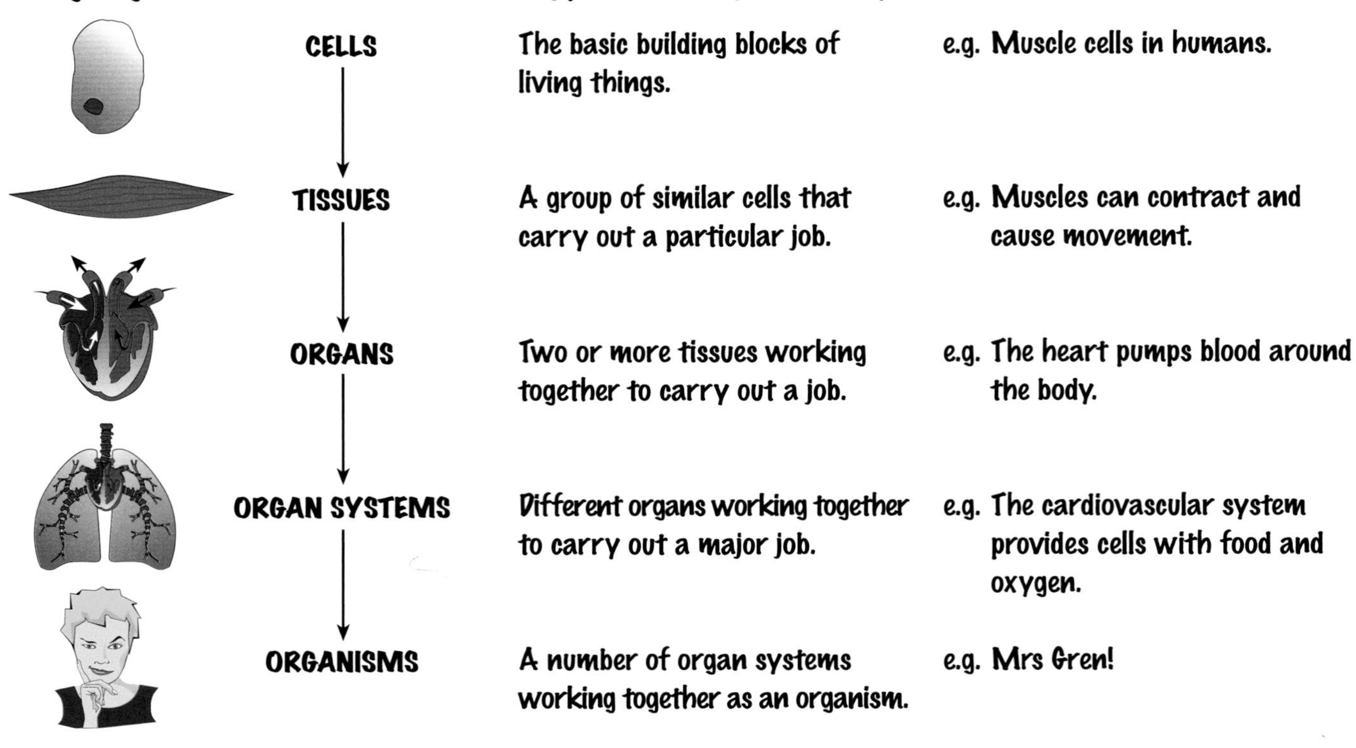

CELLS	The basic building blocks of living things.	e.g. Muscle cells in humans.
TISSUES	A group of similar cells that carry out a particular job.	e.g. Muscles can contract and cause movement.
ORGANS	Two or more tissues working together to carry out a job.	e.g. The heart pumps blood around the body.
ORGAN SYSTEMS	Different organs working together to carry out a major job.	e.g. The cardiovascular system provides cells with food and oxygen.
ORGANISMS	A number of organ systems working together as an organism.	e.g. Mrs Gren!

Examples Of Organ Systems

THE DIGESTIVE SYSTEM - breaks down and absorbs food.

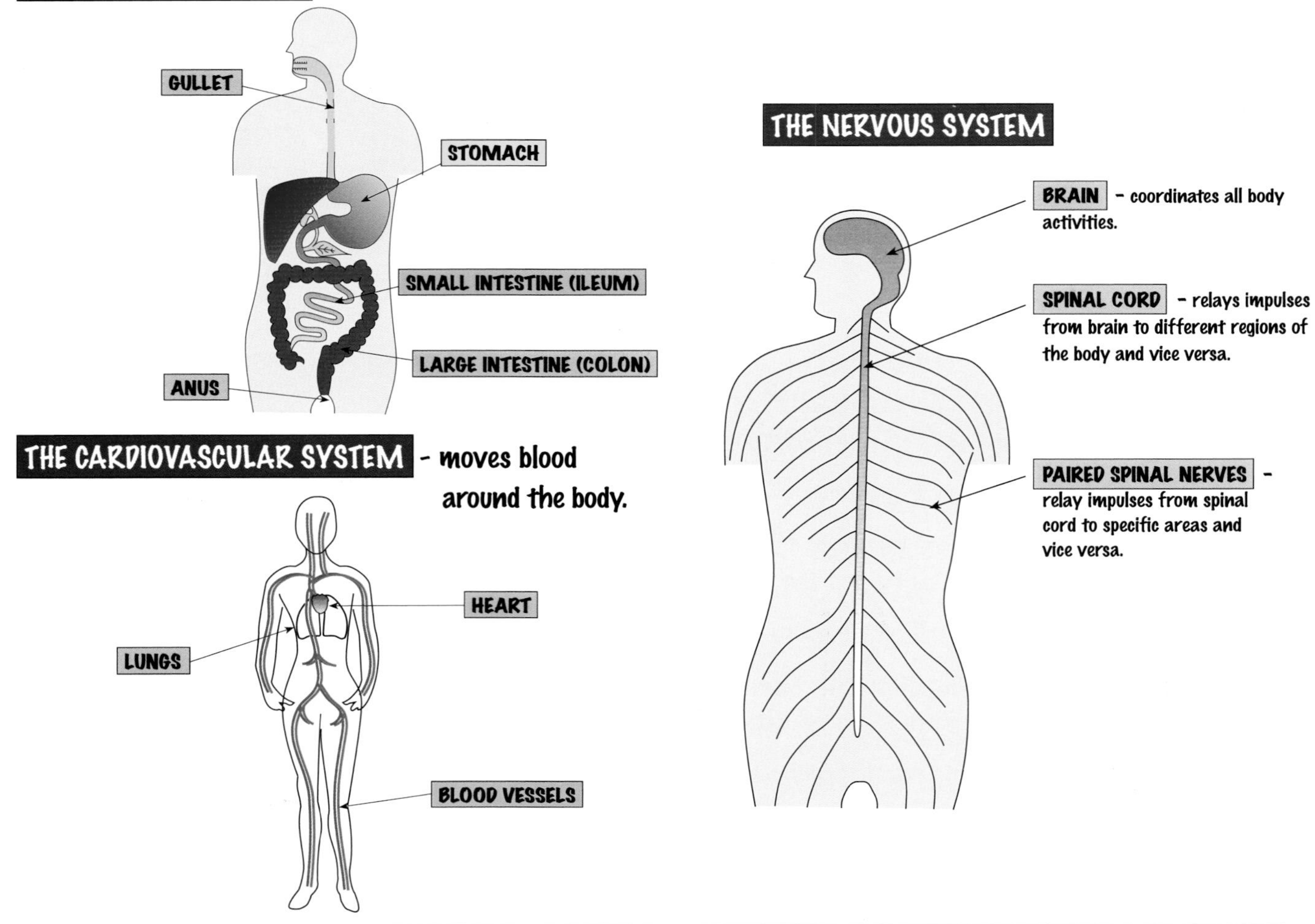

Typical Plant And Animal Cells

A PALISADE CELL FROM A LEAF

A CHEEK CELL FROM A HUMAN

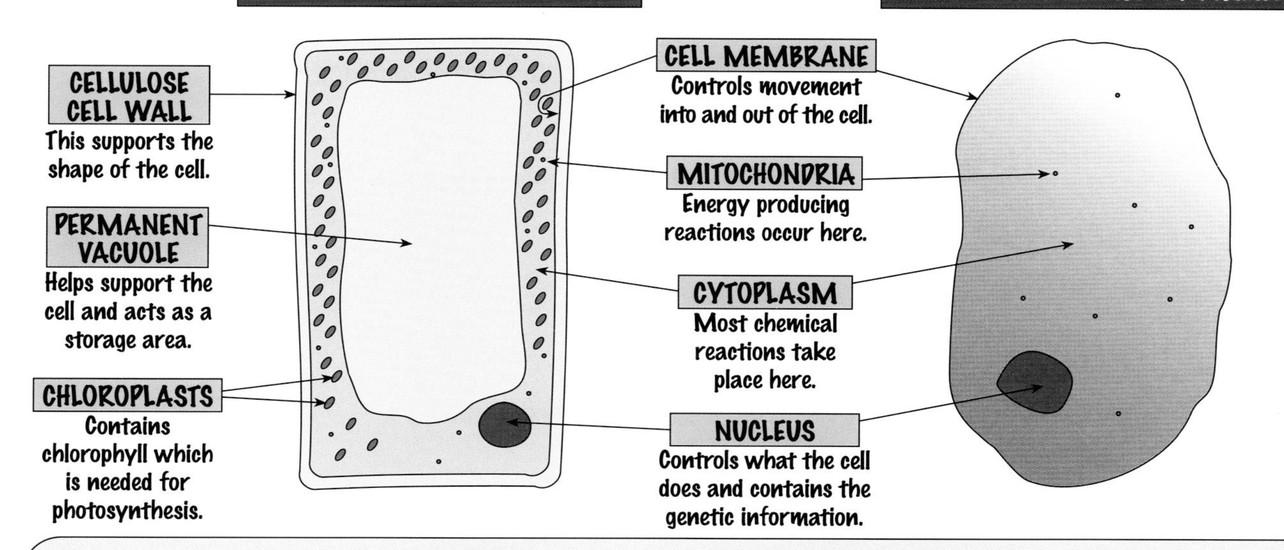

REMEMBER - A CELL WALL, PERMANENT VACUOLE AND CHLOROPLASTS ARE ONLY FOUND IN PLANT CELLS

Specialised Cells

RED BLOOD CELL

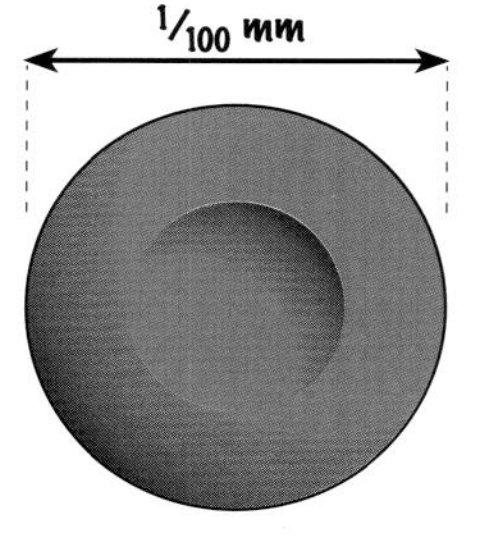

No nucleus means it can be packed with haemoglobin for carrying oxygen.

CONCAVE SHAPE Increases the surface area for transferring oxygen.

OVUM (EGG CELL)

CILIATED EPITHELIAL CELLS FROM THE WIND PIPE

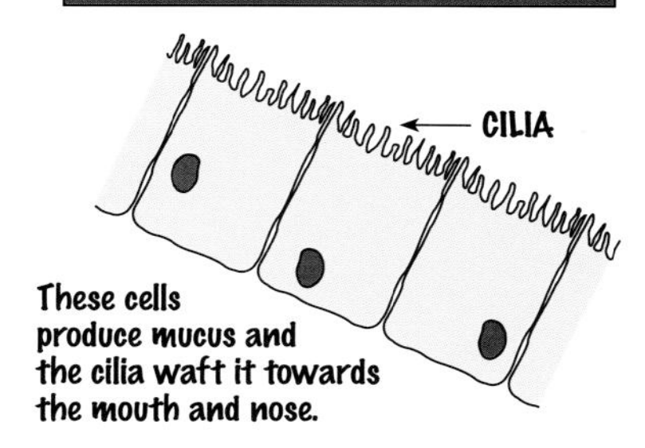

These cells produce mucus and the cilia waft it towards the mouth and nose.

SPERM CELL

Tiny short lived cell which is amazingly mobile because of its tail.

(not to same scale as ovum)

GLANDULAR CELL

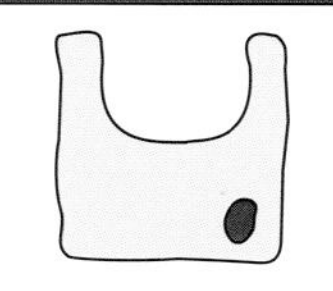

Produces digestive enzymes.

ROOT HAIR CELL

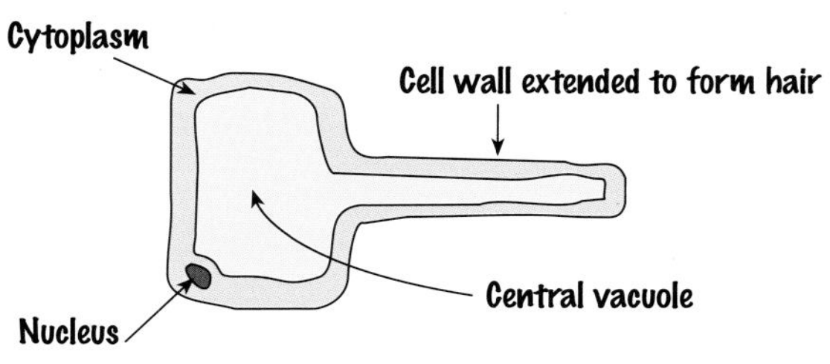

These tiny hairs increase the surface area of the cell enabling it to absorb water and ions more efficiently.

PALISADE CELL

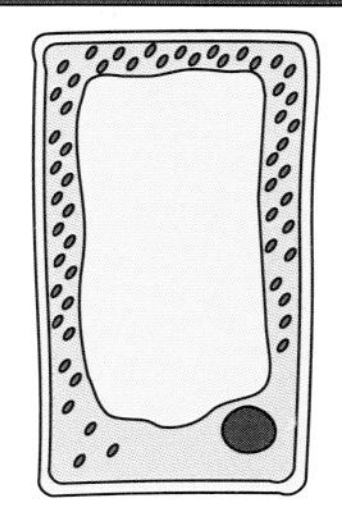

Column-shaped cells on upper surface of leaf. Packed with chloroplasts for photosynthesis.

XYLEM

Transports water through the stem and root.

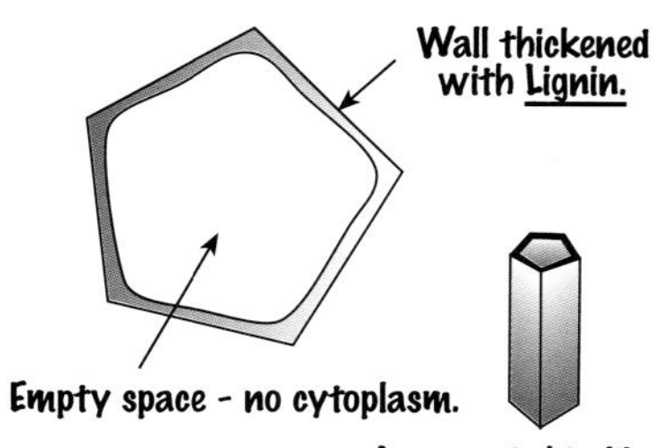

Long and thin like pipes.

Diffusion

DIFFUSION is ... **the MOVEMENT of a GAS or any SUBSTANCE IN A SOLUTION** ...
... **from a HIGHER to a LOWER CONCENTRATION.**

The GREATER the DIFFERENCE in CONCENTRATION the FASTER the RATE OF DIFFUSION.

CLASSIC EXPERIMENT

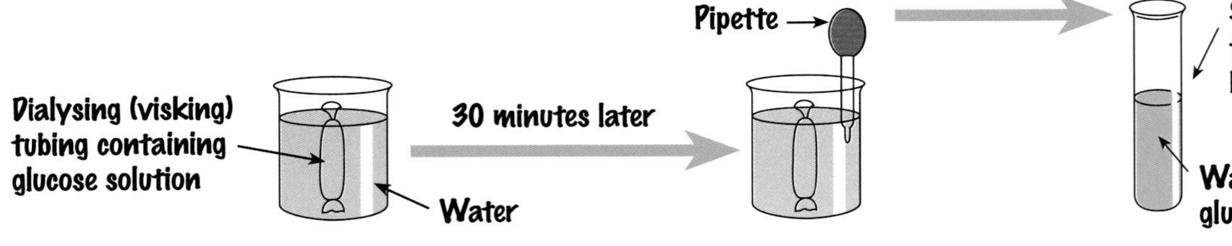

During the 30 minutes **GLUCOSE MOLECULES** from inside the dialysing tubing ...
... **MOVE** from a **HIGHER CONCENTRATION INSIDE THE TUBE** ...
... to the **WATER SURROUNDING THE TUBE** where there is a **LOWER CONCENTRATION OF GLUCOSE.**
When the water is tested for glucose using Benedict's solution (or a clinistix) a positive result is achieved.
In this example the visking tubing allows free passage of glucose molecules and water molecules.

Diffusion In The Lungs

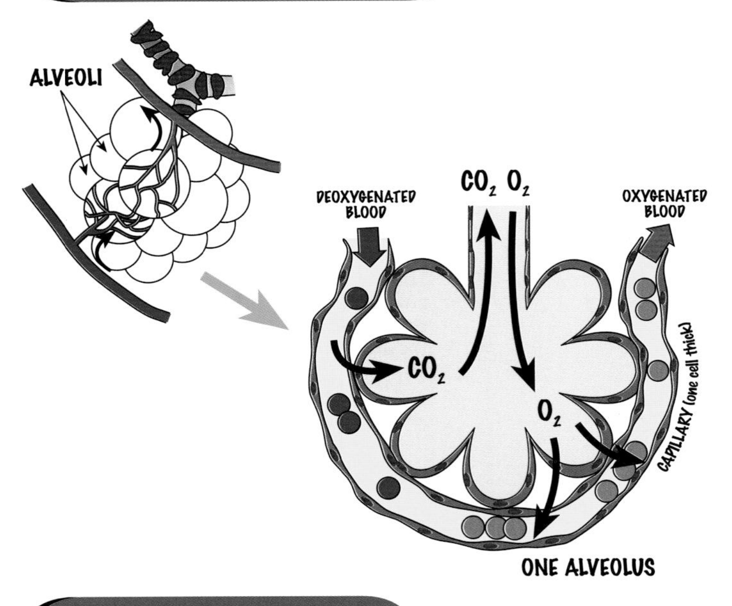

In the lungs ...
... oxygen diffuses from the alveolus into the blood ...
... and carbon dioxide diffuses from the blood into the alveolus.
BOTH SUBSTANCES move from a higher to a lower concentration.

> HIGHER/SPECIAL TIER
>
> The shape and vast number of the alveoli ...
> ... provide a **MASSIVELY INCREASED SURFACE AREA** ...
> ... for more efficient exchange of oxygen and carbon dioxide.

Diffusion In Leaves

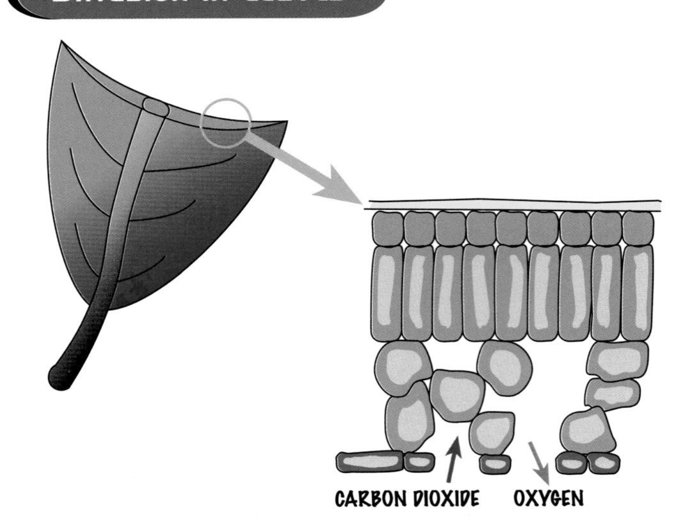

Through stomata (holes) on the underside of the leaf ...
... oxygen diffuses from inside the leaf (where it is made during photosynthesis) to the outside ...
... and carbon dioxide diffuses from the outside to the inside of the leaf.
BOTH SUBSTANCES move from a higher to a lower concentration.

> HIGHER/SPECIAL TIER
>
> The flat shape of the leaf and air spaces inside ...
> ... provide a **MASSIVE SURFACE AREA** ...
> ... for a more efficient exchange of oxygen and carbon dioxide.

HIGHER/SPECIAL TIER

Osmosis

OSMOSIS is ... the diffusion of WATER ...
... from a DILUTE SOLUTION ...
... to a MORE CONCENTRATED SOLUTION ...
... through a PARTIALLY PERMEABLE MEMBRANE.

(a partially permeable membrane is sometimes known as a SELECTIVELY PERMEABLE membrane)

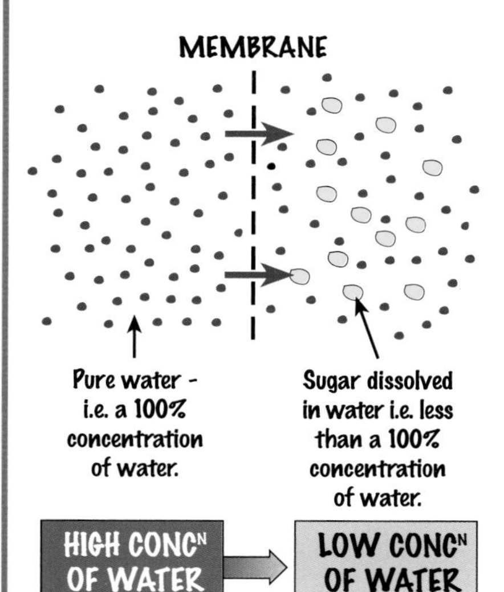

- In other words water diffuses from where it's in a HIGH CONCENTRATION to where it's in a LOW CONCENTRATION.
- The only thing that matters is the CONCENTRATION of the water. The solute molecules (e.g. sugar) can't pass through the membrane.
- The effect of all this is to gradually dilute the sugar solution.

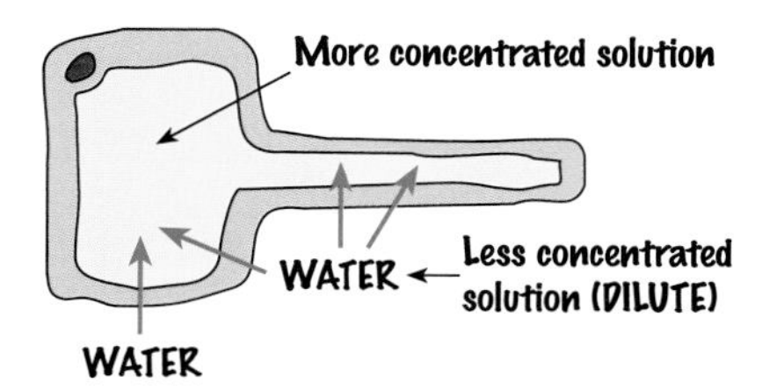

This is what happens at root hair cells, where water moves from the soil into the cell by OSMOSIS, along a CONCENTRATION GRADIENT.

Demonstrating Osmosis

CLASSIC EXPERIMENT No.1

Placed in pure water ⇦ dialysis tubing containing sugar solution ⇨ Placed in CONC^N. sugar solution

Water enters by OSMOSIS ∴ swells up

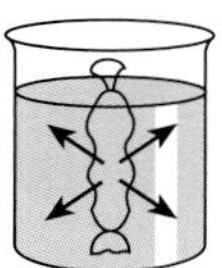

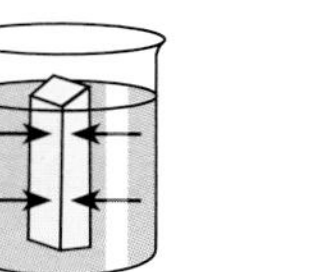

Water leaves by OSMOSIS ∴ shrivels up

CLASSIC EXPERIMENT No.2

Placed in pure water ⇦ weighed potato chip ⇨ Placed in CONC^N. sugar solution

Water enters by OSMOSIS ∴ weighs more after removal

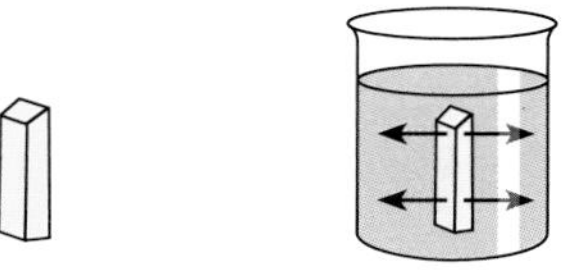

Water leaves by OSMOSIS ∴ weighs less after removal

In each case, water moves from where it's in HIGH CONCENTRATION, to where it's in LOW CONCENTRATION along a CONCENTRATION GRADIENT (A bit like a ball rolling from a high position to a low position).

Active Uptake

- Substances are sometimes absorbed AGAINST A CONCENTRATION GRADIENT.
- Plants absorb ions from very dilute solutions in this way i.e. ACTIVELY (see diagram below).
- This takes place in the opposite direction to which normal diffusion would occur.
- This process of ACTIVE UPTAKE requires the use of ENERGY FROM RESPIRATION ...

... just in the same way that pushing a ball up a hill would take energy.

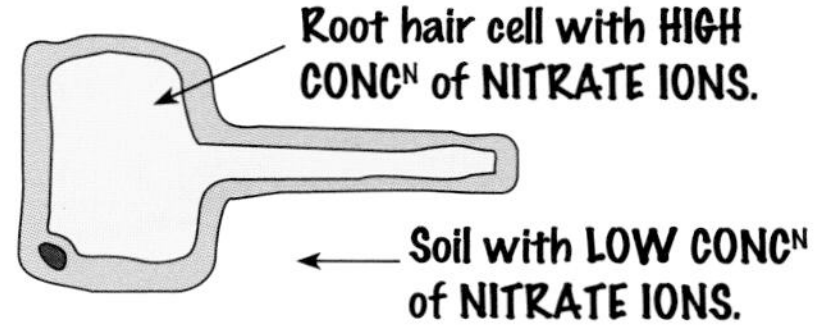

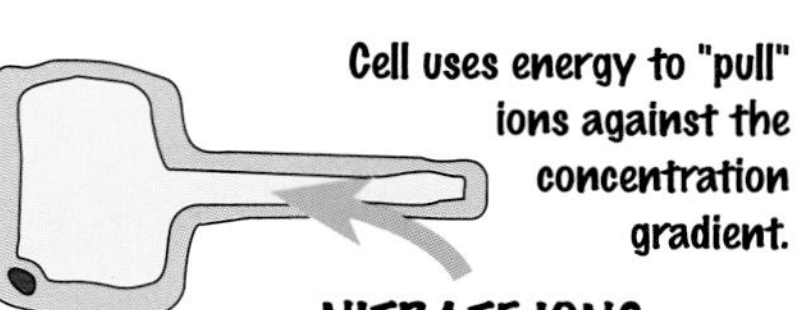

In humans sugar may be absorbed from the intestine and from the kidney tubules by ACTIVE UPTAKE.

Life Processes

- All living things can Move, Respire, Sense, Grow, Reproduce, Excrete and need Nutrition.
- These SEVEN life processes are remembered by "MRS GREN."
- Large organisms are organised in the following way:

  CELLS ⟶ TISSUES ⟶ ORGANS ⟶ ORGAN SYSTEMS ⟶ ORGANISM
- The HEART is an organ in the CIRCULATORY SYSTEM.
- The STOMACH is an organ in the DIGESTIVE SYSTEM.

Cells

- Typical plant and animal cells have a Nucleus, Cytoplasm, Cell Membrane and Mitochondria.
- Plant cells also contain a Cellulose Cell Wall, permanent Vacuole and Chloroplasts (which contain Chlorophyll).
- Cells are sometimes ADAPTED to carry out a SPECIALISED job.
- Red blood cells carry oxygen around the body. They have no nucleus, contain haemoglobin and have a large surface area.
- Root hair cells absorb water and minerals. They have a tiny hair like projection and do not contain chloroplasts.
- Diffusion is the MOVEMENT OF A GAS or any SUBSTANCE IN A SOLUTION from a HIGHER to a LOWER CONCENTRATION.
- In the lungs OXYGEN diffuses from the alveolus where it is in a HIGH concentration into the blood where it is in a LOWER concentration. Carbon dioxide diffuses in the opposite direction.

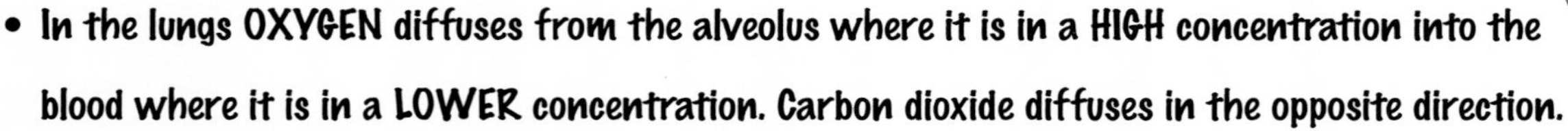

- In the leaf oxygen diffuses from inside the leaf where it is in a HIGH concentration to outside where it is in a LOWER concentration. Carbon dioxide diffuses in the opposite direction.

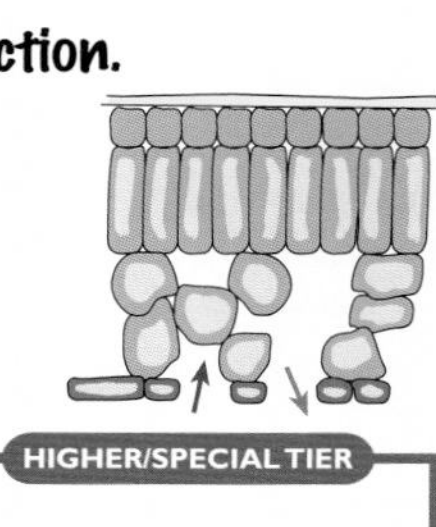

HIGHER/SPECIAL TIER

- Both the alveolus and the leaf have become specially adapted to carry out their job of exchanging gases. They both have MASSIVE SURFACE AREAS.
- OSMOSIS is the diffusion of WATER from a DILUTE SOLUTION to a MORE CONCENTRATED SOLUTION across a PARTIALLY PERMEABLE MEMBRANE.
- To absorb a substance AGAINST A CONCENTRATION GRADIENT requires energy and is called ACTIVE UPTAKE.

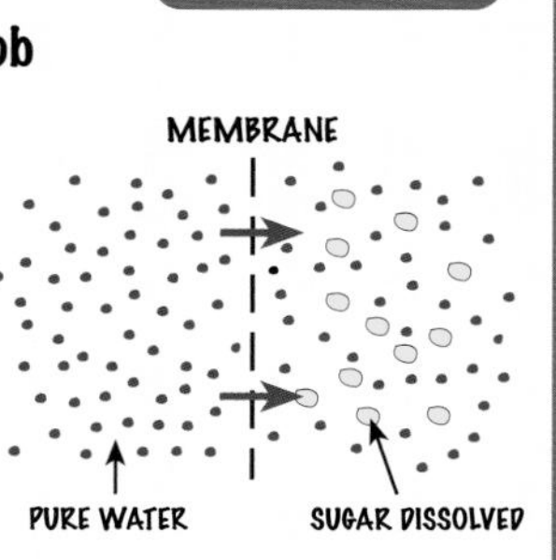

Record the FIVE 'Life Processes' and ELEVEN 'Cells' facts onto your tape.
Now - READ, COVER, WRITE and CHECK the SIXTEEN facts.

Nutrition

TEETH

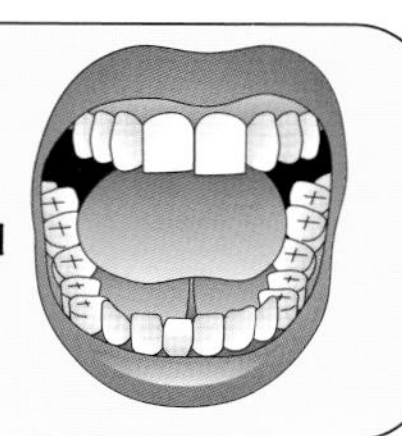

- The job of the teeth is to grind the food into a pulp.

PERISTALSIS

- A muscular contraction that moves food along the digestive system.

HEALTHY DIET

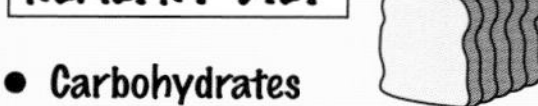

- Carbohydrates
- Proteins

- Fats

- Vitamins & Minerals, Roughage, Water

HUMAN DIGESTIVE SYSTEM

- Breaks down large, insoluble molecules into small, soluble molecules.

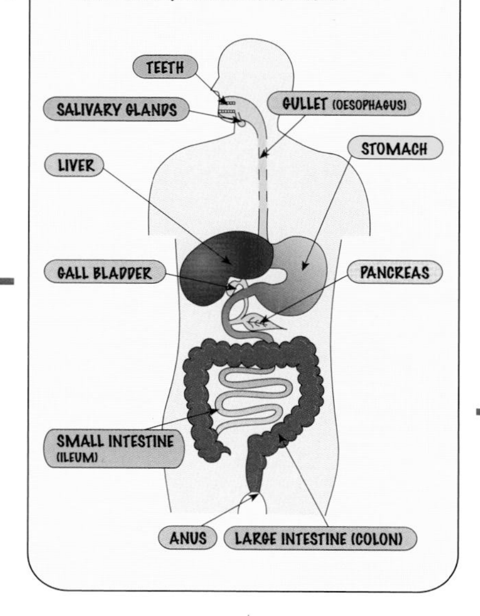

ENZYMES

- Carbohydrase (Amylase) breaks down carbohydrates to sugars.
- Protease breaks down proteins to amino acids.
- Lipase breaks down fats to fatty acids and glycerol.

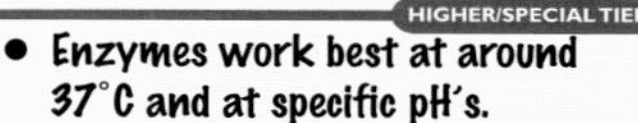

HIGHER/SPECIAL TIER

- Enzymes work best at around 37°C and at specific pH's.

ABSORPTION

HIGHER/SPECIAL TIER

- Once food has been digested it is absorbed in the small intestine.
- The small intestine has a massive surface area, good blood supply and thin walls.

VILLUS

CAPILLARIES

Disease

MICROBES

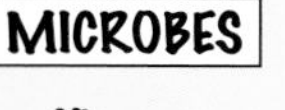

- Viruses

- Bacteria

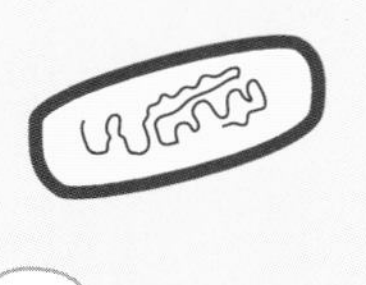

- Protozoa

- Fungi

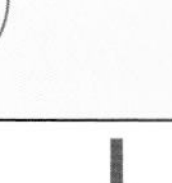

PREVENTING MICROBES ENTERING THE BODY

- Skin acts as a barrier.
- Blood clots to seal any cuts.
- Breathing system has cilia and produces mucus.

FIGHTING DISEASE

- White blood cells ingest microbes, produce antibodies and antitoxins.
- White blood cells "remember" antigens and this leads to a natural immunity.
- Immunisation boosts natural immunity.

Drugs

ALCOHOL, TOBACCO AND SOLVENTS

- Alcohol
  - a depressant that slows reactions.
  - long term effect includes liver and brain damage.

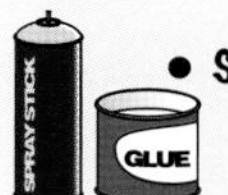

- Tobacco
  - causes emphysema, bronchitis and smokers' cough.
  - long term effect includes cancer and heart disease.
- Solvents
  - Slow reactions and hallucinations.
  - long term effect includes permanent damage to the lungs, liver, brain and kidney.

SPRAY STICK

GLUE

STIMULANTS AND DEPRESSANTS

HIGHER/SPECIAL TIER

- Stimulants increase the amount of transmitter released or they activate the receptor directly.
- Depressants prevent release of the transmitter or they block the receptors.

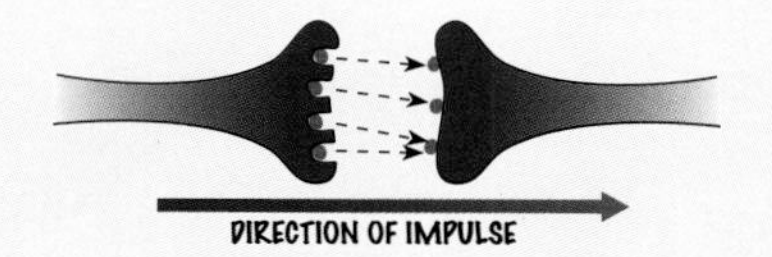

Types Of Food

To maintain a **HEALTHY DIET** a person needs to take in different types of food including: carbohydrates, proteins, fats, vitamins and minerals, roughage and water. The first three of these are broken down by the digestive system.

Human Diet

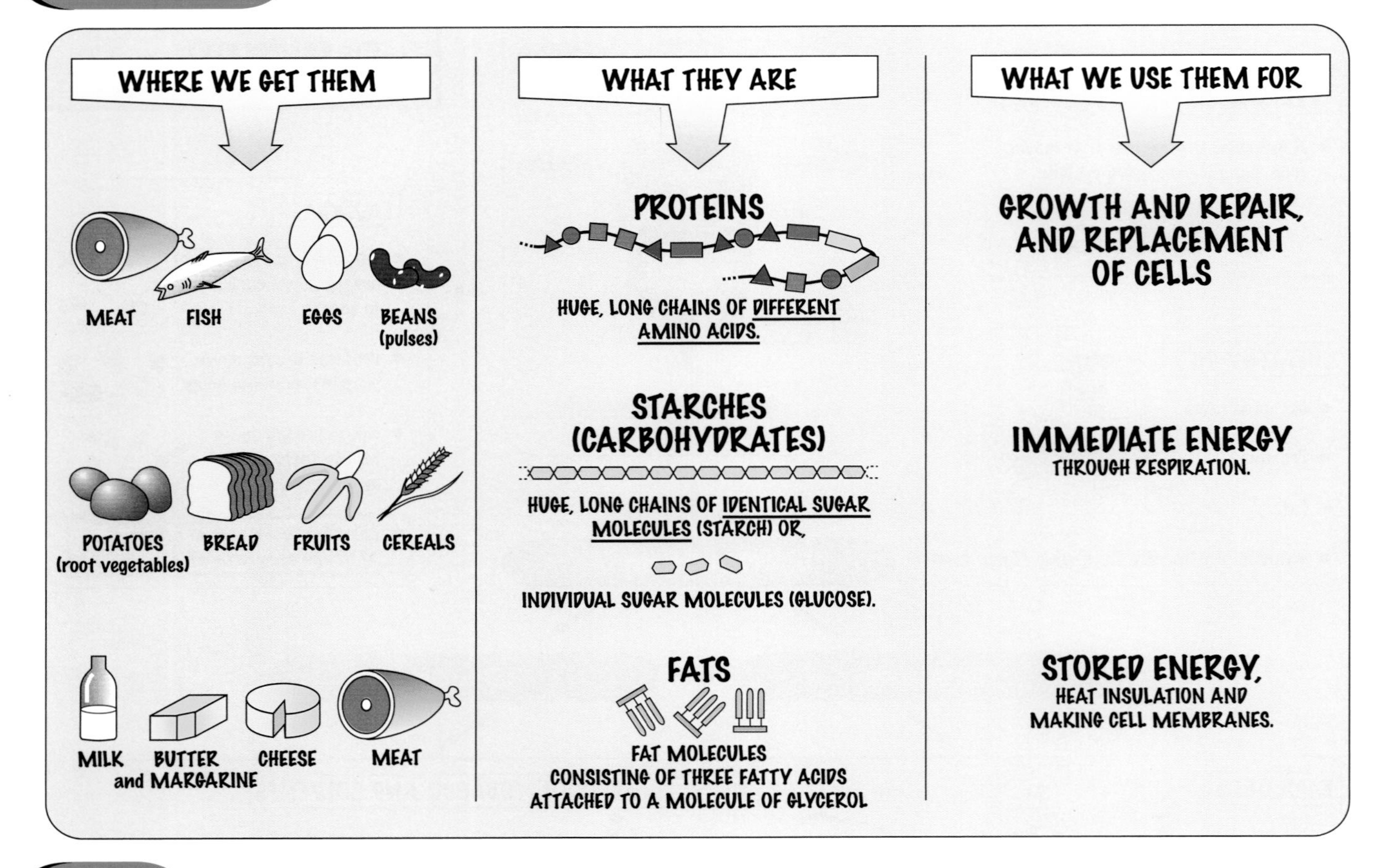

Teeth

- The job of the **DIGESTIVE SYSTEM** is to break down the **LARGE INSOLUBLE** food molecules into **SMALL, SOLUBLE** molecules ...
  ... this process is called **DIGESTION.**
  TEETH start the process of digestion by grinding the food into a **PULP.**
  This is called **MECHANICAL DIGESTION.**

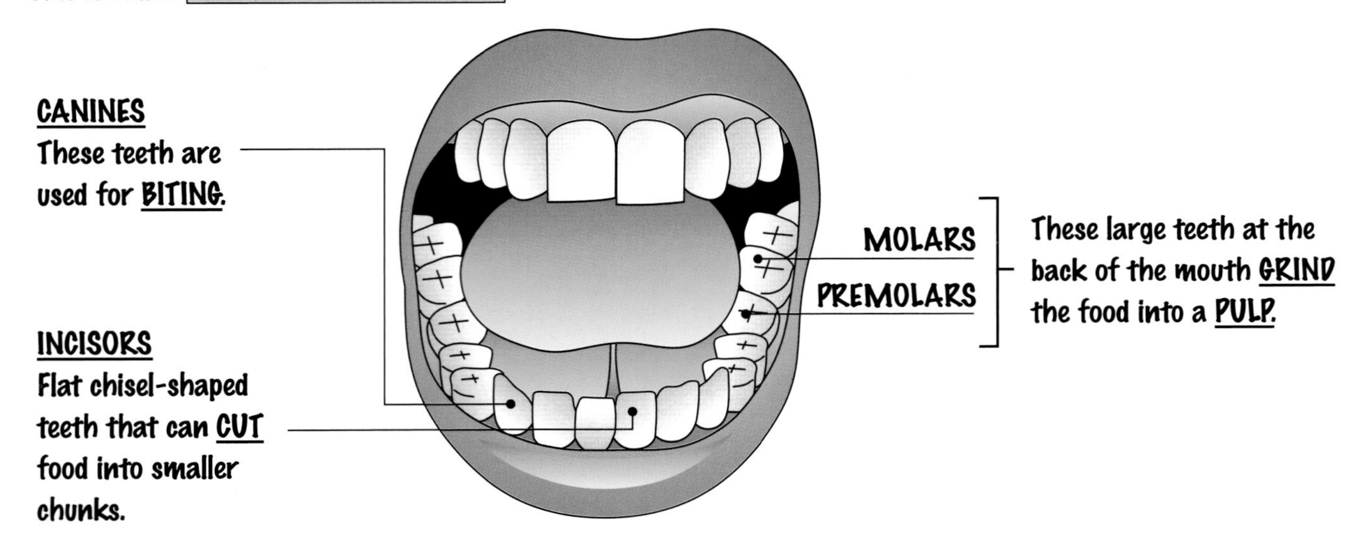

The Human Digestive System

The **DIGESTIVE SYSTEM** is really made up of a long **MUSCULAR TUBE** in which **ENZYMES** speed up (catalyse) the breakdown of **LARGE INSOLUBLE MOLECULES** into **SMALLER SOLUBLE MOLECULES.** These **SMALL SOLUBLE MOLECULES** can then pass through the walls of the small intestine and into the bloodstream.

TEETH
Used for grinding up food.

SALIVARY GLANDS
Produces saliva to soften the food and contains the enzyme **CARBOHYDRASE (AMYLASE).**

LIVER

HIGHER/SPECIAL TIER

Produces **BILE** which helps in fat digestion. Stores excess sugar as **GLYCOGEN.**

GALL BLADDER
Stores **BILE**, before releasing it into the small intestine.
Bile, ...
(a) neutralises the acid which was added in the stomach
(b) provides alkaline conditions for the enzymes of the small intestine
(c) emulsifies fats into smaller droplets so that the enzymes have a larger surface area to work on.

GULLET (OESOPHAGUS)
Carries food from the mouth to the stomach

STOMACH
Food is stored in the stomach. The stomach produces the enzyme **PROTEASE.** Hydrochloric acid is released by cells in the wall of the stomach ...
... it kills bacteria and ...
... provides the best conditions for the **PROTEASE** enzyme.

PANCREAS
Produces the enzymes ...
CARBOHYDRASE (AMYLASE)
PROTEASE, and
LIPASE

SMALL INTESTINE (ILEUM)
Produces the enzymes ...
CARBOHYDRASE (AMYLASE)
PROTEASE, and
LIPASE

The small, soluble molecules produced by digestion are **ABSORBED** by the **SMALL INTESTINE.**

ANUS
Faeces leave the body here.

LARGE INTESTINE (COLON)
Excess water from the contents of the intestines is **REABSORBED** into the blood here. **FAECES** is stored before passing out of the body.

Peristalsis

Inner circular muscle.

Outer longitudinal muscle.

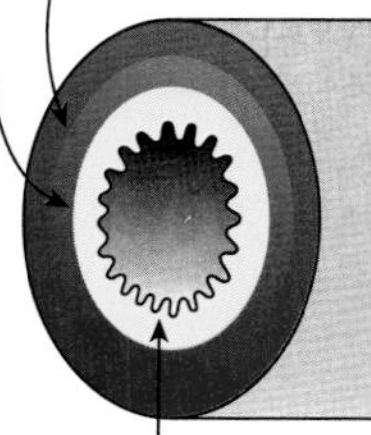

A SECTION OF THE SMALL INTESTINE WHICH IS MORE OR LESS TYPICAL OF THE DIGESTIVE SYSTEM.

An inner, folded layer of Villi and **GLANDULAR TISSUE** to make enzymes to catalyse the breakdown of the food.

The longitudinal muscles **RELAX** and the circular muscles **CONTRACT** behind the **FOOD BOLUS** ...

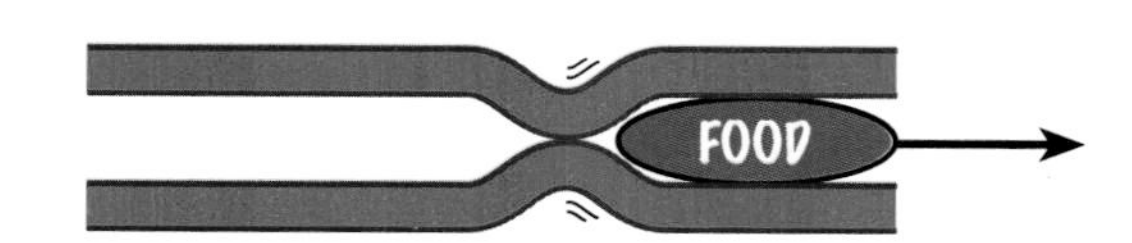

... pushing it forward through the small intestine

- There are only three enzymes involved in digestion. (Amylase is a type of carbohydrase and is mentioned in some syllabuses.)
- This diagram shows the FOUR regions which produce enzymes and the types of enzyme produced by each region.

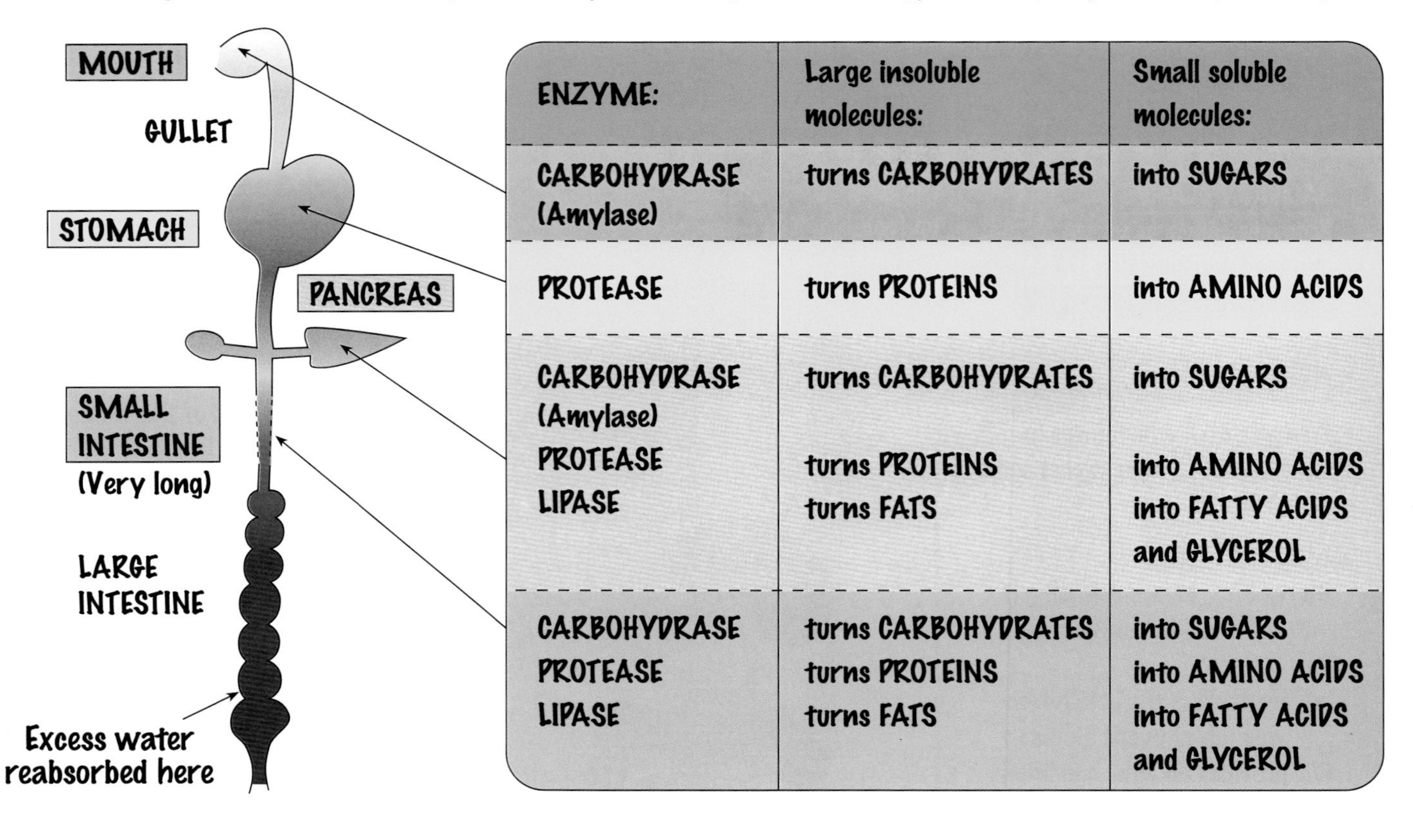

ENZYME:	Large insoluble molecules:	Small soluble molecules:
CARBOHYDRASE (Amylase)	turns CARBOHYDRATES	into SUGARS
PROTEASE	turns PROTEINS	into AMINO ACIDS
CARBOHYDRASE (Amylase) PROTEASE LIPASE	turns CARBOHYDRATES turns PROTEINS turns FATS	into SUGARS into AMINO ACIDS into FATTY ACIDS and GLYCEROL
CARBOHYDRASE PROTEASE LIPASE	turns CARBOHYDRATES turns PROTEINS turns FATS	into SUGARS into AMINO ACIDS into FATTY ACIDS and GLYCEROL

HIGHER/SPECIAL TIER

Optimum Conditions For Enzymes

- The OPTIMUM CONDITIONS are the conditions under which enzymes work best ...

  ... this is usually AROUND 37°C for most enzymes ...

  ... below this temperature the rate of reaction is SLOW ... above 40°C the enzyme becomes DENATURED.

  Denaturing means that the enzyme is permanently destroyed.
- Different enzymes work better at different pHs.

Part Of The Digestive System	Name Of Enzyme	Conditions
MOUTH	SALIVARY CARBOHYDRASE (AMYLASE)	NEUTRAL/SLIGHTLY ACIDIC
STOMACH	GASTRIC PROTEASE	VERY ACIDIC DUE TO HYDROCHLORIC ACID
EARLY PART OF SMALL INTESTINE	PANCREATIC CARBOHYDRASE (AMYLASE) PANCREATIC PROTEASE PANCREATIC LIPASE	BILE AND PANCREATIC JUICE NEUTRALISES THE STOMACH'S CONTENTS. THE CONDITIONS OVERALL ARE STILL SLIGHTLY ACIDIC
LATTER PART OF SMALL INTESTINE	CARBOHYDRASE PROTEASE LIPASE	DUE TO THE ACTION OF BILE AND PANCREATIC JUICE THE CONDITIONS ARE APPROXIMATELY NEUTRAL

Because Proteins, Carbohydrates and Fats are LARGE INSOLUBLE MOLECULES, they must be broken down into SMALLER SOLUBLE MOLECULES before they can be ABSORBED.

PROTEASE ENZYMES

catalyse the breakdown of PROTEINS into AMINO ACIDS.

PROTEINS

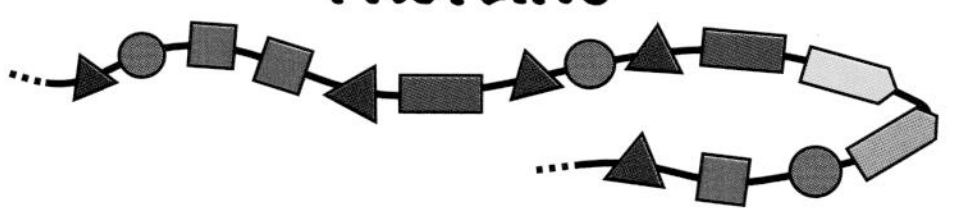

CARBOHYDRASE (AMYLASE) ENZYMES

catalyse the breakdown of CARBOHYDRATES (e.g. starch) into SUGARS (e.g. glucose).

CARBOHYDRATES (e.g. Starch)

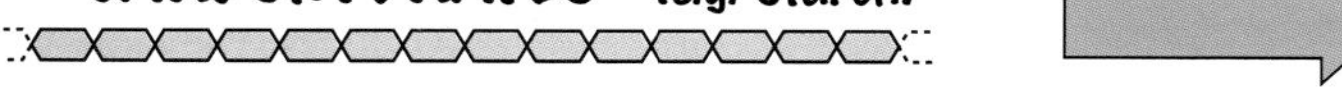

LIPASE ENZYMES

catalyse the breakdown of FATS into FATTY ACIDS and GLYCEROL.

FATS

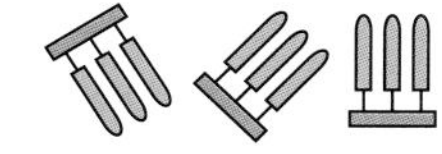

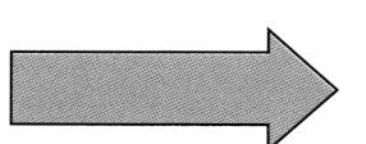

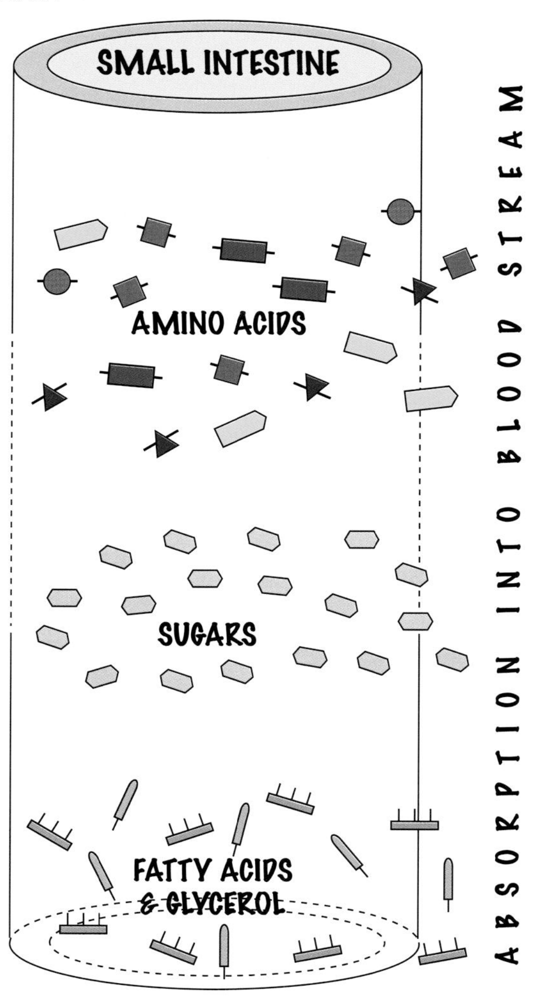

LOOK CAREFULLY AT THE PREVIOUS PAGE TO SEE WHERE THESE ENZYMES ARE MADE.

HIGHER/SPECIAL TIER

Absorption In The Small Intestine

The surface of the small intestine is covered by thousands of tiny finger-like projections called villi.

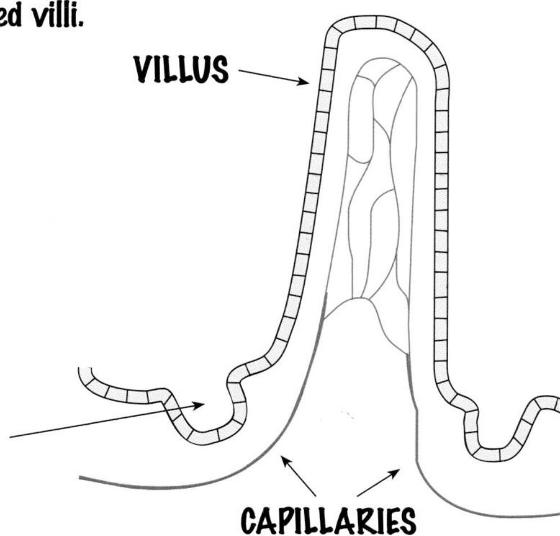

The small intestine is very well adapted for ABSORPTION by having:

- a **MASSIVE SURFACE AREA** due to its length and the presence of villi.
- a **VERY GOOD BLOOD SUPPLY.**
- **THIN WALLS** which are permeable to SUGARS (e.g. glucose), AMINO ACIDS, FATTY ACIDS and GLYCEROL.

Microbes

NAME OF MICROBE (SIZE)	DIAGRAM (NOT TO SCALE)	HOW THEY WORK	DISEASES CAUSED
Virus - (0.0001mm)	protein coat, genes	• Reproduce very rapidly INSIDE LIVING CELLS damaging the cell • Can produce TOXINS (poisons)	Measles, Colds, Flu, Mumps, Polio
Bacteria - (0.001mm)	membrane, cell wall, cytoplasm, genetic material	• Reproduce very rapidly (over 2 million produced in 7 hours). • Can produce TOXINS (poisons)	Whooping Cough, Pneumonia, Tetanus, Cholera, Tuberculosis
Protozoa - (0.01mm)	membrane, cytoplasm, nucleus	• Some have complex life stages in two hosts. • Can produce TOXINS (poisons)	Malaria (passed to humans by the female mosquito)
Fungi - (0.01mm)	reproductive body, hyphae (thread)	• Reproduce INSIDE LIVING CELLS damaging the cell • Can produce TOXINS (poisons)	Athlete's Foot Ringworm

A Comparison Between Viruses And Bacteria

VIRUSES	BACTERIA
Have a simple PROTEIN COAT. No membrane or cell wall.	Consist of CYTOPLASM and a MEMBRANE surrounded by a CELL WALL.
The genetic material is NOT contained within a NUCLEUS.	The genetic material is NOT contained within a NUCLEUS.
Smaller than bacteria.	Very small.
Reproduce very quickly - BUT ONLY INSIDE LIVING CELLS, WHICH ARE THEN DAMAGED.	Reproduce very quickly.

- Microbes can ENTER THE BODY through NATURAL OPENINGS (e.g. the nose or mouth) ...
  ... and through BREAKS IN THE SKIN (cuts, bites).
- If LARGE NUMBERS OF MICROBES enter the body due to UNHYGIENIC CONDITIONS ...
  ... or contact with INFECTED PEOPLE ...
  ... the MICROBES can REPRODUCE RAPIDLY and make the person unwell.

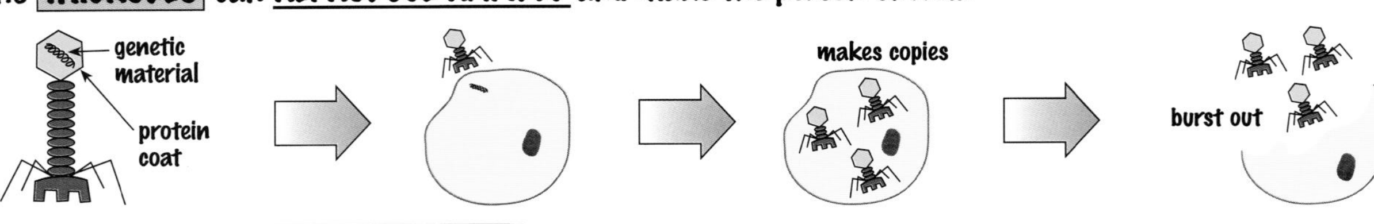

Our Defence Against Microbes

1. The blood produces CLOTS that seal cuts.
2. The BREATHING ORGANS produce a STICKY, LIQUID MUCUS, which covers the lining of these organs and traps microbes.
3. The SKIN acts as a barrier to invading microbes.
4. The WHITE CELLS - Deal with microbes once they're in.
   A microbe invades the body and starts to multiply ...
   ... causing the body's WHITE CELLS to multiply in response (see overleaf).

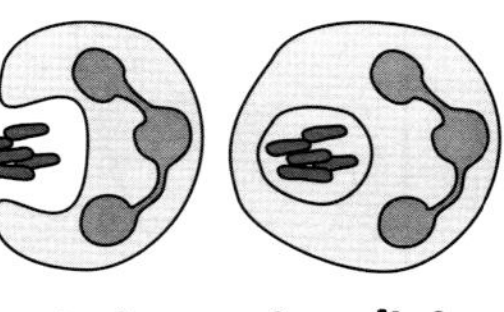

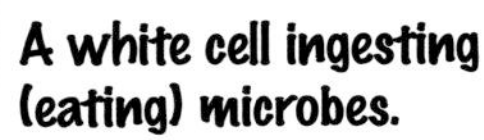
A white cell ingesting (eating) microbes.

- DISINFECTANTS can kill microbes but are too toxic or corrosive to be used on living tissue.
- GERMICIDES and ANTISEPTICS can be applied to living tissue to kill microbes.

The **WHITE BLOOD CELLS** form part of the body's **IMMUNE SYSTEM.**

White Blood Cells work by ...

... **INGESTING MICROBES** ...

... **PRODUCING ANTITOXINS** to NEUTRALISE TOXINS produced by the microbes ...

... **PRODUCING ANTIBODIES** to DESTROY PARTICULAR MICROBES.

Ingesting Microbes

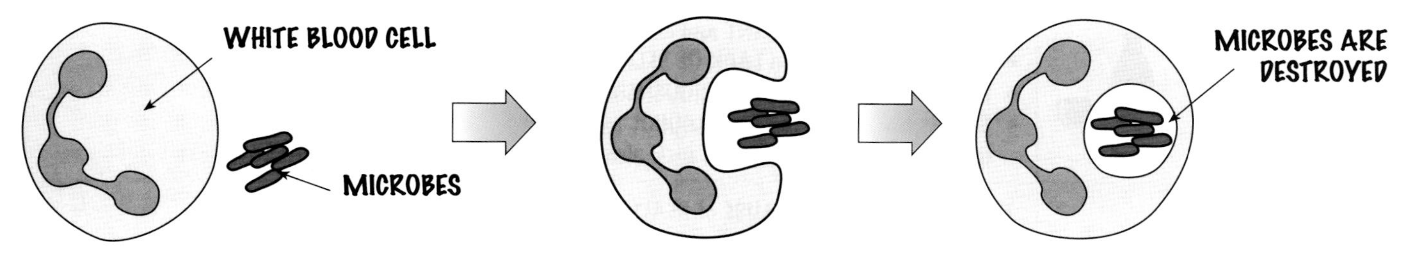

Microbes invade the body ...

... the white blood cell starts to surround the microbes.

The microbes are INGESTED by the white blood cell.

Producing Antitoxins

White Blood Cells produce **ANTITOXINS** that NEUTRALISE HARMFUL TOXINS (Poisons) produced by microbes.

Producing Antibodies

- WHITE BLOOD CELLS recognise the microbes as ANTIGENS (foreign bodies) ...
  ... and produce ANTIBODIES to destroy the ANTIGENS.
- The reason we feel ILL is because it takes TIME for the WHITE BLOOD CELLS to produce ANTIBODIES to the microbes.
- The PRODUCTION OF ANTIBODIES is much faster if a person has already had the infectious disease.
  The WHITE BLOOD CELLS seem to 'remember' the antigen and in the future can produce ANTIBODIES more rapidly providing the person with a **NATURAL IMMUNITY.**

Immunisation

The body's NATURAL IMMUNITY can be increased by **IMMUNISATION.**

STEP 1: A WEAKENED or DEAD ANTIGEN is injected into a person.

STEP 2: The body PRODUCES ANTIBODIES to fight the antigen.

STEP 3: The body's NATURAL IMMUNITY IS INCREASED because the white cells are now sensitised to this particular antigen and will react quickly to future infections.

Rejection Of Transplanted Organs

REJECTION OF TRANSPLANTED ORGANS occurs ...

... because the WHITE BLOOD CELLS recognise the TRANSPLANTED ORGAN as a FOREIGN BODY ...

... and produce ANTIBODIES to act against it.

DRUGS are chemical substances that **ALTER THE WAY THE BODY WORKS.**
Some drugs can be obtained from LIVING THINGS, others are SYNTHETIC (MAN-MADE).

Some drugs are called **MEDICINES** and these are taken to **CURE ILLNESSES** or **EASE THE SYMPTOMS** produced during an illness. Examples include PAIN-KILLERS and ANTIBIOTICS (which destroy bacteria and some other microbes).

Alcohol, Tobacco And Solvents

NAME OF DRUG	FURTHER NOTES
ALCOHOL Contains the chemical ethanol.	• ALCOHOL is a DEPRESSANT and causes SLOW REACTIONS. • ALCOHOL can lead to a LACK OF SELF CONTROL. • EXCESS can lead to UNCONSCIOUSNESS and even COMA or DEATH. • The LONG TERM effects of ALCOHOL can be LIVER DAMAGE (due to the liver removing the toxic alcohol from the body) or BRAIN DAMAGE.
TOBACCO Contains the chemicals Nicotine Tar Carbon Monoxide	TOBACCO is a MAJOR CAUSE of HEALTH PROBLEMS: • EMPHYSEMA - alveoli damage by excessive coughing. • BRONCHITIS - increased infection due to INCREASED mucus production. • 'SMOKERS COUGH' - chemicals in the cigarette smoke damage the CILIA (hair-like projections) lining the breathing tubes. The CILIA cannot work properly to remove the mucus, tar and dirt from the lungs. In the morning, after a time without cigarette smoke, the CILIA BEGIN TO WORK and the mucus and tar are removed out of the lungs and coughed up. • ARTERIAL and HEART DISEASE - damage to blood vessels that can lead to HEART ATTACKS, STROKES and even AMPUTATIONS.
SOLVENTS Different kinds of vapours are given off by solvents.	• SOLVENTS lead to SLOWED REACTIONS and HALLUCINATIONS. • SOLVENTS can affect a person's BEHAVIOUR and cause CHARACTER CHANGES. • SOLVENTS may cause PERMANENT DAMAGE to the LUNGS, LIVER, BRAIN or KIDNEYS.

- Some drugs are **ADDICTIVE** for example NICOTINE. Smokers develop a psychological 'need' to have the drug and therefore want to smoke more cigarettes.
- If an addict stops taking an ADDICTIVE DRUG they can suffer **PSYCHOLOGICAL PROBLEMS,** for example CRAVING the drug, and **PHYSICAL PROBLEMS,** like sweating, the shakes, feeling sick or vomiting. These are termed **WITHDRAWAL SYMPTOMS.**

Stimulants And Depressants

- Both **STIMULANTS** and **DEPRESSANTS** act at the place where nerves join, called the **SYNAPSE.** (See P.36)
  - CAFFEINE is a STIMULANT
  - ALCOHOL/SOLVENTS are DEPRESSANTS

HIGHER/SPECIAL TIER

At the end of a neurone are small amounts of a transmitter that when stimulated move across the synapse to activate the receptors on the next neurone.

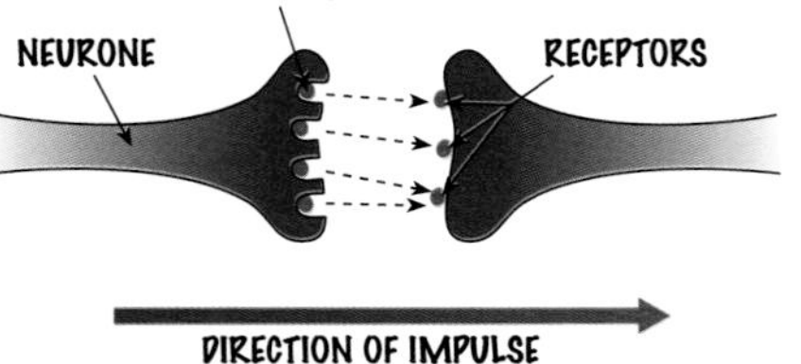

- **STIMULANTS** act by INCREASING THE AMOUNT of TRANSMITTER RELEASED or by ACTIVATING THE RECEPTOR DIRECTLY.
- **DEPRESSANTS** act by PREVENTING RELEASE OF THE TRANSMITTER or by BLOCKING THE RECEPTORS.
- **DRUG TOLERANCE** is caused by the continual taking of the same drug so that it NO LONGER AFFECTS THE BODY in the same way and HIGHER DOSES of the drug are required.

Nutrition

- To maintain a healthy diet humans require a balanced intake of different types of food including carbohydrates, proteins and fats.
- The Digestive System breaks down large insoluble molecules into small, soluble molecules.
- The teeth start the process of digestion by grinding the food to a pulp.
- Food is pushed along the gut by a wave of muscle contraction called peristalsis.
- Carbohydrase (Amylase) enzymes catalyse the break down of starch into sugars.
- Protease enzymes catalyse the breakdown of proteins into amino acids.
- Lipase enzymes catalyse the breakdown of proteins into amino acids.

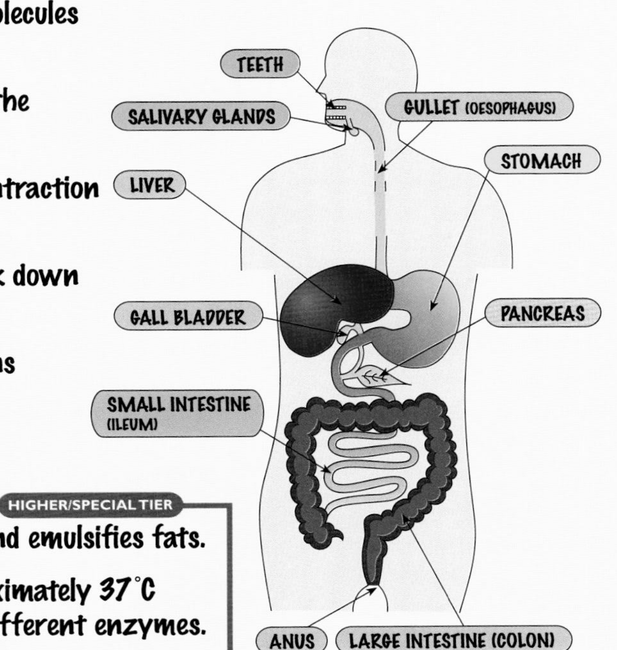

HIGHER/SPECIAL TIER

- Bile neutralises the acidic contents of the stomach and emulsifies fats.
- The best temperature for enzymes to work is approximately 37°C (Body temperature) but the optimum pH varies for different enzymes.

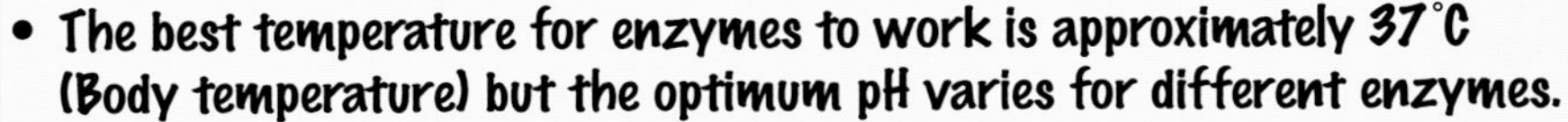

- The small intestine is adapted for absorption of small, soluble food molecules due to having villi, a good blood supply and thin walls.

Disease

- Microbes that can cause disease include: viruses, bacteria, protozoa and fungi.
- Disinfectants, germicides and antiseptics are all used to kill microbes.
- Barriers to microbes entering the body include the skin, the blood's ability to clot and sticky mucus and cilia in the breathing system.
- The white Blood Cells work by ingesting microbes, producing antitoxins and antibodies.
- Once antibodies have been produced by the body a person develops a natural immunity to a disease. This is the basis of immunisation.

Drugs

- Alcohol, tobacco and solvents are all forms of drugs which can alter the way the body works and if taken in excess will damage the body.
- Addiction is a craving produced after taking a drug for some time and can lead to withdrawal symptoms if the drug is no longer taken.

HIGHER/SPECIAL TIER

- Stimulants and depressants act on the synapses between nerves.
- Drug tolerance is when the body is no longer affected by the usual dose of the drug.

Record the TEN 'Nutrition' facts, FIVE 'Disease' facts and FOUR 'Drugs' facts onto your tape.

Now - READ, COVER, WRITE and CHECK the NINETEEN facts.

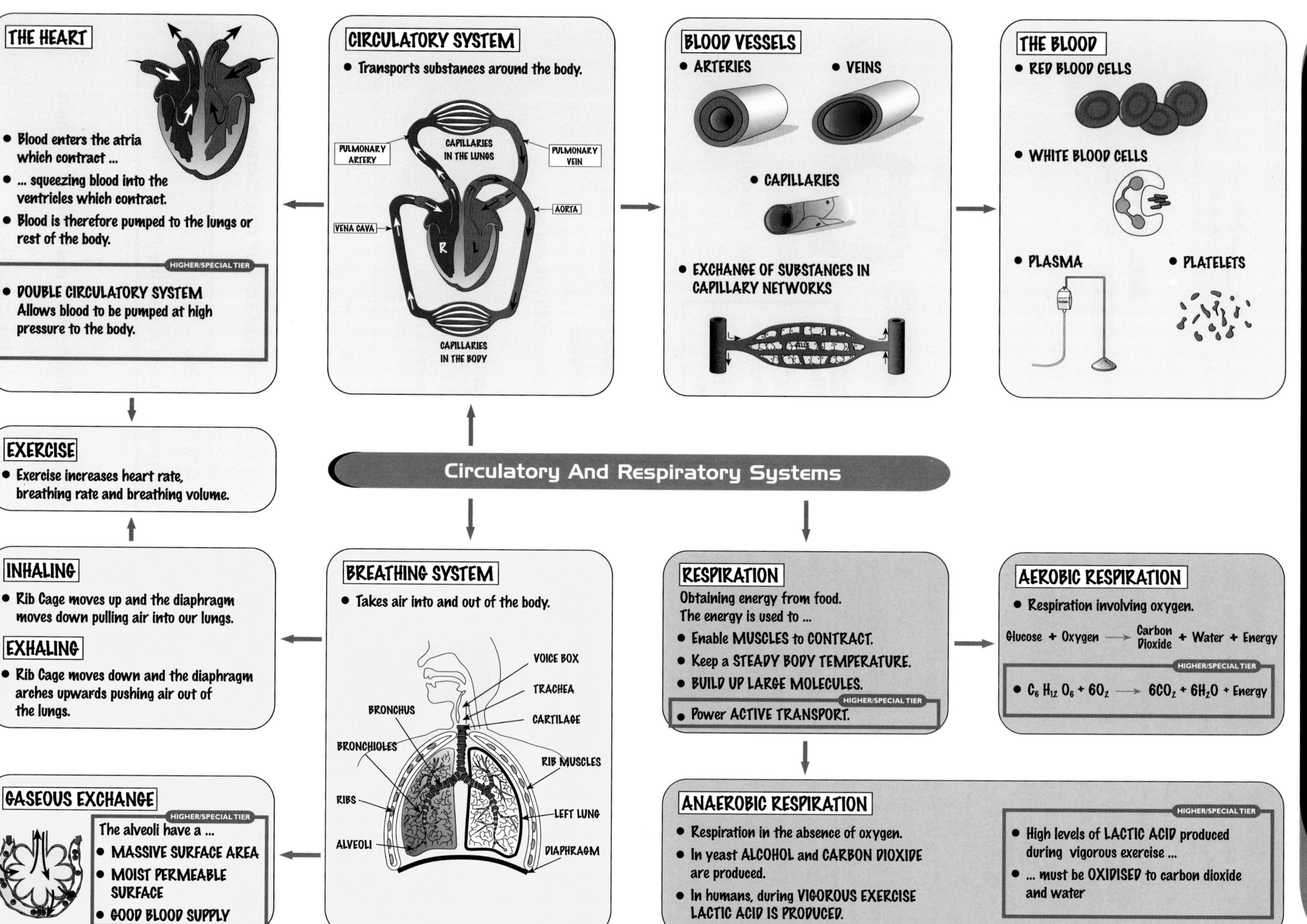
Circulatory And Respiratory Systems
THE HEART
Blood enters the atria which contract ...
... squeezing blood into the ventricles which contract.
Blood is therefore pumped to the lungs or rest of the body.
HIGHER/SPECIAL TIER
DOUBLE CIRCULATORY SYSTEM
Allows blood to be pumped at high pressure to the body.
CIRCULATORY SYSTEM
Transports substances around the body.
PULMONARY ARTERY
CAPILLARIES IN THE LUNGS
PULMONARY VEIN
AORTA
VENA CAVA
R
L
CAPILLARIES IN THE BODY
BLOOD VESSELS
ARTERIES
VEINS
CAPILLARIES
EXCHANGE OF SUBSTANCES IN CAPILLARY NETWORKS
THE BLOOD
RED BLOOD CELLS
WHITE BLOOD CELLS
PLASMA
PLATELETS
EXERCISE
Exercise increases heart rate, breathing rate and breathing volume.
INHALING
Rib Cage moves up and the diaphragm moves down pulling air into our lungs.
EXHALING
Rib Cage moves down and the diaphragm arches upwards pushing air out of the lungs.
GASEOUS EXCHANGE
HIGHER/SPECIAL TIER
The alveoli have a ...
MASSIVE SURFACE AREA
MOIST PERMEABLE SURFACE
GOOD BLOOD SUPPLY
BREATHING SYSTEM
Takes air into and out of the body.
VOICE BOX
TRACHEA
CARTILAGE
BRONCHUS
BRONCHIOLES
RIB MUSCLES
RIBS
LEFT LUNG
ALVEOLI
DIAPHRAGM
RESPIRATION
Obtaining energy from food.
The energy is used to ...
Enable MUSCLES to CONTRACT.
Keep a STEADY BODY TEMPERATURE.
BUILD UP LARGE MOLECULES.
HIGHER/SPECIAL TIER
Power ACTIVE TRANSPORT.
AEROBIC RESPIRATION
Respiration involving oxygen.
Glucose + Oxygen → Carbon Dioxide + Water + Energy
HIGHER/SPECIAL TIER
$C_6H_{12}O_6 + 6O_2 \rightarrow 6CO_2 + 6H_2O$ + Energy
ANAEROBIC RESPIRATION
Respiration in the absence of oxygen.
In yeast ALCOHOL and CARBON DIOXIDE are produced.
In humans, during VIGOROUS EXERCISE LACTIC ACID IS PRODUCED.
HIGHER/SPECIAL TIER
High levels of LACTIC ACID produced during vigorous exercise ...
... must be OXIDISED to carbon dioxide and water

The CIRCULATORY SYSTEM transports substances around the body.
The CIRCULATORY SYSTEM can be divided into ... the HEART and BLOOD VESSELS
... and the BLOOD.

The Layout Of The System

Blood low in oxygen (DEOXYGENATED)

Blood rich in oxygen (OXYGENATED)

LUNGS
In the LUNGS
CARBON DIOXIDE diffuses OUT of the blood ...
... and OXYGEN diffuses IN to the blood.

CAPILLARIES IN THE LUNGS

PULMONARY VEIN carries OXYGENATED BLOOD from the lungs to the heart.

PULMONARY ARTERY carries DEOXYGENATED BLOOD from the heart to the lungs.

AORTA
The Aorta is the main artery that leaves the heart and supplies OXYGENATED BLOOD TO THE BODY.

VENA CAVA
The body's veins join together to form this main vein carrying DEOXYGENATED BLOOD BACK TO THE HEART.

R L

Blood containing high levels of oxygen and food flows to the cells in the body.

CAPILLARIES IN THE BODY

Blood containing high levels of carbon dioxide and waste returns to the heart.

CAPILLARIES
Oxygen and food are supplied to the cells. Carbon dioxide and waste are removed from the cells.

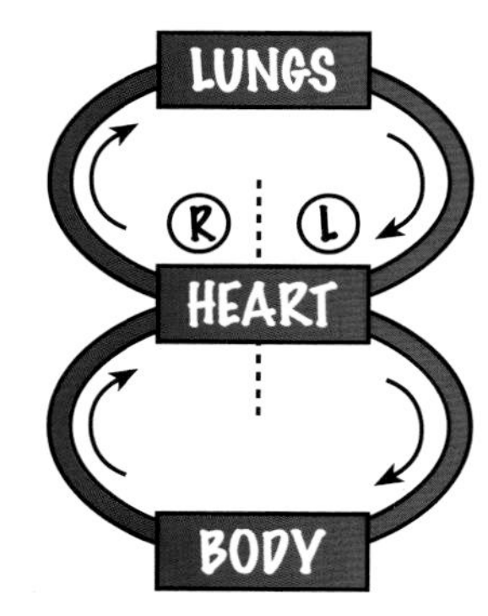

The Double Circulation

There are TWO SEPARATE CIRCULATORY SYSTEMS ...

One which carries blood from the HEART to the LUNGS and then back to the HEART ...

... and one which carries blood from the HEART to ALL OTHER PARTS OF THE BODY and then back to the HEART.

- This means that blood flows around a 'figure of eight' circuit and passes through the heart TWICE on each circuit.
- Blood travels AWAY from the heart through the ARTERIES ...
- ... and returns to the heart through the VEINS.

The LEFT SIDE of the heart pumps blood which is RICH IN OXYGEN and delivers it to all other parts of the BODY.

The RIGHT SIDE of the heart pumps blood which is LOW IN OXYGEN to the LUNGS, to pick up OXYGEN.

HIGHER/SPECIAL TIER

The advantage of this DOUBLE CIRCULATION SYSTEM ...
... is that BLOOD can be pumped TO THE BODY AT HIGHER PRESSURE, than it is pumped to the lungs.
This produces a MUCH GREATER RATE OF FLOW to the body.

The Heart In More Detail

The **HEART** is the main organ in the circulatory system and **PUMPS BLOOD** around the body.

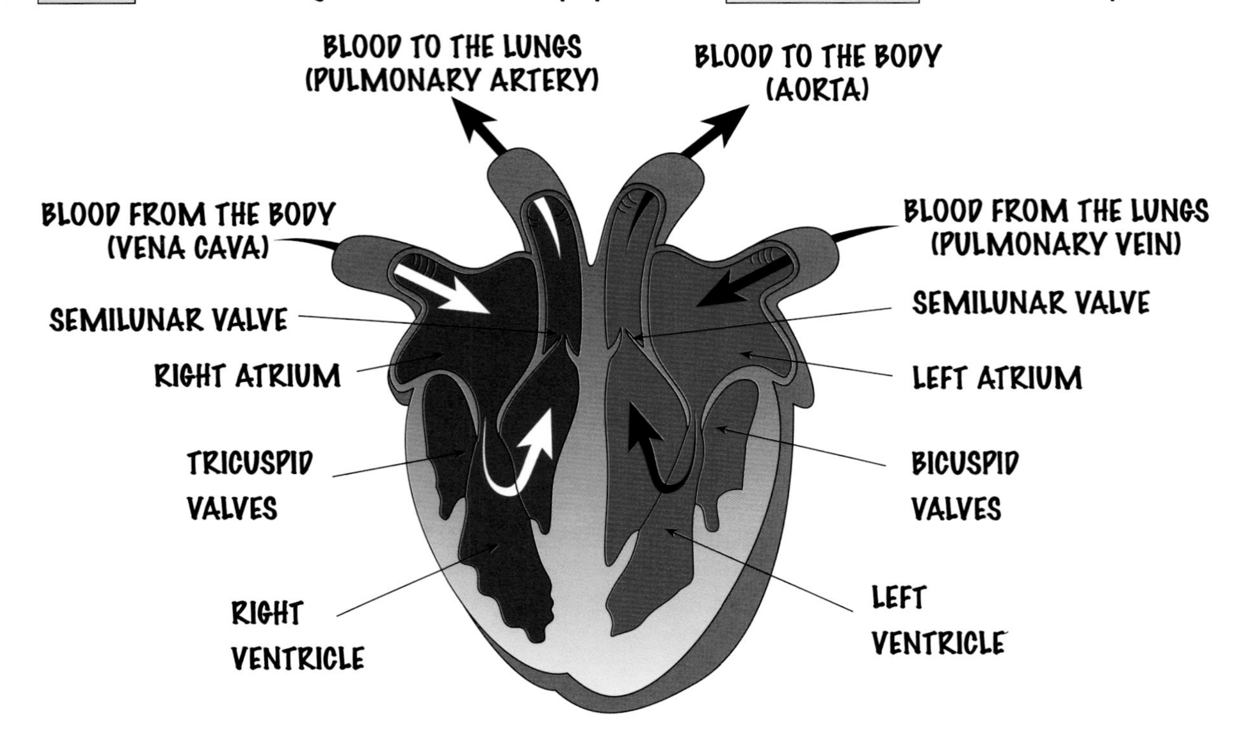

- Most of the wall of the heart is made of **MUSCLE.**
- **ATRIA** are the smaller, **LESS MUSCULAR** upper chambers, which receive blood coming back to the heart through **VEINS.**
- **VENTRICLES** are the larger, **MORE MUSCULAR** lower chambers. The **LEFT** is more muscular than the right since it has to pump blood around the whole body.
- **VALVES** make sure that the blood flows in the right direction, and can't flow backwards.

How The Heart Pumps Blood

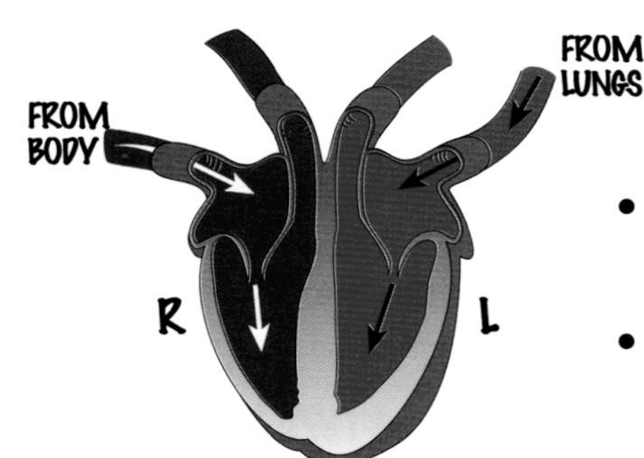

- When the HEART MUSCLE RELAXES, blood flows into the **ATRIA** from the **LUNGS** and the rest of the **BODY.**
- The **ATRIA** then CONTRACT squeezing blood into the **VENTRICLES.**

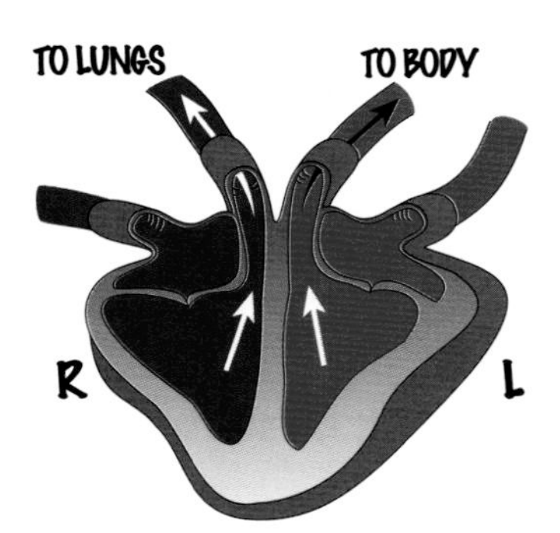

- When the **VENTRICLES CONTRACT** (squeezes) ...
  ... blood is forced out of the lower chambers into two arteries ...
  ... these carry blood to the body and the lungs.
- The blood can't flow backwards because of **VALVES** in the heart.
- The heart muscle now relaxes and the whole process starts again.

There are three types of blood vessels ... **ARTERIES**, **VEINS** and **CAPILLARIES**.
They form the "plumbing" of the circulatory system.

Arteries

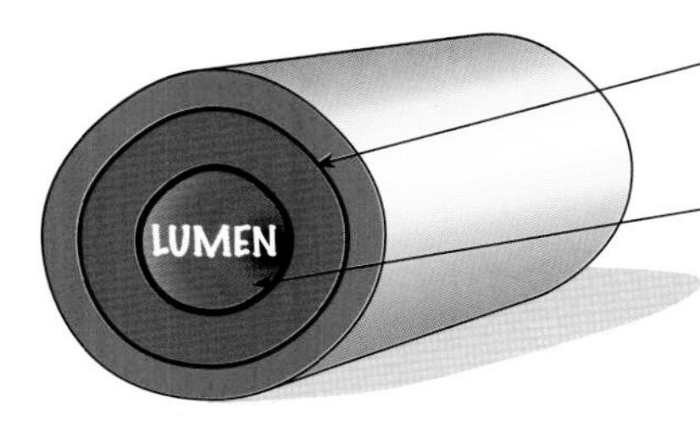

- Thick wall containing **ELASTIC** and **MUSCLE** fibres to cope with the much higher pressure in these vessels.
- Much smaller lumen compared to the thickness of the wall.
- No valves.
- Carry blood AWAY from the heart.
- Substances from the blood **CANNOT** pass through the artery walls.

Veins

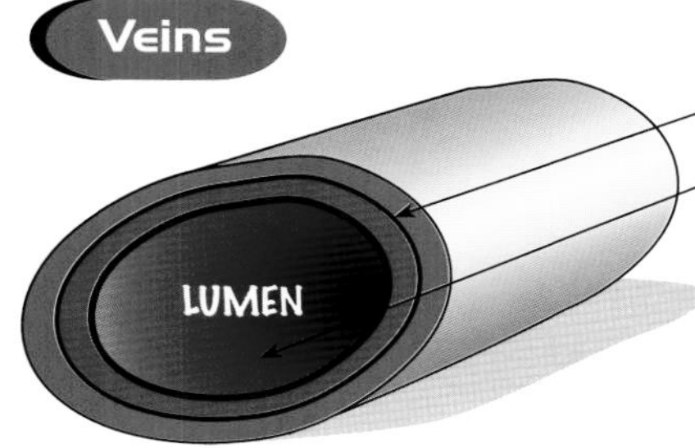

- Thinner wall containing **LESS ELASTIC** and **MUSCLE** fibres.
- Much bigger lumen compared to the thickness of the wall.
- Have VALVES to prevent backflow of blood.
- Carry blood TOWARDS the heart.
- Substances **CANNOT** pass through the veins' walls.

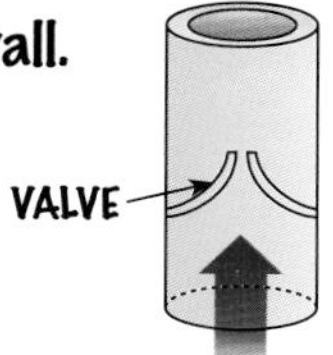

Capillaries

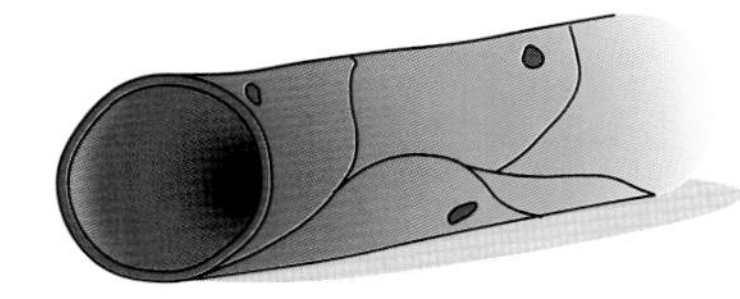

- Narrow, thin-walled vessels, just **ONE CELL THICK.**
- Microscopic - (too small to see without a microscope).
- **EXCHANGE OF SUBSTANCES** between cells and blood ONLY takes place here.
- Connect arteries to veins.

Exchange Of Substances At The Capillaries

Arteries branch into tiny one cell thick capillaries which pass close to each cell before reuniting to form a vein.

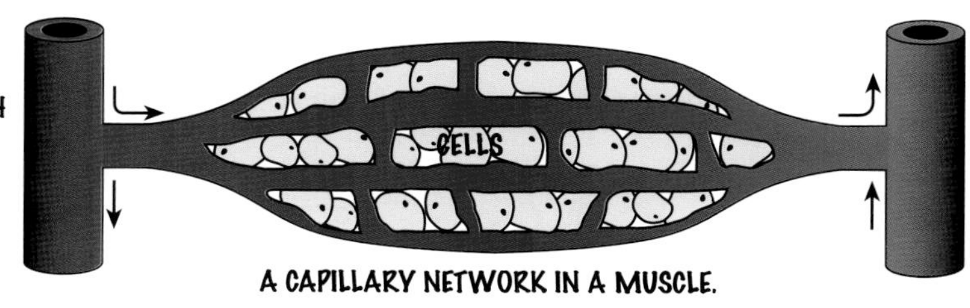

A CAPILLARY NETWORK IN A MUSCLE.

ONLY AT THE CAPILLARIES can SUBSTANCES BE EXCHANGED with the body's cells.
Food and oxygen is passed from the blood to the cells and carbon dioxide and other waste are passed from the cells to the blood.

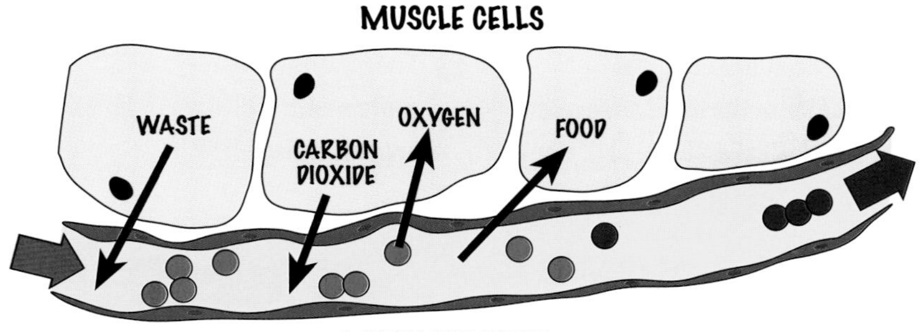

A CAPILLARY VESSEL (one cell thick)

The BLOOD is a FLUID that TRANSPORTS FOOD AND OXYGEN to cells and REMOVES WASTE PRODUCTS. It also forms part of the body's defence mechanism.

The Red Blood Cells

The bi-concave shape of the cells gives them a bigger surface area through which to absorb oxygen.

- They have no nucleus so that they can be packed with HAEMOGLOBIN.
- HAEMOGLOBIN is a substance which combines easily with oxygen when there's plenty of oxygen about.
- In the lungs, where there's lots of oxygen ...
  ... HAEMOGLOBIN + OXYGEN ⟶ OXYHAEMOGLOBIN.
- In the tissues where oxygen is being used up ...
  ... OXYHAEMOGLOBIN ⟶ HAEMOGLOBIN + OXYGEN.
- Haemoglobin's reversible reaction with oxygen ensures that oxygen is transported to where it's needed.

The White Blood Cells

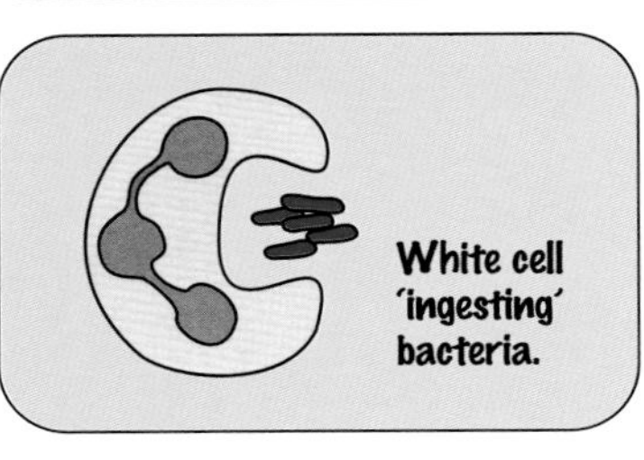

White cell 'ingesting' bacteria.

... have a NUCLEUS which may be quite variable in shape.

They help to DEFEND the body against INVADING MICROBES ...

... by ingesting microbes and ...

... releasing antibodies and antitoxins into the plasma (See P.21).

The Plasma

... is a straw-coloured liquid containing a suspension of blood cells.

Plasma transports ...

1. CARBON DIOXIDE from the organs to the lungs.
2. SOLUBLE PRODUCTS OF DIGESTION (e.g. glucose) from the small intestine to the organs.
3. UREA from the liver to the kidneys.
4. Chemical messengers called HORMONES.
5. WATER to and from various parts of the body.

The Platelets

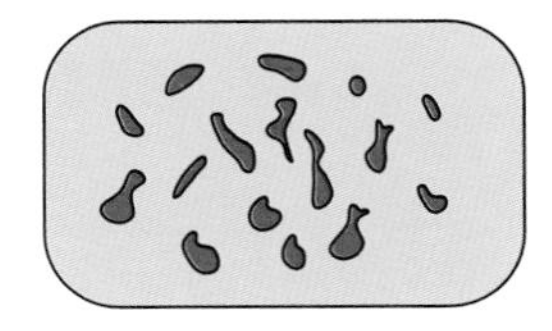

... are tiny pieces of cells which have no nucleus.
They are an important factor in HELPING THE BLOOD TO CLOT when a blood vessel has been damaged.

HIGHER/SPECIAL TIER

1. When the skin is cut the PLATELETS in the blood are exposed to air and RELEASE AN ENZYME.

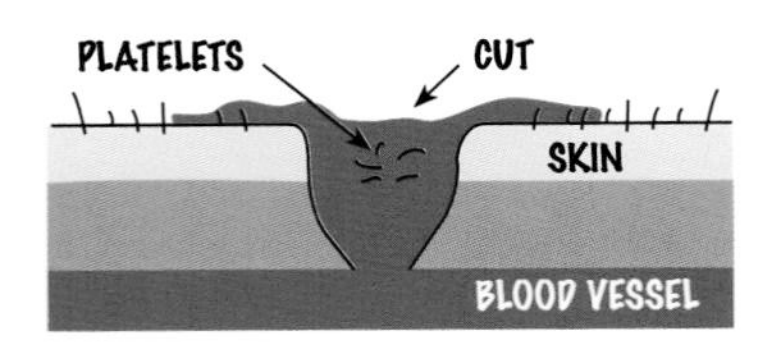

2. The enzyme converts a SOLUBLE protein into INSOLUBLE FIBRES of protein called FIBRIN.

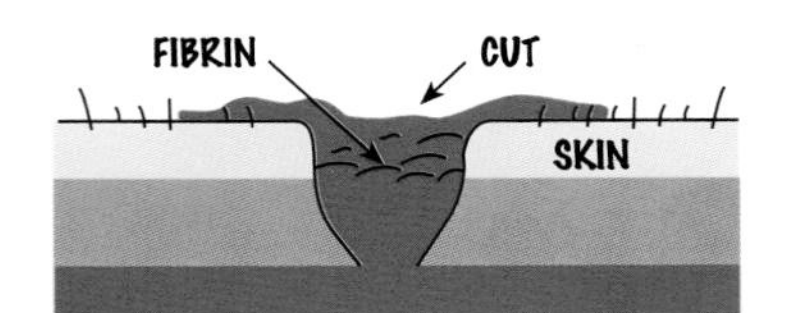

3. The FIBRIN forms a MESH that traps red blood cells and a CLOT forms. This hardens to form a SCAB.

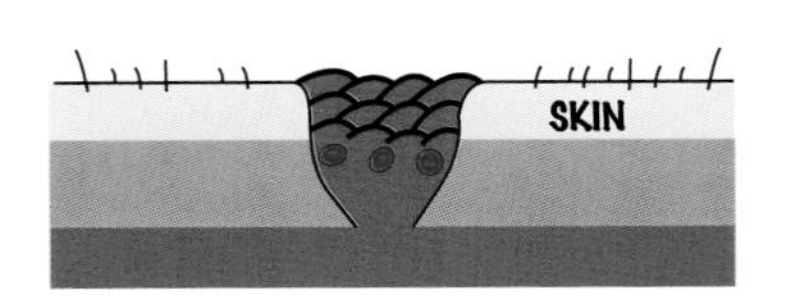

The **RESPIRATORY SYSTEM** takes air into and out of the lungs to allow **OXYGEN TO PASS INTO THE BLOOD** and **CARBON DIOXIDE TO PASS OUT OF THE BLOOD.**
The **LUNGS** are the major organ in the **BREATHING SYSTEM.**

Contents Of The Thorax (Chest Cavity)

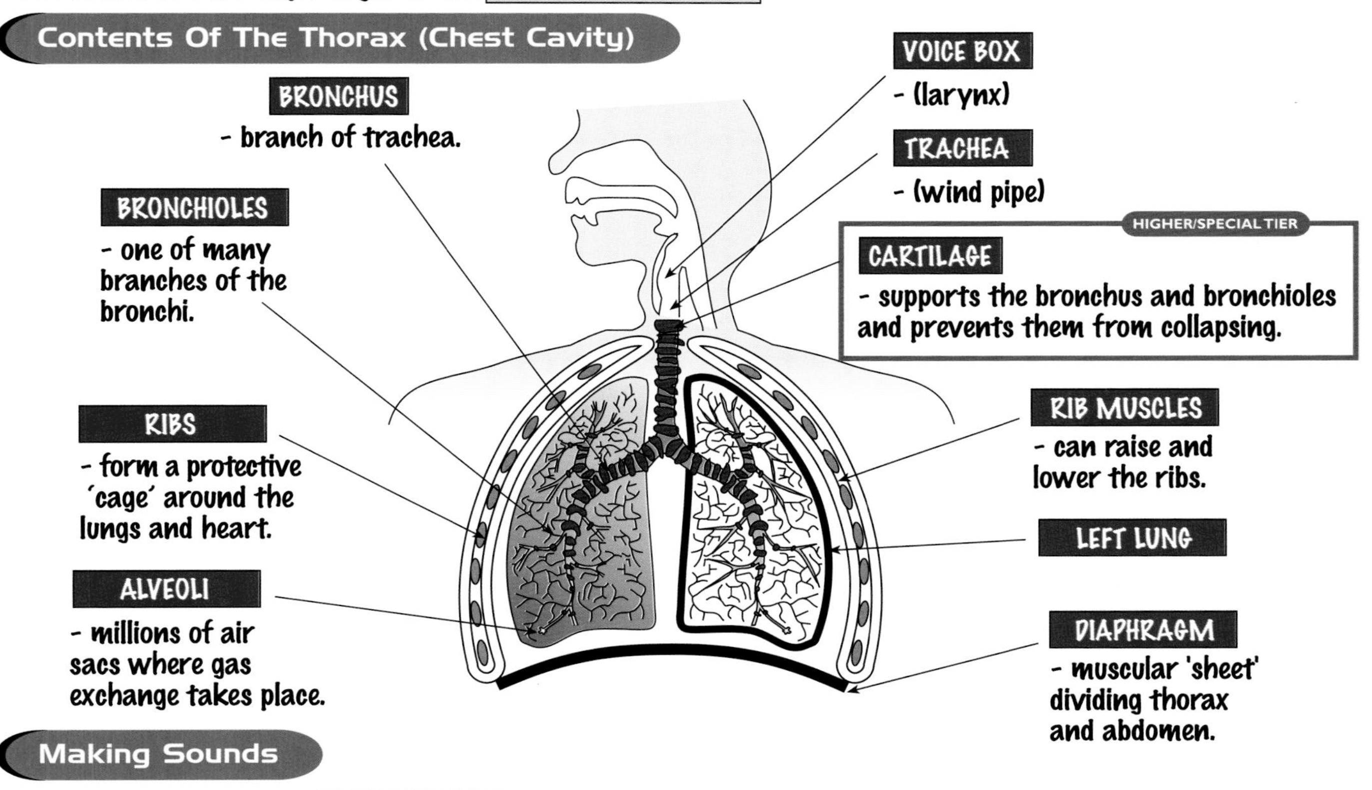

Making Sounds

The **VOICE BOX** contains **VOCAL CORDS** which are fine ligaments.
The **VOCAL CORDS** are controlled by muscles which alter the **TENSION** and the **DISTANCE** between the cords.
As **AIR** passes over the **VOCAL CORDS** the cords vibrate and produce different **SOUNDS.**

Gas Exchange Between The Alveoli And Capillaries

In the **ALVEOLUS** ...

- **CARBON DIOXIDE DIFFUSES** from the **BLOOD INTO THE ALVEOLUS.**
- **OXYGEN DIFFUSES** from the **ALVEOLUS INTO THE BLOOD.**

This process is called **GAS EXCHANGE.**

The blood **LEAVING THE LUNGS** is now **RICH IN OXYGEN** and returns to the heart to be pumped around the body.

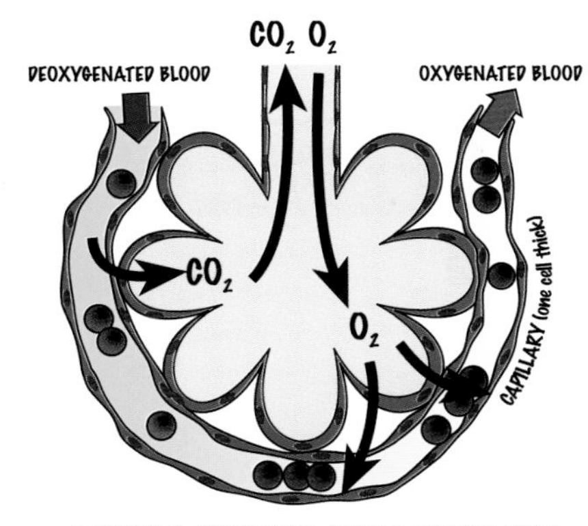

A SINGLE ALVEOLUS AND A CAPILLARY

HIGHER/SPECIAL TIER

BRANCH OF THE PULMONARY VEIN
CAPILLARIES
ALVEOLI
BRANCH OF THE PULMONARY ARTERY

- The **TRACHEA** divides into two tubes called the **BRONCHI** ...
... which divide many times to form the **BRONCHIOLES** ...
... which continue to divide until they form tiny air sacs called the **ALVEOLI.**

The **ALVEOLI** are **SPECIALLY ADAPTED** for their job of exchanging gases.

- They have a **MASSIVE SURFACE AREA,** ...
... a **MOIST, PERMEABLE SURFACE** (only one cell thick) ...
... and a **VERY GOOD BLOOD SUPPLY.**

In ventilation we must first make the volume of the thorax (chest) larger, in order to breathe air in. Then we make the volume smaller again in order to breathe air out ...

Inhaling

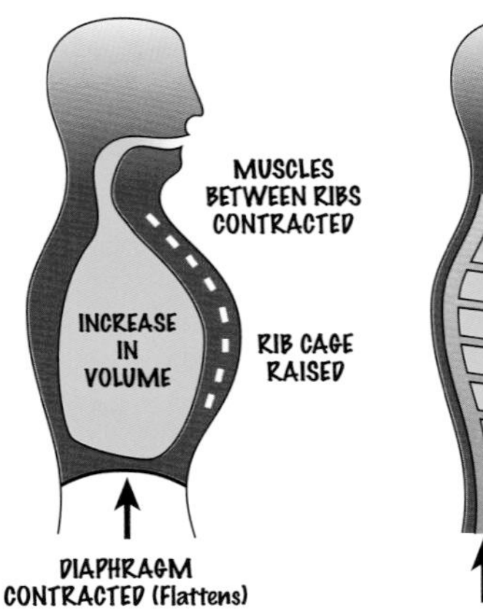

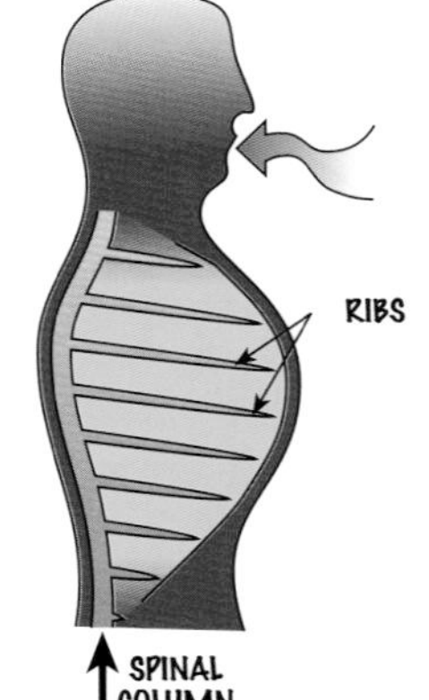

TWO things happen to make the volume of the thorax larger ...

1. The **DIAPHRAGM** contracts, and therefore flattens.
2. The muscles between the ribs contract causing each of the ribs to swing upwards and outwards - rather like the handle of a bucket.

This increase in the volume of the thorax causes air to enter the lungs.

Exhaling

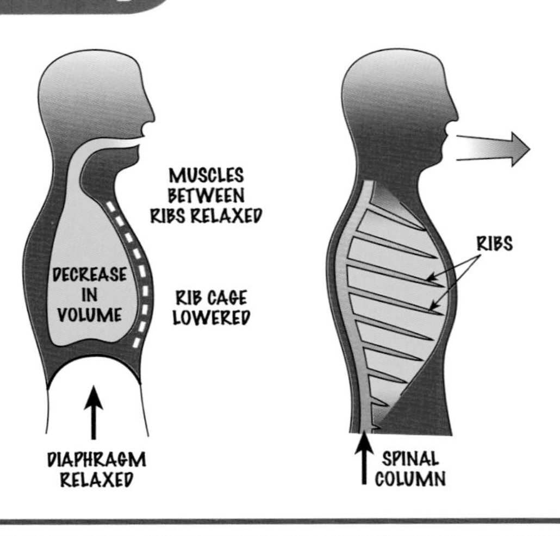

TWO things happen to reduce the volume of the thorax ...

1. The **DIAPHRAGM** relaxes and resumes its former position.
2. The muscles between the ribs relax causing the ribs to swing downwards and inwards.

This decrease in the volume of the thorax causes air to leave the lungs.

HIGHER/SPECIAL TIER

Ventilation In Terms Of Pressure And Volume

INHALING

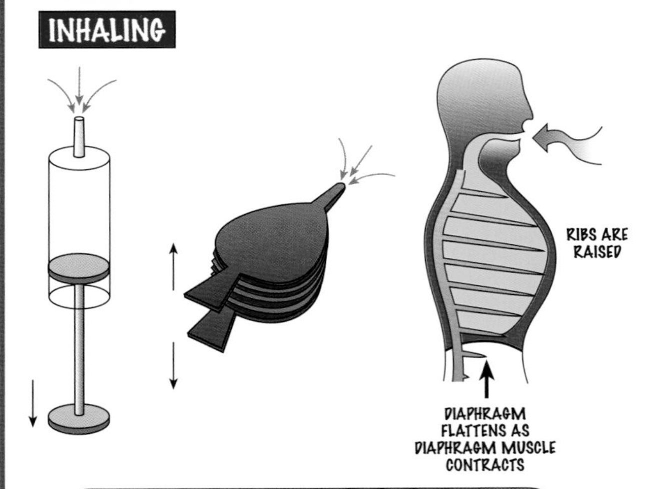

AN INCREASE IN VOLUME CAUSES A DECREASE IN PRESSURE - and air enters, because atmospheric pressure is higher than the pressure of air in the lungs.

EXHALING

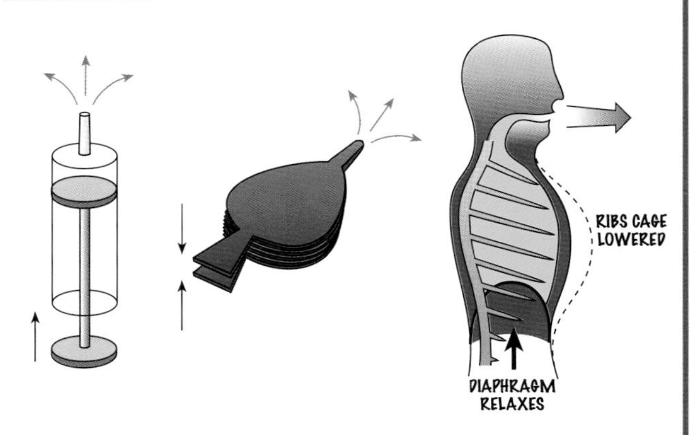

A DECREASE IN VOLUME CAUSES AN INCREASE IN PRESSURE - and air is forced out, because atmospheric pressure is lower than the pressure of air in the lungs.

Changes In Oxygen And Carbon Dioxide

- The AIR we BREATHE OUT ...
  ... contains LESS OXYGEN.
  and MORE CARBON DIOXIDE ...
  ... than the air we breathe in.
- AIR we BREATHE OUT has ...
  ... more MOISTURE and a HIGHER TEMPERATURE ...
  ... than the air we breathe in.

Type of Air	% of Oxygen	% of Carbon Dioxide	% of Nitrogen
Inhaled Air	21	0.03	78
Exhaled Air	17	4	78

Effect Of Exercise On The Heart Rate And Breathing

- During exercise ...
  ... the PULSE RATE INCREASES ...
  ... the BREATHING RATE INCREASES and ...
  ... the VOLUME OF EACH BREATH INCREASES.
- This means that ...
  ... OXYGEN and FOOD are delivered to the cells faster and ...
  ... WASTE and CARBON DIOXIDE are removed more quickly.

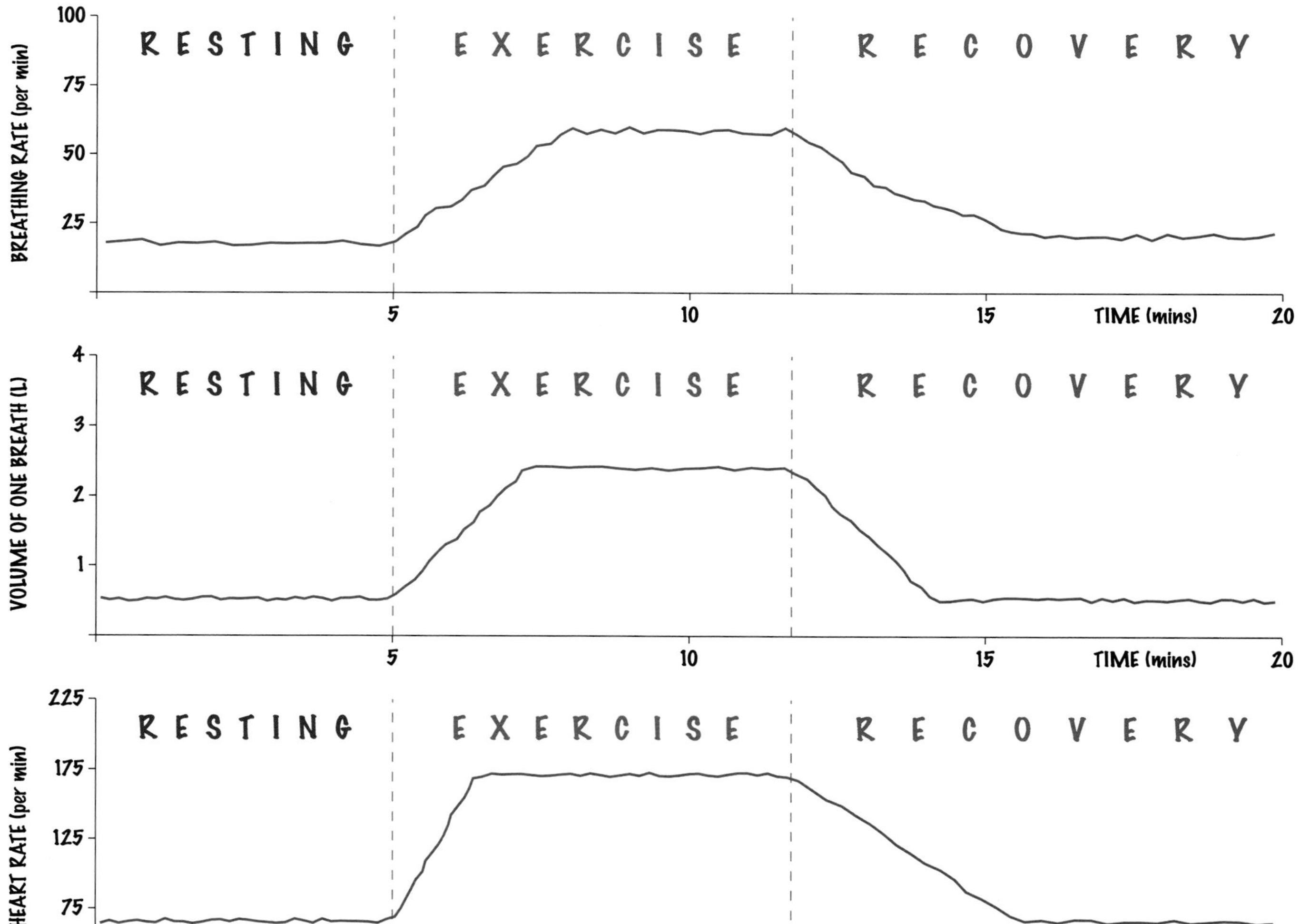

- The fitter a person is, the quicker he will return to his resting 'rates' after exercise i.e. he recovers more quickly.

Aerobic Respiration

- AEROBIC RESPIRATION is THE RELEASE OF ENERGY FROM THE BREAKDOWN OF GLUCOSE ...
  ... BY COMBINING IT WITH OXYGEN ... INSIDE LIVING CELLS.

THE EQUATION: **GLUCOSE + OXYGEN**  **CARBON DIOXIDE + WATER + ENERGY**

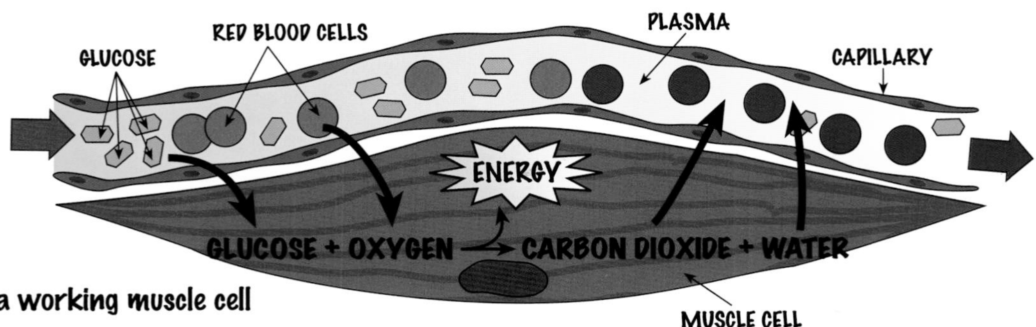

EXAMPLE: a working muscle cell

- The energy is contained INSIDE THE GLUCOSE molecule, and comes from the food we eat.
- The oxygen has come from the atmosphere, via the lungs.
- The two are combined together inside living cells to produce ENERGY.
- Respiration is a process that goes on in every cell in the body ...
  ... to release energy from food.
- The more work a cell does, the more energy it needs ...
  ... and therefore the more glucose and oxygen it requires.
- This is why we breathe harder and our hearts pump faster when we exercise.
- But remember ... respiration DOESN'T mean breathing in and out ...
  ... that's ventilation and is dealt with on page 30!

AEROBIC RESPIRATION PRODUCES LOTS MORE ENERGY THAN ANAEROBIC RESPIRATION.

How Cells Use Energy

The energy released during respiration is used in the following ways ...

REMEMBER THE "M"s

- **METABOLISM** - building up larger molecules from smaller ones and vice versa.
- **MUSCLE CONTRACTION** - energy for the muscle cells and the nerves which supply them.
- **MAINTENANCE OF TEMPERATURE** - 'Waste' energy given off as heat.

HIGHER/SPECIAL TIER

- **MEMBRANES** across which materials are **ACTIVELY** transported against a diffusion gradient (see p.13).

The Role Of Mitochondria

Mitochondria are found in greater numbers in fast respiring cells ...

... because they are the SITE OF AEROBIC RESPIRATION.

They absorb glucose and oxygen and provide energy which is transferred in cells.

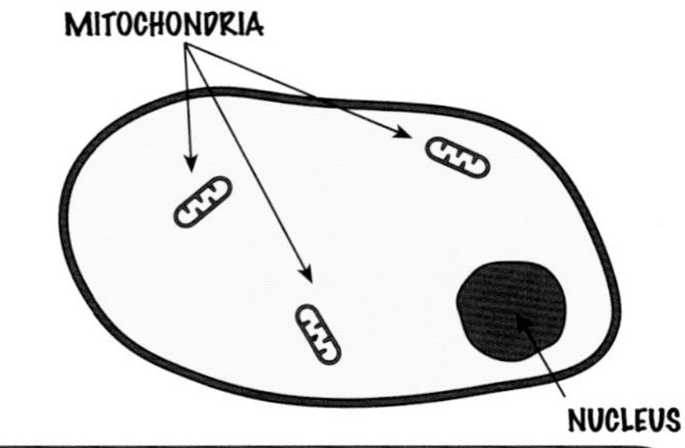

The symbol equation for AEROBIC RESPIRATION is ...

$$C_6H_{12}O_6 + 6O_2 \longrightarrow 6CO_2 + 6H_2O + \text{ENERGY}$$

Anaerobic Respiration

In a nutshell, this means:-

- THE RELEASE OF A LITTLE BIT OF ENERGY FROM THE INCOMPLETE BREAKDOWN OF GLUCOSE.
- .... in the ABSENCE OF OXYGEN ...
- ... INSIDE THE CYTOPLASM OF LIVING CELLS.

THE EQUATION: GLUCOSE ⟹ A BIT OF ENERGY + LACTIC ACID

It's quite important to realise that ANAEROBIC RESPIRATION ...
... is NOT an alternative to AEROBIC RESPIRATION.

ANAEROBIC RESPIRATION is just the first few stages of a much longer sequence of chemical reactions which can only be fully completed in the presence of a good oxygen supply.

This type of respiration leaves lots of energy 'untouched' in the lactic acid!
It provides about 1/20 th as much energy as aerobic respiration from each glucose molecule ...
... but that might be critical in an emergency!

When It Happens

- Anaerobic respiration happens when the muscles are working so hard that ...
- ... the lungs and bloodstream can't deliver enough OXYGEN, to respire the available glucose aerobically.
- Therefore the GLUCOSE can only be partly broken down, releasing a much smaller amount of energy ...
- ... and LACTIC ACID as a waste product. It can only operate for a short time.

HIGHER/SPECIAL TIER

- Accumulation of lactic acid gives you that "rubbery" legs feeling ...
- ... and you incur an "OXYGEN DEBT" that must be repaid by continued deep breathing after exercise.
- This oxidises some of the lactic acid to carbon dioxide and water, which provides enough energy to convert the remaining lactic acid back to glycogen for storage.

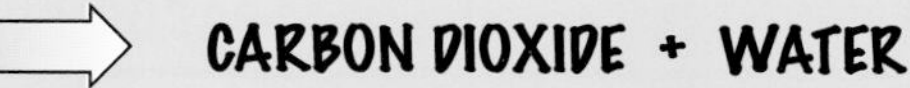

- Because the breakdown of glucose is incomplete MUCH LESS ENERGY IS PRODUCED by this method.

Anaerobic Respiration In Yeast

1. THE BREWING INDUSTRY

In yeast anaerobic respiration produces ALCOHOL and CARBON DIOXIDE.

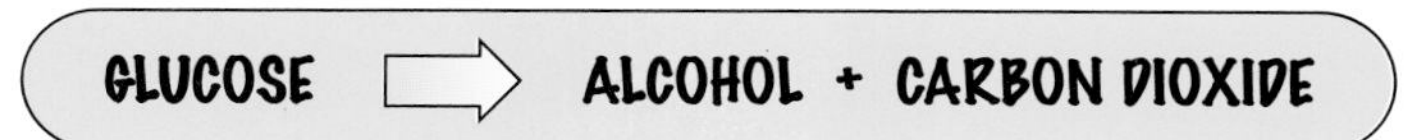

The level of alcohol eventually builds up and kills the yeast that formed it.
This limits the alcoholic strength of wines etc. which are produced by FERMENTATION.

2. THE BAKING INDUSTRY

This same reaction is used to produce CARBON DIOXIDE in dough ...
... in order to make bread rise.
The alcohol is evaporated off by heating.

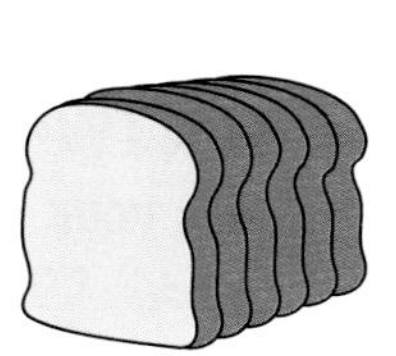

Circulation

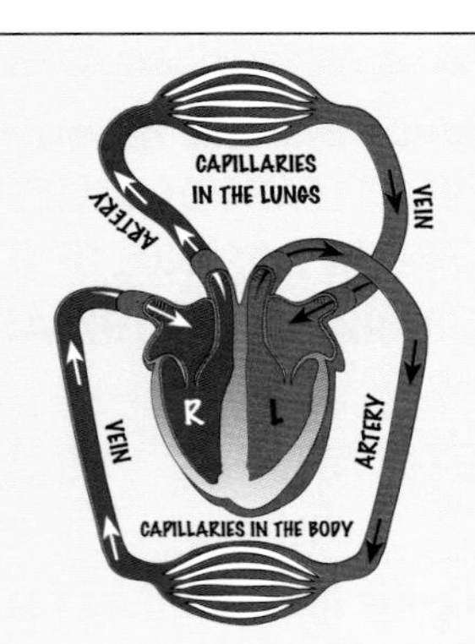

- The CIRCULATORY SYSTEM transports substances around the body.
- It consists of two loops - one taking blood from the heart to the lungs and back, and the other taking blood around the body.

HIGHER/SPECIAL TIER

- The advantage of the double circulatory system is the higher pressure and greater rate of bloodflow around the body.

- The HEART pumps blood around the body and consists of four chambers - two atria and two ventricles.
- VALVES in the heart prevent blood flowing backwards.
- The ARTERIES have thick walls and no valves - they take blood AWAY from the HEART.
- The VEINS have thinner walls and valves to prevent back flow of blood - they take blood TOWARDS the heart.

- CAPILLARIES are very thin - walled blood vessels and allow exchange of substances.
- RED BLOOD CELLS contain HAEMOGLOBIN and transport oxygen around the body.
- WHITE BLOOD CELLS defend the body by INGESTING MICROBES and producing ANTIBODIES and ANTITOXINS.
- PLASMA transports carbon dioxide, soluble products of digestion, urea and hormones.
- PLATELETS take part in the process that CLOTS THE BLOOD

Breathing

- The BREATHING SYSTEM takes air into and out of the body.
- When a person INHALES the RIB CAGE moves UPWARDS and the DIAPHRAGM FLATTENS.

HIGHER/SPECIAL TIER

- This increases the volume of the thorax and reduces the internal pressure.

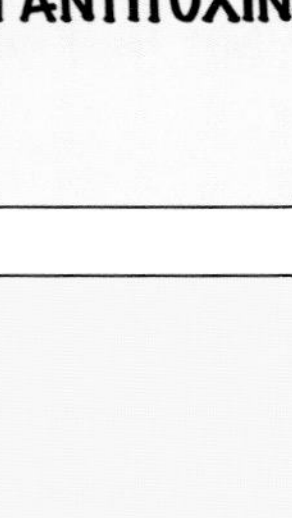

- When a person EXHALES the RIB CAGE moves DOWNWARDS and the DIAPHRAGM ARCHES UPWARDS.

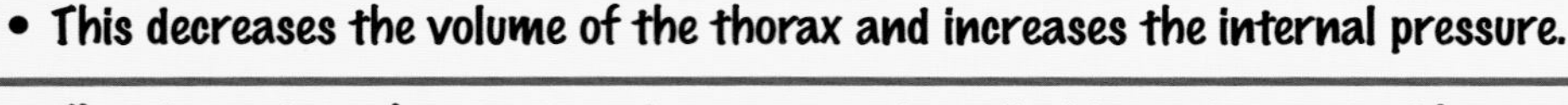

HIGHER/SPECIAL TIER

- This decreases the volume of the thorax and increases the internal pressure.

- The air we breathe out contains more carbon dioxide, moisture, and less oxygen than the air we breath in. It is also warmer.
- In the alveolus OXYGEN diffuses INTO the blood and CARBON DIOXIDE diffuses OUT.

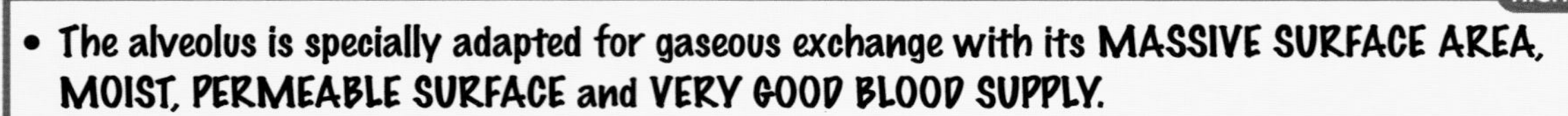

HIGHER/SPECIAL TIER

- The alveolus is specially adapted for gaseous exchange with its MASSIVE SURFACE AREA, MOIST, PERMEABLE SURFACE and VERY GOOD BLOOD SUPPLY.

- A fit person's PULSE RATE and BREATHING VOLUME return to normal quickly after exercise.

Respiration

- RESPIRATION involving Oxygen is called AEROBIC RESPIRATION and can be summarised as:

GLUCOSE + OXYGEN ⟹ CARBON DIOXIDE + WATER + ENERGY

- Energy released during respiration is used to: enable MUSCLES TO CONTRACT, keep a STEADY BODY TEMPERATURE, BUILD UP LARGE MOLECULES and for ACTIVE TRANSPORT.
- ANAEROBIC RESPIRATION is the release of energy from food in the ABSENCE of OXYGEN.

HIGHER/SPECIAL TIER

- An OXYGEN DEBT produced DURING VIGOROUS EXERCISE is due to the build up of LACTIC ACID which must be oxidised to Carbon Dioxide and water during recovery.

Record the TWELVE 'Circulation', NINE 'Breathing' and the FOUR 'Respiration' facts onto your tape.
Now - READ, COVER, WRITE and CHECK the TWENTY FIVE facts.

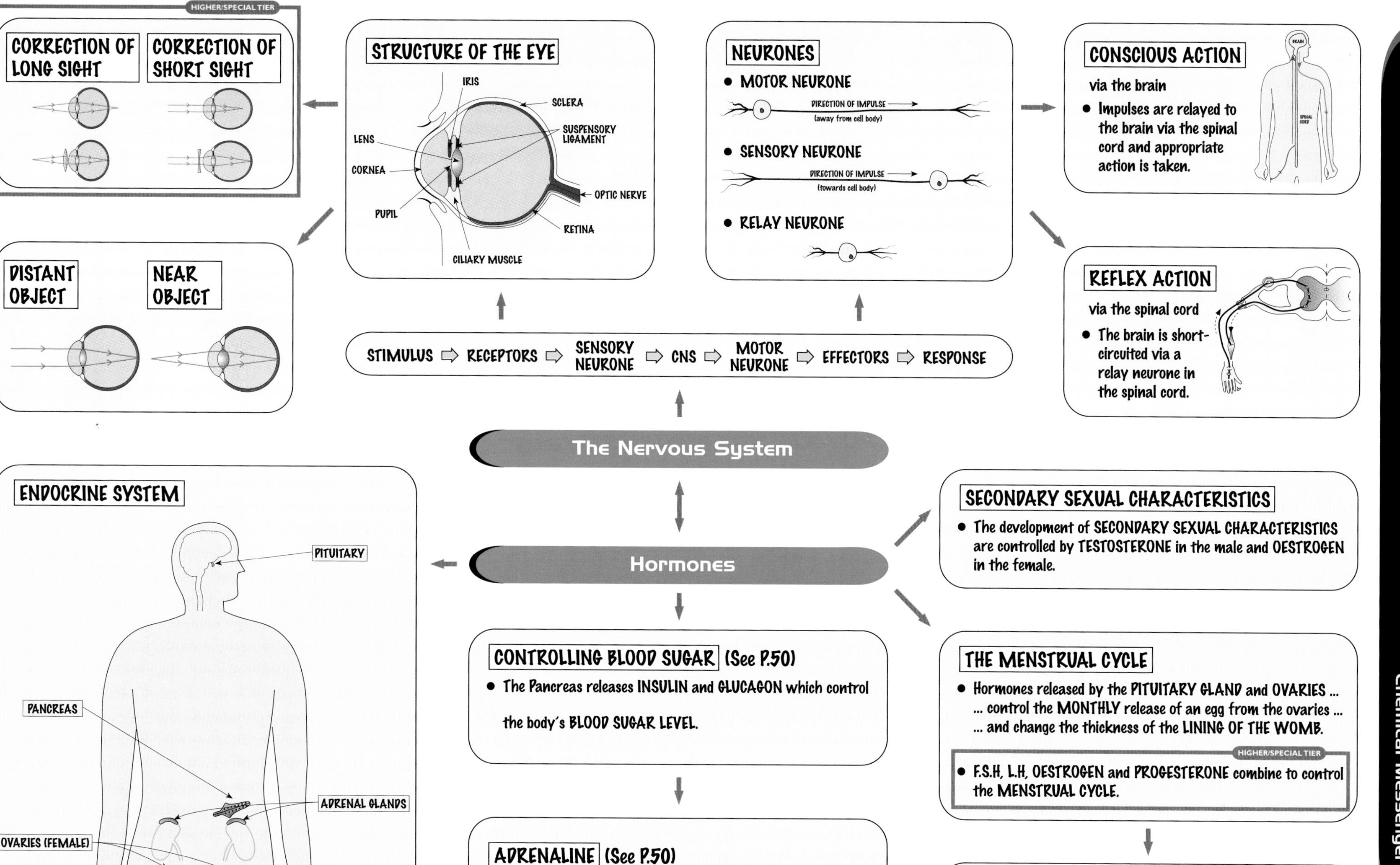
HIGHER/SPECIAL TIER
CORRECTION OF LONG SIGHT
CORRECTION OF SHORT SIGHT
DISTANT OBJECT
NEAR OBJECT
STRUCTURE OF THE EYE
IRIS
SCLERA
LENS
SUSPENSORY LIGAMENT
CORNEA
OPTIC NERVE
PUPIL
RETINA
CILIARY MUSCLE
NEURONES
MOTOR NEURONE
DIRECTION OF IMPULSE
(away from cell body)
SENSORY NEURONE
DIRECTION OF IMPULSE
(towards cell body)
RELAY NEURONE
CONSCIOUS ACTION
via the brain
Impulses are relayed to the brain via the spinal cord and appropriate action is taken.
BRAIN
SPINAL CORD
REFLEX ACTION
via the spinal cord
The brain is short-circuited via a relay neurone in the spinal cord.
STIMULUS ⇨ RECEPTORS ⇨ SENSORY NEURONE ⇨ CNS ⇨ MOTOR NEURONE ⇨ EFFECTORS ⇨ RESPONSE
The Nervous System
Hormones
ENDOCRINE SYSTEM
PITUITARY
PANCREAS
ADRENAL GLANDS
OVARIES (FEMALE)
TESTES (MALE)
SECONDARY SEXUAL CHARACTERISTICS
The development of SECONDARY SEXUAL CHARACTERISTICS are controlled by TESTOSTERONE in the male and OESTROGEN in the female.
CONTROLLING BLOOD SUGAR (See P.50)
The Pancreas releases INSULIN and GLUCAGON which control the body's BLOOD SUGAR LEVEL.
THE MENSTRUAL CYCLE
Hormones released by the PITUITARY GLAND and OVARIES ...
... control the MONTHLY release of an egg from the ovaries ...
... and change the thickness of the LINING OF THE WOMB.
HIGHER/SPECIAL TIER
F.S.H, L.H, OESTROGEN and PROGESTERONE combine to control the MENSTRUAL CYCLE.
ADRENALINE (See P.50)
Prepares the body for stressful situations.
HIGHER/SPECIAL TIER
Increases blood sugar level and pulse rate.
CONTROLLING FERTILITY
Hormones can be used to ...
... PROMOTE the RELEASE OF EGGS
... INHIBIT the RELEASE OF EGGS
HIGHER/SPECIAL TIER
(F.S.H.)
(OESTROGEN)

Reflex Action

- The nervous system consists of the **BRAIN**, the **SPINAL CORD**, the **PAIRED PERIPHERAL NERVES** and **RECEPTORS**.
- It allows organisms to **REACT TO THEIR SURROUNDINGS** and ...
  ... to **COORDINATE THEIR BEHAVIOUR**.
- The **FIVE SENSES**, namely **SEEING**, **HEARING**, **TASTING**, **SMELLING** and **TOUCHING** play a very important part in these processes.

Components Of The Nervous System

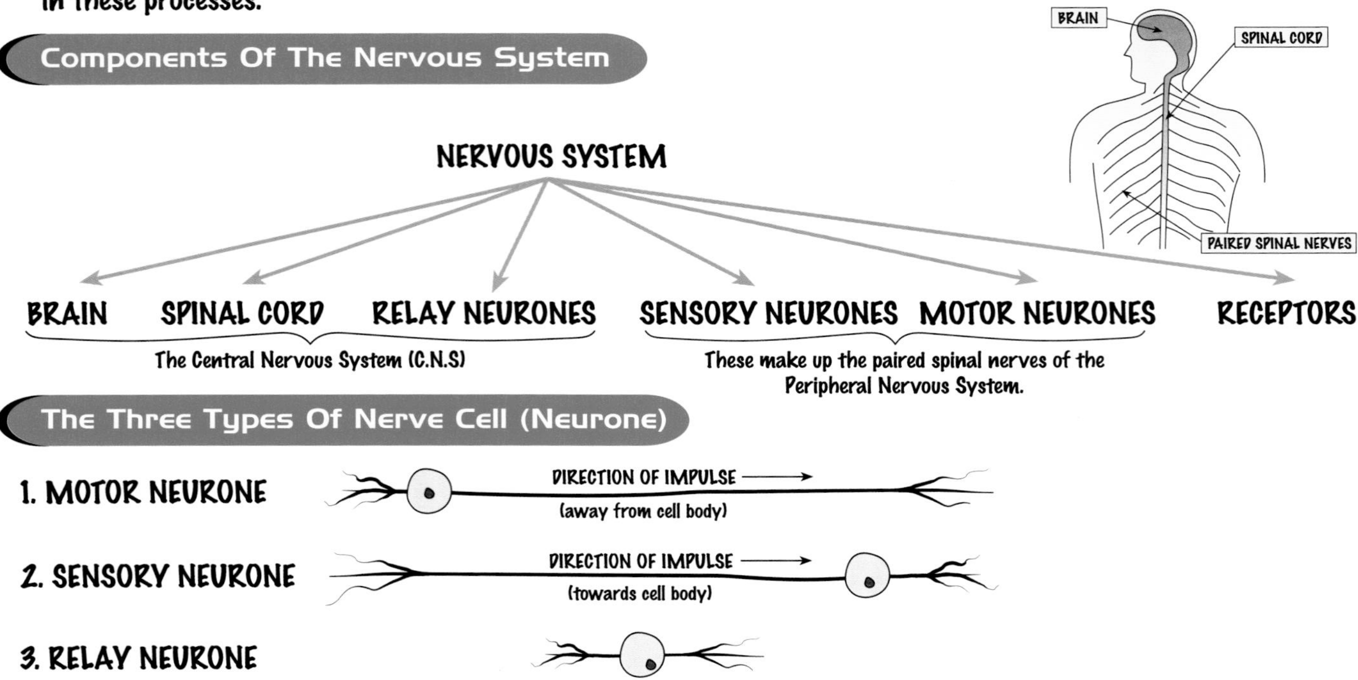

The Three Types Of Nerve Cell (Neurone)

1. **MOTOR NEURONE**
2. **SENSORY NEURONE**
3. **RELAY NEURONE**

HIGHER/SPECIAL TIER

Neurones In More Detail

NEURONES are **SPECIALLY ADAPTED CELLS** that can carry an **ELECTRICAL SIGNAL**, e.g. a **NERVE IMPULSE**.

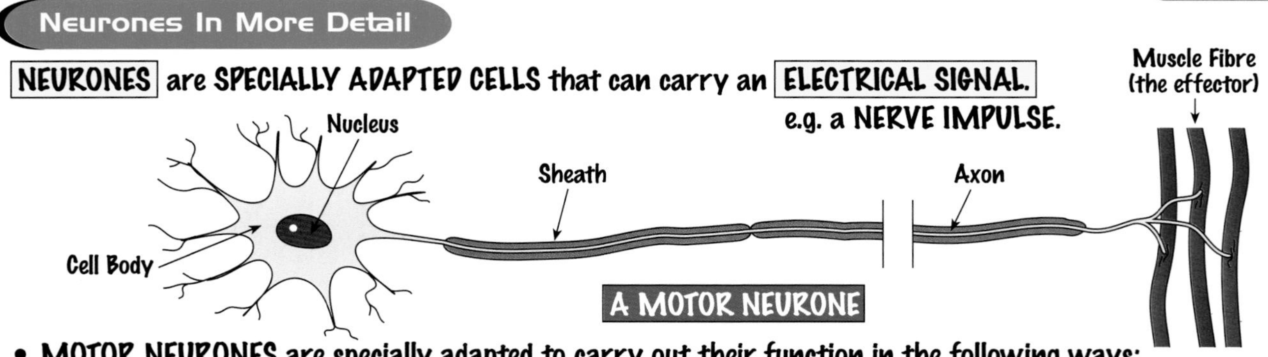

- **MOTOR NEURONES** are specially adapted to carry out their function in the following ways:
  They are **ELONGATED** (long) to **MAKE CONNECTIONS** from one part of the body to another.
  They have an **INSULATING SHEATH** which **SPEEDS UP THE NERVE IMPULSE** ...
  They have **BRANCHED ENDINGS** which allows a **SINGLE NEURONE** to act on **MANY MUSCLE FIBRES**.
  The cell body has many connections to allow communication with other neurones.

Connections Between Neurones

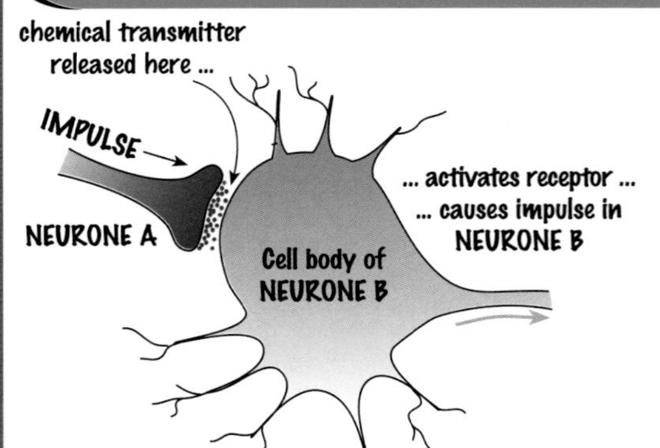

- Neurones do **NOT TOUCH EACH OTHER** ...
- ... there is a very small gap between them ...
- ... called a **SYNAPSE**.
- When an electrical impulse reaches this gap via neurone A a **CHEMICAL TRANSMITTER** ...
- ... is released and activates receptors on **NEURONE B** ...
- ... which causes an electrical **IMPULSE** to be generated in **NEURONE B**.
- The **CHEMICAL TRANSMITTER** is then **IMMEDIATELY DESTROYED**.

Types Of Receptor

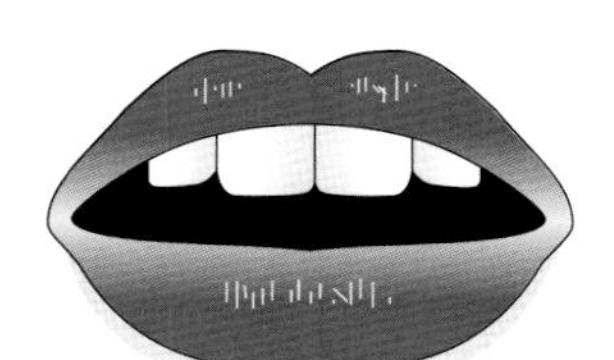

- LIGHT RECEPTORS IN THE EYES.
- SOUND RECEPTORS IN THE EARS.
- CHANGES OF POSITION RECEPTORS IN THE EARS (for balance).
- TASTE RECEPTORS ON THE TONGUE.
- SMELL RECEPTORS IN THE NOSE.
- PRESSURE AND TEMPERATURE RECEPTORS IN THE SKIN.

The pathways for receiving information and then acting upon it is:

Examples Of Responses To Stimuli

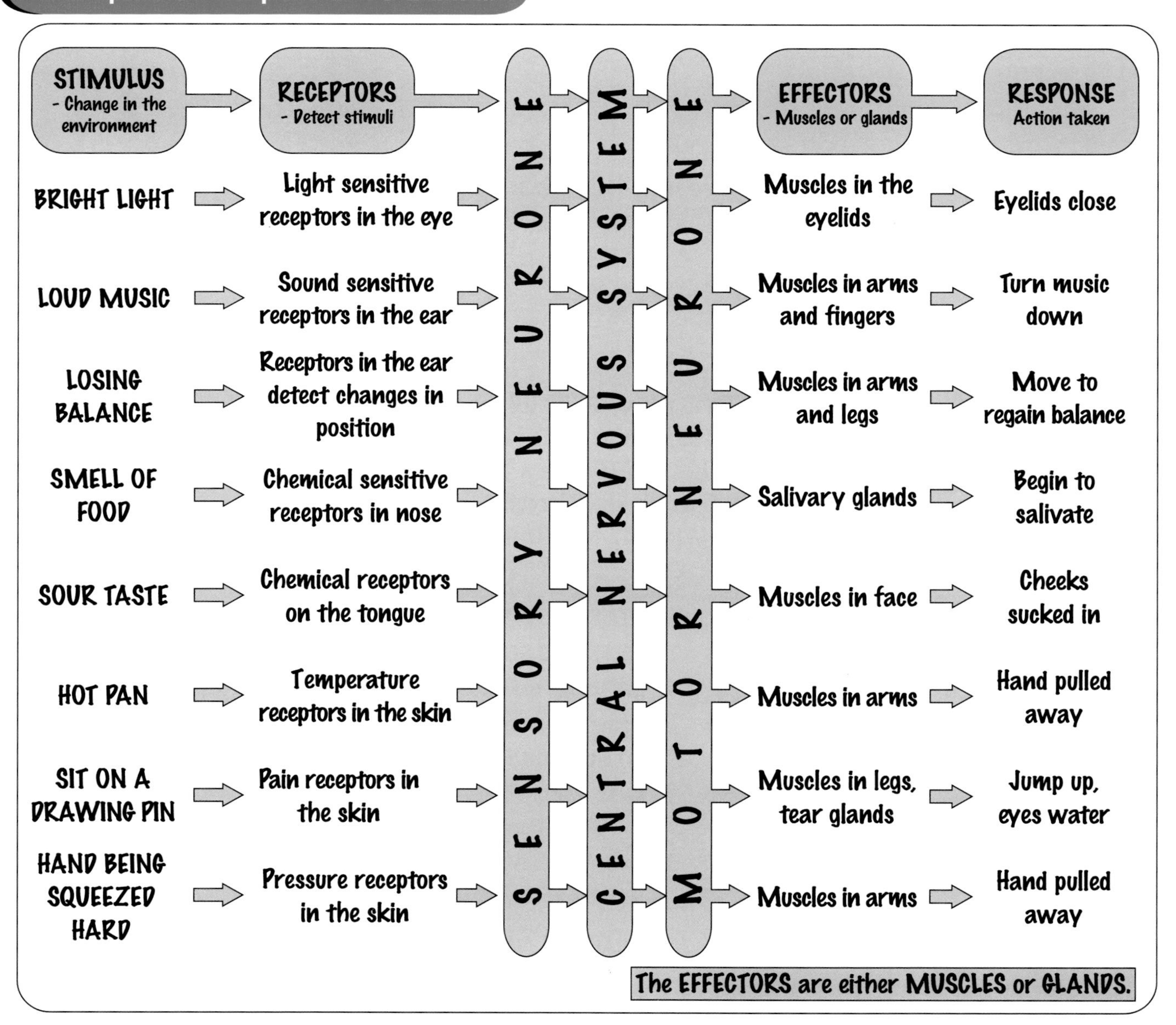

These responses can be either ...

... CONSCIOUS RESPONSES, or ...

... REFLEX RESPONSES (see next page).

Conscious Action

After receiving a stimulus the body can make a considered response, i.e. it acts consciously in making its response

4. The brain (part of the Central Nervous System) thinks about this and decides to flick the insect away with the left hand ...

3. ... spinal cord (part of the Central Nervous System). Here, another SENSORY NEURONE carries the impulse to the brain.

2. ... these cause an impulse to travel along a SENSORY NEURONE to the ...

1. RECEPTORS in the skin of your thigh detect an insect crawling on you ...

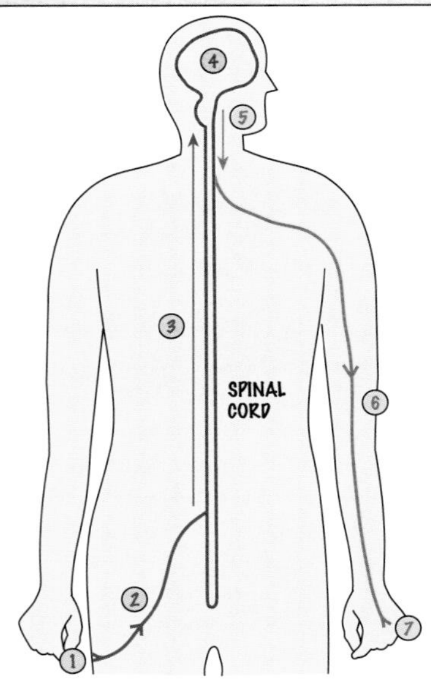

5. An impulse is sent down a MOTOR NEURONE in the spinal cord ...

6. ... and causes an impulse to be sent out of the spinal cord via another MOTOR NEURONE ...

7. ... to a muscle (an EFFECTOR) in the hand. This causes the hand to move and flick away the insect (a RESPONSE).

This pathway for receiving information and then acting upon it is:

STIMULUS	RECEPTOR	SENSORY NEURONE	COORDINATOR (ANALYSER)	MOTOR NEURONE	EFFECTOR	RESPONSE
Insect crawling on skin	Pressure receptor in skin	Nerve from skin receptor	Brain via spinal cord	Nerve to muscle	Muscle in hand	Flick insect away

Reflex Action

Reflexes are usually DEFENCE MECHANISMS which SPEED UP your RESPONSE TIME by SHORT CIRCUITING THE BRAIN, e.g. BLINKING, COUGHING, WITHDRAWAL FROM PAIN.

- The SPINAL CORD acts as the COORDINATOR via a third special neurone within it.
- This is called a RELAY NEURONE which 'short circuits' the brain ...
- ... by passing IMPULSES from a SENSORY NEURONE directly to a MOTOR NEURONE.

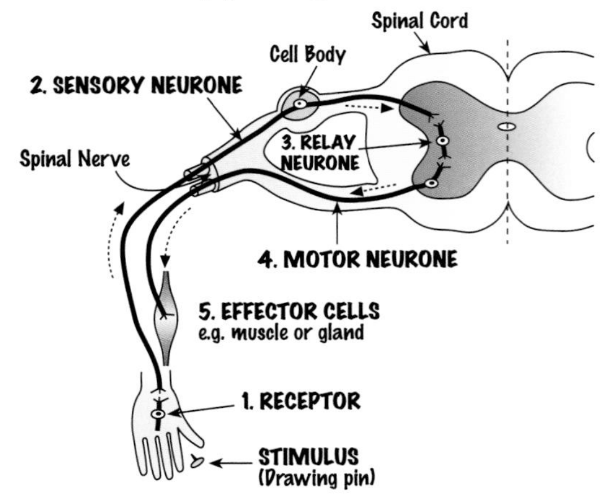

STAGES OF REFLEX ACTION

STAGES OF REFLEX ACTION

1. RECEPTORS STIMULATED by a SHARP DRAWING PIN.
2. IMPULSES pass along a SENSORY NEURONE into the SPINAL CORD.
3. Sensory neurone SYNAPSES with a RELAY NEURONE, 'short circuiting' the BRAIN.
4. Relay neurone SYNAPSES with a MOTOR NEURONE, sending IMPULSES down the MOTOR NEURONE.
5. These impulses reach MUSCLES causing them to CONTRACT ... bringing about a RESPONSE e.g. moving the hand away.

THIS HAPPENS AUTOMATICALLY - WITHOUT CONSCIOUS THOUGHT.

This pathway can be analysed in the following way.

STIMULUS	RECEPTOR	SENSORY NEURONE	COORDINATOR (ANALYSER)	MOTOR NEURONE	EFFECTOR	RESPONSE
Drawing pin	Pain receptor	Nerve from receptor	Relay neuron in spinal cord	Nerve to muscle	Muscle in hand	Withdraw hand

The Eye is quite a complicated sense organ which focusses light onto light-sensitive receptor cells in the retina. These are then stimulated and cause nerve impulses to pass along sensory neurones to the brain.

The Structure Of The Eye

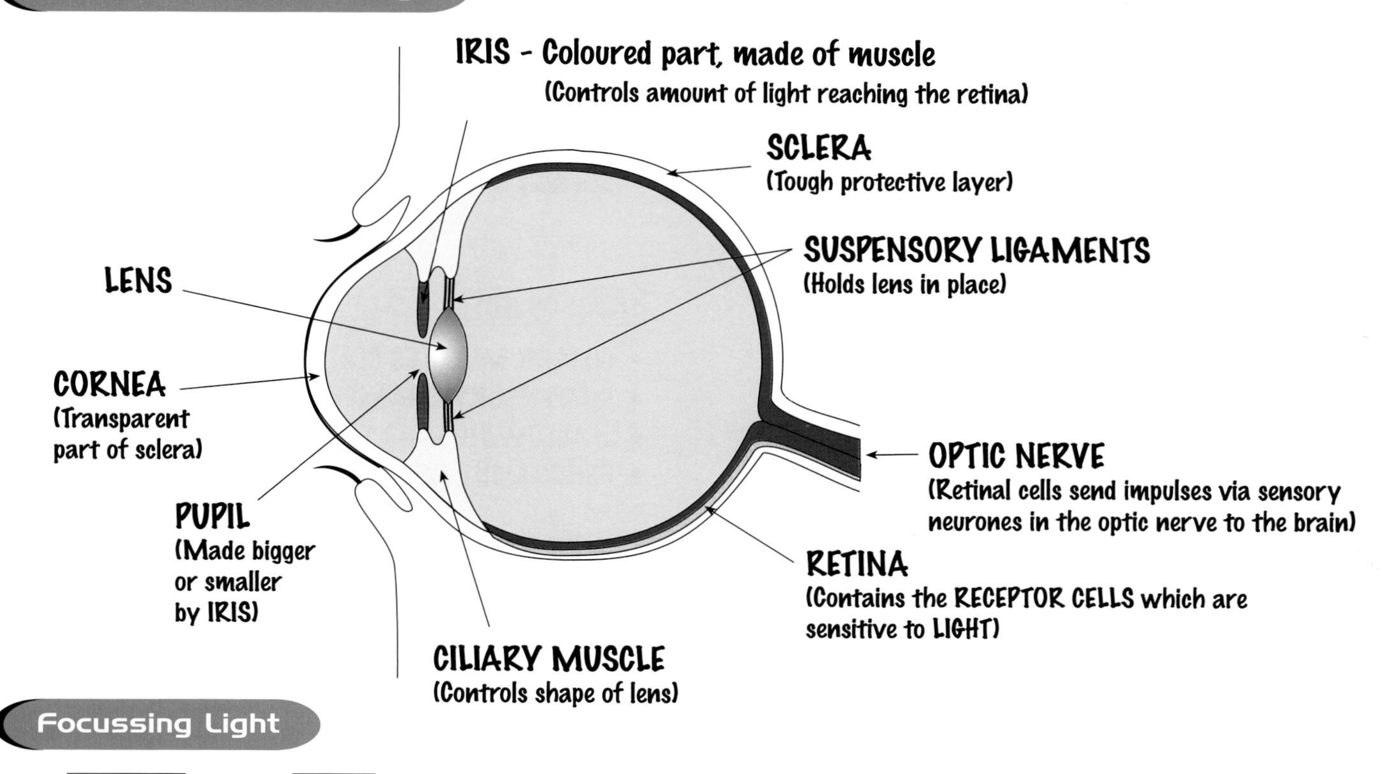

Focussing Light

The CORNEA and the LENS, focus rays of light ...
... so that an IMAGE is formed on the RETINA.

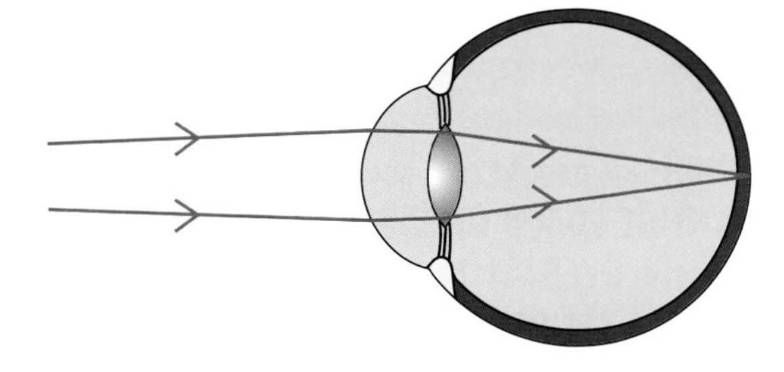

Rays of light are BENT (REFRACTED) BY THE CORNEA.
The rays of light are then ...
... further BENT (REFRACTED) BY THE LENS ...
... to produce a CLEAR IMAGE ...
... on the RETINA.

Controlling The Amount Of Light Entering The Eye

The IRIS consists of muscle tissue which by contraction of various muscle fibres ...
... CONTROLS THE SIZE OF THE PUPIL ...
... and therefore the AMOUNT OF LIGHT ENTERING THE EYE.

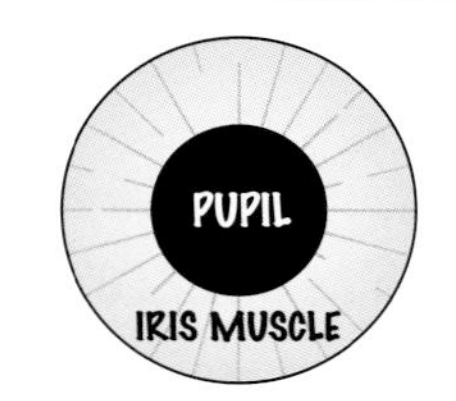

RESPONSE TO DIM LIGHT

RESPONSE TO MODERATE LIGHT

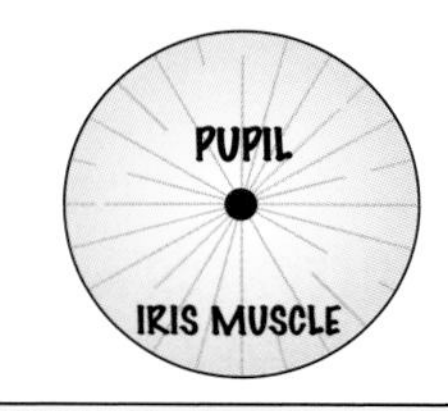

RESPONSE TO BRIGHT LIGHT

HIGHER/SPECIAL TIER

In DIM LIGHT ...
... RADIAL MUSCLES IN THE IRIS CONTRACT ...
... and CIRCULAR MUSCLES RELAX ...
... INCREASING THE SIZE OF THE PUPIL.

In BRIGHT LIGHT ...
... CIRCULAR MUSCLES IN THE IRIS CONTRACT ...
... and RADIAL MUSCLES RELAX ...
... DECREASING THE SIZE OF THE PUPIL.

HIGHER/SPECIAL TIER

Focussing On Objects At Different Distances

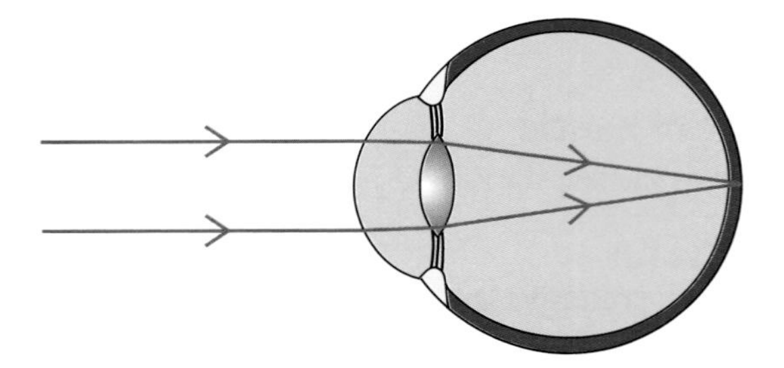

DISTANT OBJECT

- CILIARY MUSCLES RELAX.
- SUSPENSORY LIGAMENTS PULL TIGHT.
- LENS IS PULLED 'THINNER.'
- DOESN'T BEND LIGHT AS MUCH.

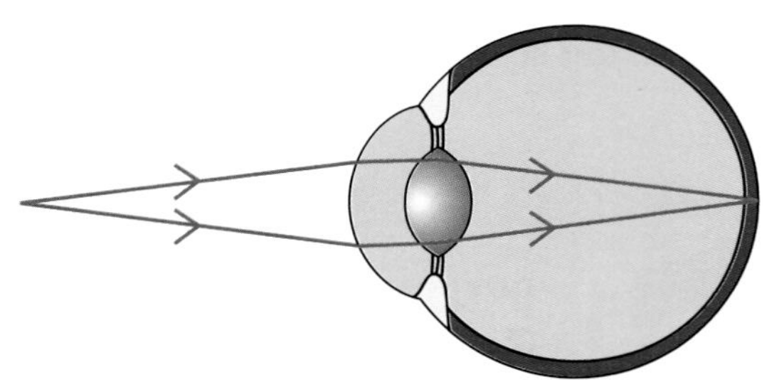

NEAR OBJECT

- CILIARY MUSCLES CONTRACT.
- SUSPENSORY LIGAMENTS GO SLACK ...
- ... ALLOWING LENS TO BECOME 'FATTER'.
- BENDS LIGHT MUCH MORE.

It's important to understand that the **FLUID** in the eye retains the shape of the eye and keeps the **SUSPENSORY LIGAMENTS TIGHT**. The **CILIARY MUSCLES** have to work to overcome this tension which is why eyes get tired after lots of focussing on near objects, e.g. reading.

Apparent And Actual Size

- The **APPARENT SIZE** of an object depends on its **ACTUAL SIZE** and its **DISTANCE FROM THE EYE**.
- A **NEARBY GATE** may **APPEAR** to be **BIGGER** than an oak tree although the **REVERSE IS TRUE**.

Long Sightedness

- **LONG SIGHTED** people can see objects in the **DISTANCE** but ...
  ... **CANNOT FOCUS ON NEAR OBJECTS** ...
  ... because the **EYEBALL IS TOO SHORT** ...
  ... or the **LENS DOES NOT BEND THE RAYS ENOUGH**.

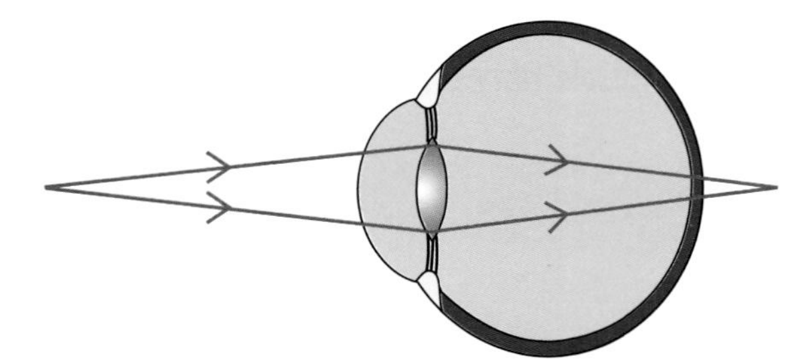

- **LONG SIGHTEDNESS** can be **CORRECTED** ...
  ... using a **CONVEX LENS**.

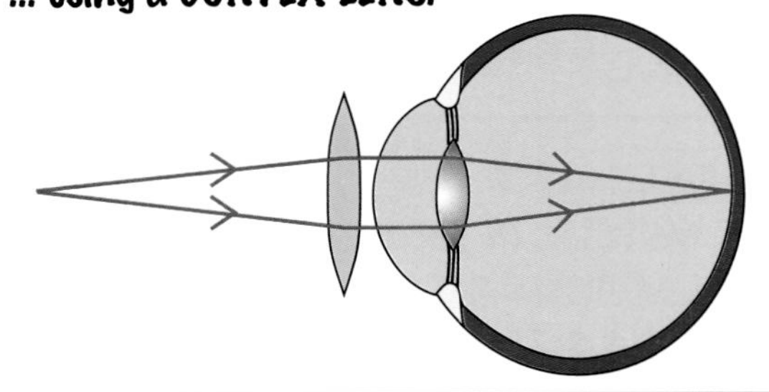

Short Sightedness

- **SHORT SIGHTED** people can see **NEAR OBJECTS** ...
  ... but **CANNOT FOCUS ON DISTANT OBJECTS** ...
  ... because the **EYEBALL IS TOO LONG** ...
  ... or the **LENS BENDS THE RAYS TOO MUCH**.

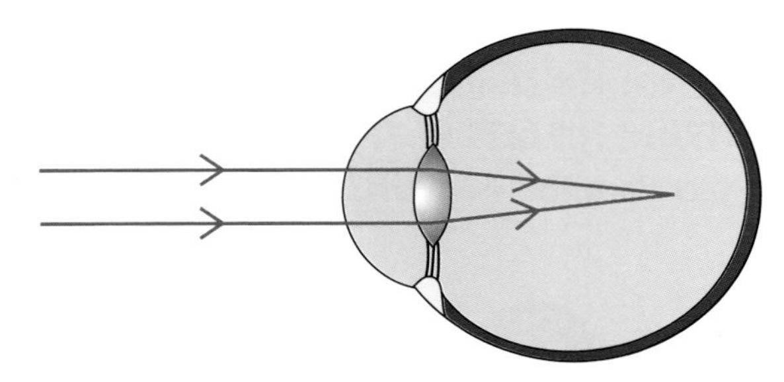

- **SHORT SIGHTEDNESS** can be **CORRECTED** ...
  ... using a **CONCAVE LENS**.

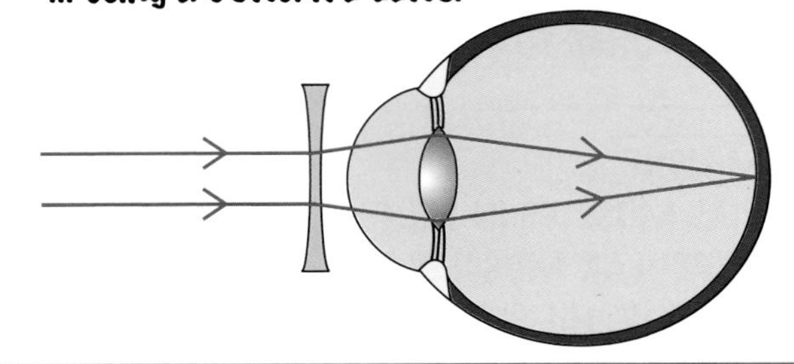

Hormones are chemicals released by the endocrine glands. They are released directly into the blood and travel to their TARGET ORGANS. The actions of hormones are usually slower and more general than those of the Nervous System and their effects tend to be longer lasting. They coordinate things that need constant regulation (see Homeostasis).

The Major Human Endocrine Glands

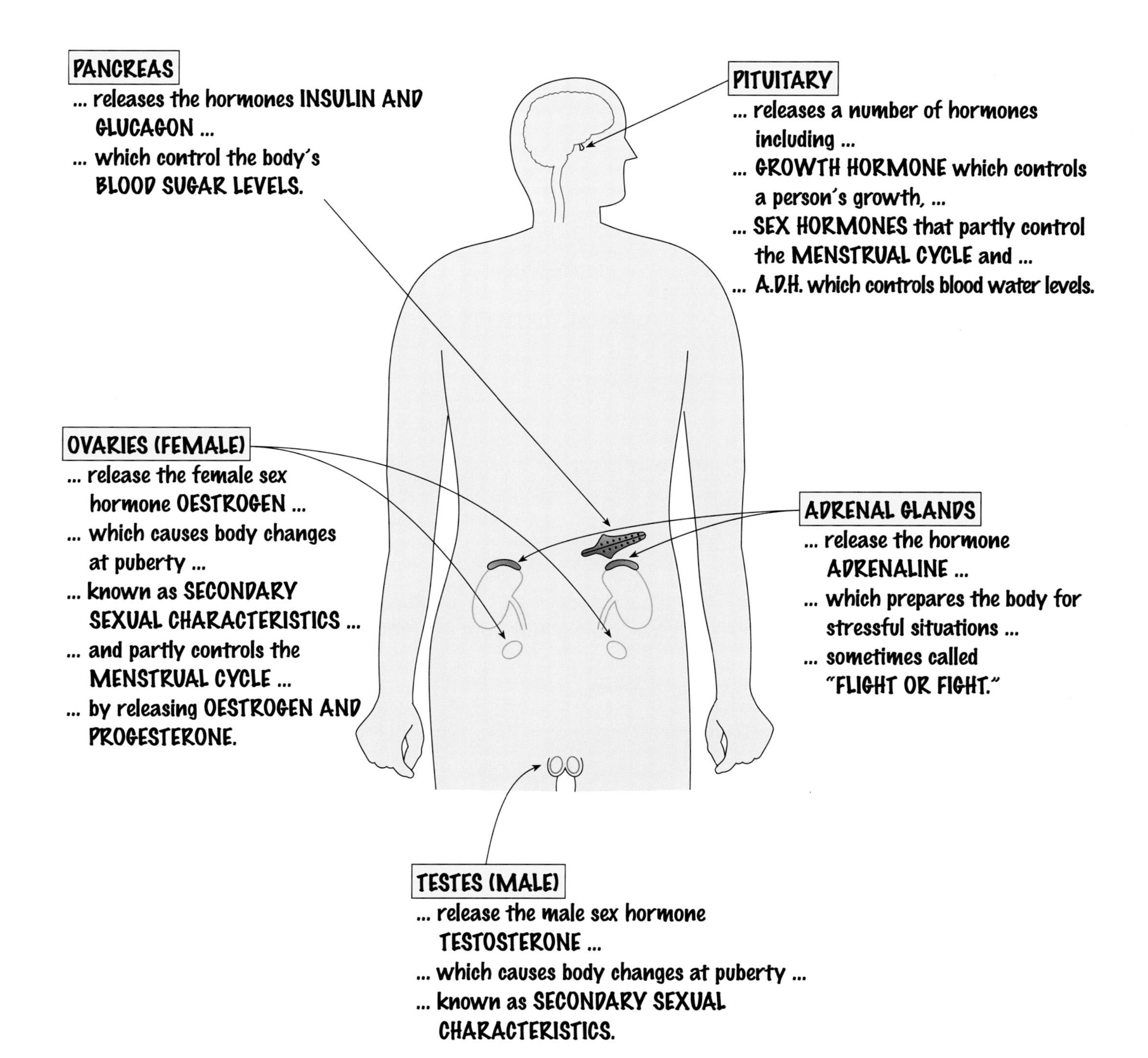

Hormonal Control Compared To Nervous Control

Hormonal control is SLOWER, MORE GENERAL IN ITS EFFECT, AND LONGER ACTING.

Nervous control is FASTER, MORE SPECIFIC IN ITS EFFECT, IMMEDIATE AND SHORTER ACTING.

Secondary Sexual Characteristics

- Between the ages of 10 and 16 in girls, and 12 and 17 in boys ...
- ... the sex organs begin to produce the SEX HORMONES which cause ...
- ... the development of the SECONDARY SEXUAL CHARACTERISTICS (PUBERTY).

GIRL	SEX	BOY
OESTROGEN	HORMONE	TESTOSTERONE
OVARIES	ENDOCRINE GLAND	TESTES
• OVULATION AND MENSTRUATION STARTS (i.e. PERIODS). • GROWTH OF BREASTS, UTERUS AND PELVIS. • GROWTH OF PUBIC HAIR, AND ARMPIT HAIR. • DEVELOPMENT OF SOFTER, ROUNDER SHAPE. • FEELINGS OF ATTRACTION TO OPPOSITE SEX.	EFFECT ON TARGET ORGANS. i.e. DEVELOPMENT OF SECONDARY SEXUAL CHARACTERISTICS.	• PRODUCTION OF SPERM. • GROWTH OF MUSCLES AND PENIS. • VOICE BECOMES DEEPER. • GROWTH OF PUBIC HAIR, FACIAL HAIR AND BODY HAIR. • FEELINGS OF ATTRACTION TO OPPOSITE SEX.

All these changes take place relatively slowly unlike a NERVOUS RESPONSE!
Oestrogen together with other hormones also plays a large part in the menstrual cycle.

The Menstrual Cycle

Between the ages of approximately 13 and 50, a woman is fertile and the lining of her uterus is replaced every month. This is a PERIOD. We can represent the changes in the uterus wall which occur over 28 days like this ...

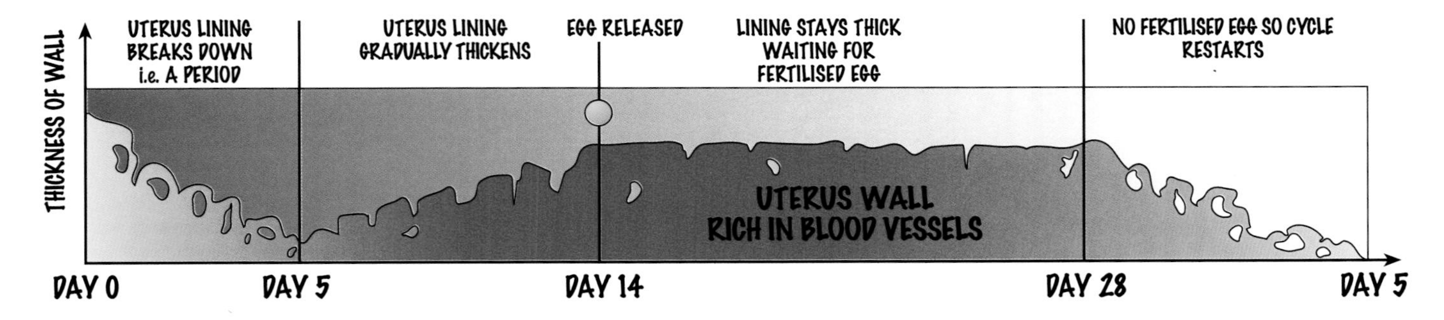

There are two hormones involved in these changes:

- OESTROGEN which stimulates the lining of the uterus to thicken and is indirectly responsible for the release of an egg, and
- PROGESTERONE which preserves the uterus lining until the end of the cycle.

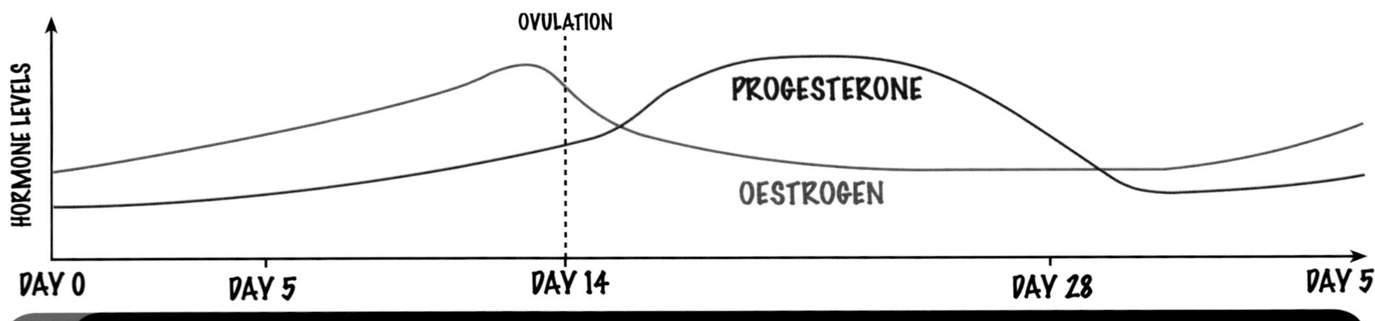

Fertility in women can be artificially controlled by giving ...

- Hormones that stimulate the release of eggs from the ovaries (FERTILITY DRUGS)
- Hormones that prevent the release of eggs from the ovaries (CONTRACEPTIVE PILLS)

- However, a woman produces hormones naturally that cause the release of an egg from her ovaries, ...
- ... and also cause the changes in the thickness of the lining of her womb.
- These hormones are produced by the PITUITARY GLAND and the OVARIES.

HIGHER/SPECIAL TIER

Natural Control Of Fertility: F.S.H. Oestrogen And L.H.

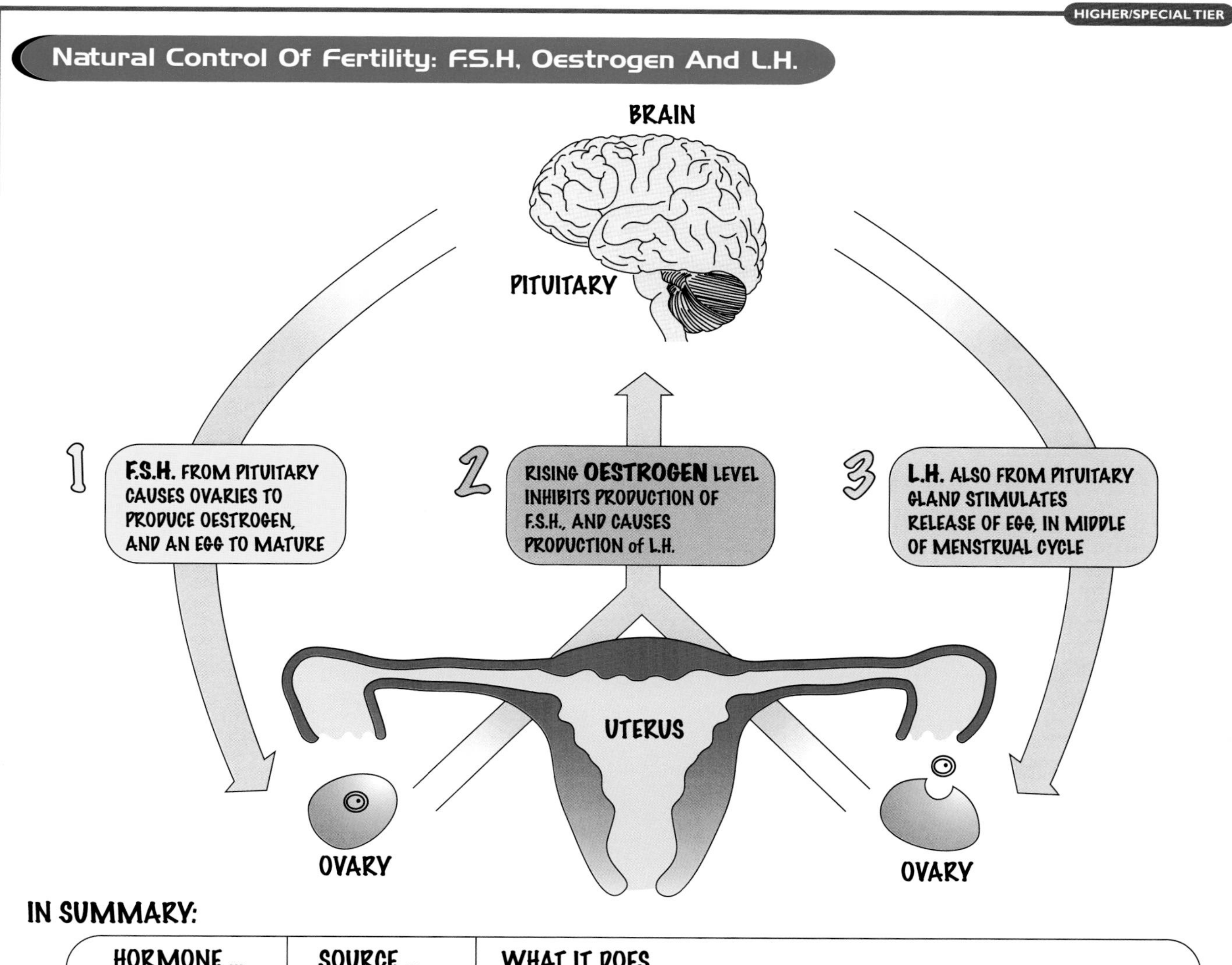

IN SUMMARY:

HORMONE ...	SOURCE ...	WHAT IT DOES ...
F.S.H.	PITUITARY	CAUSES EGG TO MATURE and OVARIES TO PRODUCE OESTROGEN.
OESTROGEN	OVARIES	INHIBITS PRODUCTION OF F.S.H. and CAUSES PRODUCTION OF L.H.
L.H	PITUITARY	STIMULATES RELEASE OF EGG.

Artificial Control Of Fertility

F.S.H. and OESTROGEN can be given to women in order to achieve opposing results!

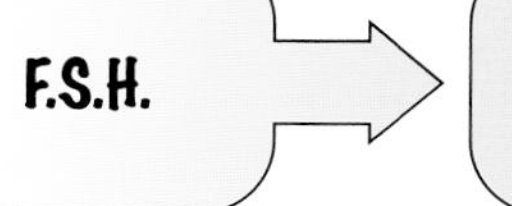

- Given as a FERTILITY DRUG ...
- ... to women who don't produce enough of it ...
- ... to stimulate eggs to mature and be released.

INCREASING FERTILITY

OESTROGEN

- Given as an ORAL CONTRACEPTIVE ...
- ... to inhibit F.S.H. production ...
- ... so that no eggs mature.

REDUCING FERTILITY

Nervous System

- **The NERVOUS SYSTEM** allows humans to **REACT QUICKLY** to their surroundings and **CO-ORDINATE THEIR BEHAVIOUR.**
- **NERVE PATHWAYS** involve:

STIMULUS ⇨ RECEPTORS ⇨ SENSORY NEURONE ⇨ CENTRAL NERVOUS SYSTEM ⇨ MOTOR NEURONE ⇨ EFFECTORS ⇨ RESPONSE

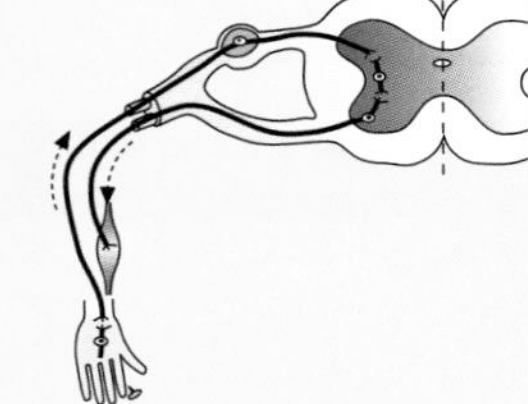

- **RECEPTORS** can be found in the **EYES, EARS, NOSE, TONGUE** and **SKIN.**
- **A REFLEX ACTION** is usually a defence mechanism which speeds up a response by **SHORT CIRCUITING** the brain.
- **SENSORY NEURONES** and **MOTOR NEURONES** are specially adapted cells that carry electrical signals called nerve impulses.

HIGHER/SPECIAL TIER

- **NEURONES** are elongated, have an insulating sheath and a branched ending.
- **SYNAPSES** are very small gaps between neurones that ensure nerve impulses only travel in one direction.

- The **CORNEA** and **LENS** focus rays of light on the **RETINA.**
- Muscles in the iris alter the size of the pupil, so the pupil is large in dim light and small in bright light.

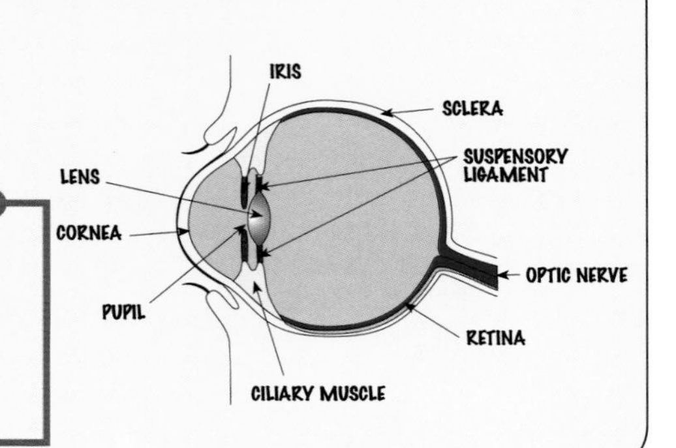

HIGHER/SPECIAL TIER

- To focus **DISTANT OBJECTS** the **LENS** is pulled **THINNER.**
- To focus **NEAR OBJECTS** the **LENS** is allowed to become **FATTER.**
- **A CONVEX LENS** is used to correct **LONG SIGHTEDNESS.**
- **A CONCAVE LENS** is used to correct **SHORT SIGHTEDNESS.**

Hormones

- **HORMONES** are chemicals released by a number of glands that make up the **ENDOCRINE SYSTEM.**
- Hormones are transported by the blood to their target organs.
- Hormones usually act more slowly and generally than the nervous system.
- **TESTOSTERONE** in males and **OESTROGEN** in females control the development of secondary sexual characteristics.
- The hormone **INSULIN LOWERS BLOOD SUGAR LEVELS** and the hormone **GLUCAGON INCREASES BLOOD SUGAR LEVELS.**

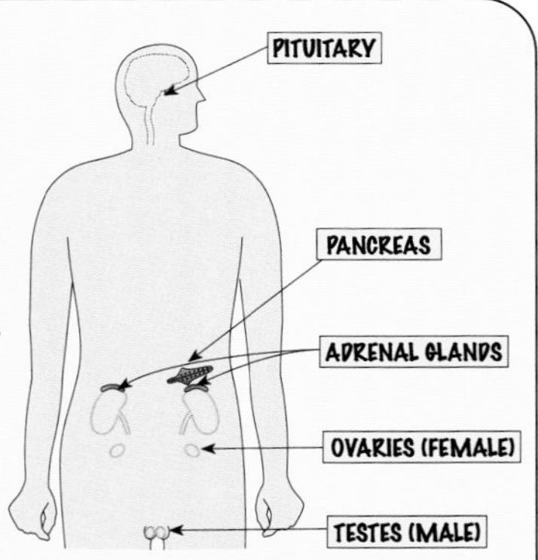

HIGHER/SPECIAL TIER

- **ADRENALINE** is a hormone that helps the body cope with stressful situations. It increases blood sugar levels and pulse rate.

- The **MONTHLY RELEASE OF AN EGG** and changes in the thickness of the **LINING OF THE WOMB** in a woman's body are controlled by hormones released by the **PITUITARY GLAND** and **OVARIES.**
- Hormones in **FERTILITY DRUGS** can stimulate the release of eggs from the ovaries.
- Hormones in **CONTRACEPTIVE PILLS** can prevent the release of eggs from the ovaries.

Record the **THIRTEEN** 'Nervous System' and the **NINE** 'Hormones' facts onto your tape.
Now - **READ, COVER, WRITE** and **CHECK** the **TWENTY TWO** facts.

HIGHER/SPECIAL TIER

TRANSPLANT

- A suitably COMPATIBLE KIDNEY can be surgically placed into a RECIPIENT'S BODY.
- The main problem with transplants is the threat of rejection.

HIGHER/SPECIAL TIER

DIALYSIS

- Blood from a patient runs into a DIALYSIS MACHINE.
- WASTE from the blood DIFFUSES through a semi-permeable membrane into DIALYSIS FLUID.

HIGHER/SPECIAL TIER

NEPHRON

- Waste is removed by the kidney:
  - ULTRAFILTRATION
  - SELECTIVE REABSORPTION
  - RELEASE AS URINE

BOWMAN'S CAPSULE, GLOMERULUS, RENAL TUBULE, COLLECTING DUCT, CAPILLARY NETWORK, URINE

EXCRETORY SYSTEM

AORTA, VENA CAVA, DIAPHRAGM, KIDNEY, RENAL ARTERY, RENAL VEIN, BLADDER, URETER, URETHRA

- All UREA is removed by the kidneys ...
- ... but water and ion levels are kept within fairly narrow limits.

HIGHER/SPECIAL TIER

EFFECT OF A.D.H.

- Produced by the pituitary gland.
- Blood water level too high → Less A.D.H. → Less water reabsorbed → lots of dilute urine
- Blood water level too low → More A.D.H. → More water reabsorbed → small amount of concentrated urine.

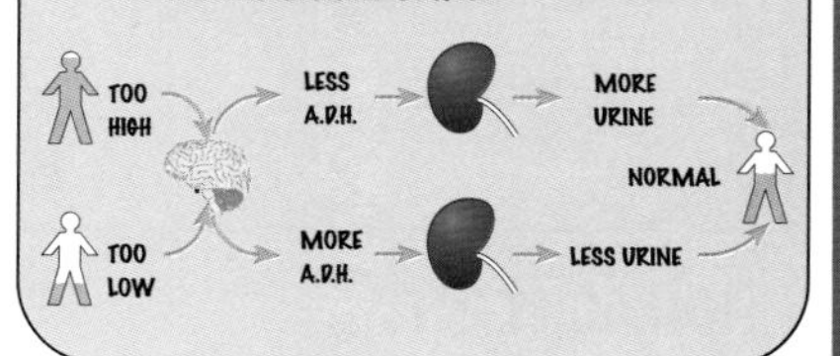

Control Of Water and Ion Content

Control Of Blood Sugar

BLOOD SUGAR LEVEL

- Blood sugar level is controlled by the hormones INSULIN and GLUCAGON which are produced by the pancreas.

LOWER ← INSULIN ← BLOOD SUGAR → GLUCAGON → HIGHER

HIGHER/SPECIAL TIER

CONTROL OF BLOOD SUGAR

Blood sugar level is TOO LOW → GLUCAGON RELEASED → INSOLUBLE GLYCOGEN converted to GLUCOSE in the liver and released into the blood. → NORMAL BLOOD SUGAR LEVEL

PANCREAS MONITORS BLOOD SUGAR LEVELS.

LIVER IS THE TARGET ORGAN ACTED ON BY HORMONES.

Blood sugar level is TOO HIGH → INSULIN RELEASED → GLUCOSE from the blood converted to INSOLUBLE GLYCOGEN in the liver. → NORMAL BLOOD SUGAR LEVEL

DIABETES

- Glucagon and Insulin control the amount of glucose in the blood.
- Diabetics don't produce enough INSULIN and so may have to monitor their diet, or actually inject insulin.

Thermoregulation

CONTROL OF BODY TEMPERATURE

- Temperature is maintained at 37°C ...
  ... because enzymes work best at this temperature.
- Thermoregulatory centre in the brain monitors and controls the temperature.

TEMPERATURE DECREASED BY

- Sweating
- Dilation of skin capillaries

TEMPERATURE INCREASED BY

- Shivering
- Constriction of skin capillaries

HIGHER/SPECIAL TIER

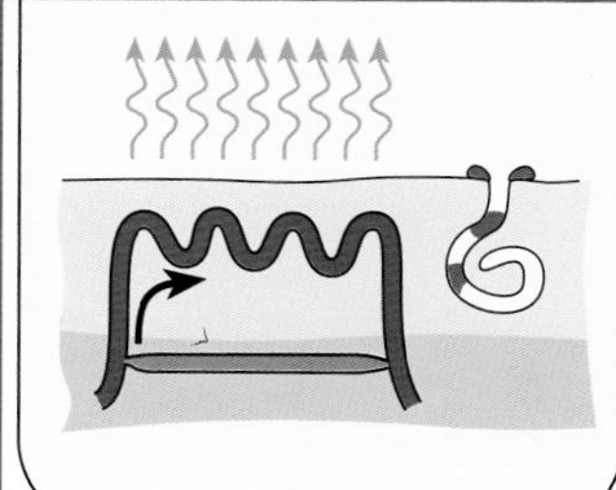

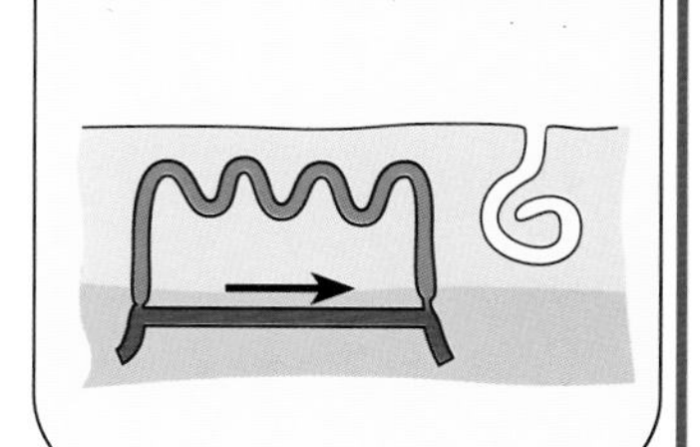

HOMEOSTASIS is the maintenance of a fairly **CONSTANT INTERNAL ENVIRONMENT** ...
... by **BALANCING BODILY INPUTS AND OUTPUTS** and ...
... removing **WASTE PRODUCTS**.

Waste Products Which Have To Be Removed

CARBON DIOXIDE (See page 29)	• Produced by **RESPIRATION**. Removed via the **LUNGS** when we breathe out. HIGHER/SPECIAL TIER • High levels of Carbon dioxide in the blood are detected by the brain and the person's breathing rate increases.
UREA	• Produced by **LIVER** breaking down excess amino acids. Removed by **KIDNEYS** and transferred to bladder before being released.

Internal Conditions Which Have To Be Controlled

WATER CONTENT	Water lost by • Breathing via lungs. (water vapour). • Sweating. • Excess via kidneys in urine. Water gained by • Drinking and from food.
ION CONTENT (Sodium, Potassium etc.)	Ions are lost by • Sweating. • Excess via kidneys in urine. Ions are gained by • Eating (particularly salty foods). • Drinking.
TEMPERATURE (Ideally at 37°C) - because this is the temperature at which **ENZYMES** work best!	Temperature increased by:- • Shivering (muscles make heat by respiration). • 'Shutting down' skin capillaries so less heat is lost from the surface of the skin. Temperature decreased by:- • Sweating (the water lost on a hot day must be replaced). • 'Opening up' skin capillaries so more heat is lost from the surface of the skin.
BLOOD GLUCOSE (See page 50)	Blood glucose increased by:- • Hormone **GLUCAGON** (from the **PANCREAS**) and ... • Hormone **ADRENALINE** (from the **ADRENAL GLANDS**). Blood glucose decreased by:- • Hormone **INSULIN** (from the **PANCREAS**).

The Excretory System

The **MAJOR ORGAN** in the **EXCRETORY SYSTEM** is the **KIDNEY**.

The job of the **KIDNEY** is to remove **EXCESS WATER** and the waste substance **UREA** from the body.

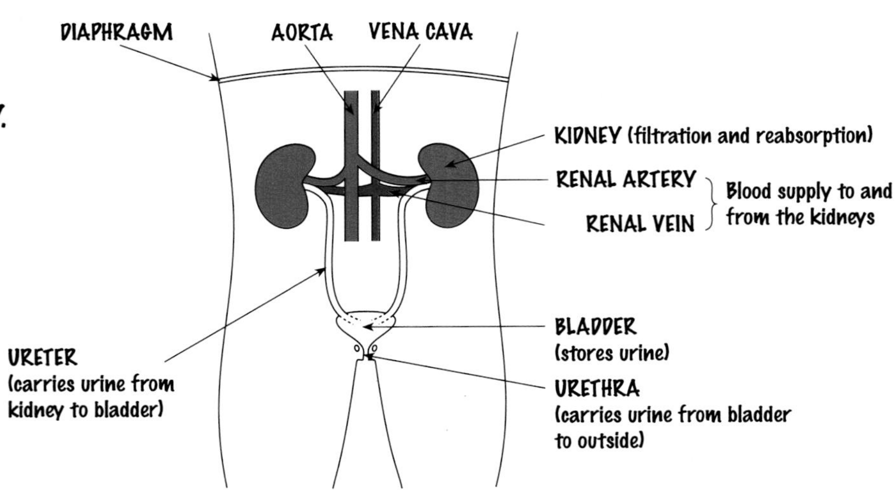

HIGHER/SPECIAL TIER

The Role Of The Kidney

- The Kidney's job is to ...
  ... **REGULATE THE AMOUNT OF WATER AND IONS IN THE BLOOD** ...
  ... and to **REMOVE <u>ALL</u> UREA.**
- The functional unit of the kidney is the **NEPHRON**. There are over a million of these in each kidney.

The Nephron

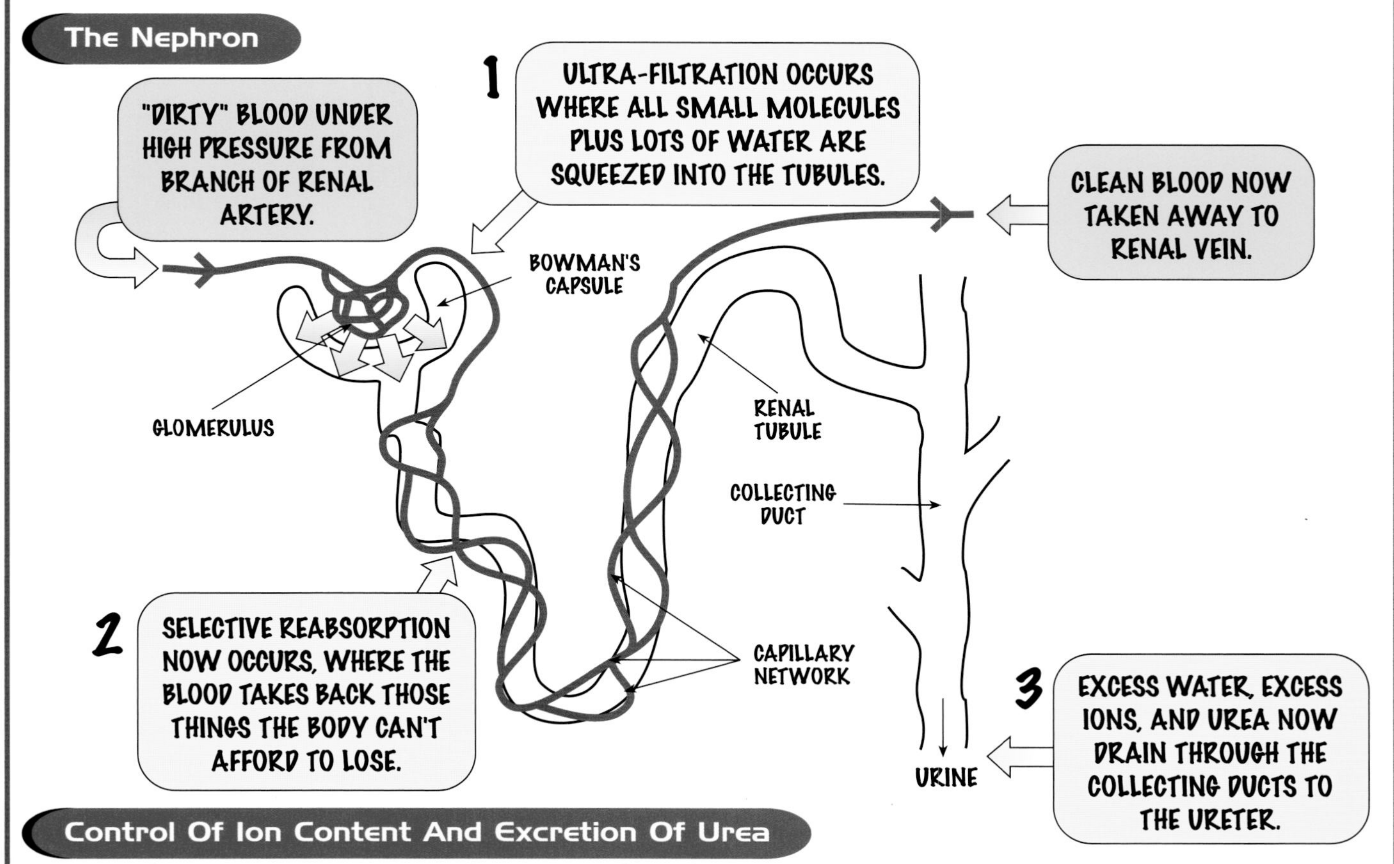

Control Of Ion Content And Excretion Of Urea

- It's perhaps easier to understand if we look at the exchange between the **CAPILLARIES** and the **RENAL TUBULES**.
- Try to learn the **THREE** main stages. They're the key to understanding how the kidney works.

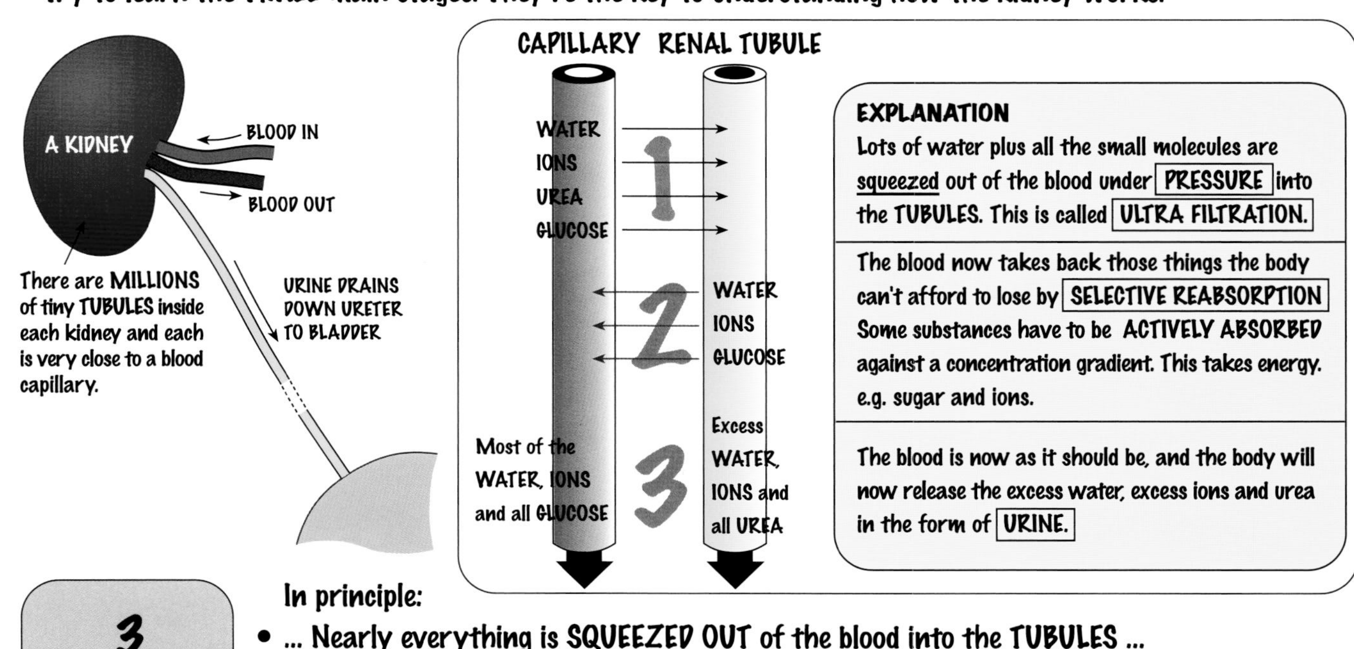

3 STAGES

In principle:

- ... Nearly everything is **SQUEEZED OUT** of the blood into the **TUBULES** ...
- ... the substances we want to keep are **REABSORBED** back into the Blood ...
- ... unwanted substances are **RELEASED** as **URINE**.

HIGHER/SPECIAL TIER

Control Of Water Content - Effect Of A.D.H. On The Kidney

The amount of water reabsorbed by the kidneys in Stage 2 on the previous page is controlled by the hormone A.D.H. which is produced by the **PITUITARY GLAND** in the brain. A.D.H. directly affects the permeability (to water) of the renal tubules. This is a classical example of **NEGATIVE FEEDBACK.**

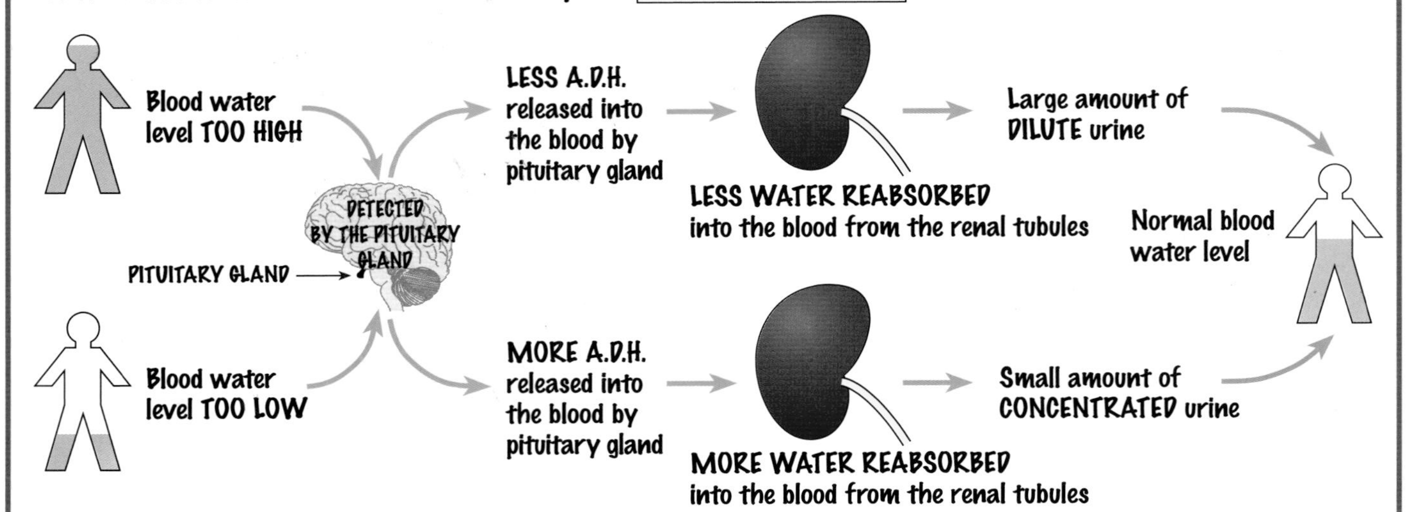

Kidney Failure

- If one kidney fails then there is no reason why a person shouldn't lead a normal life.
- However, if both kidneys fail then either <u>**DIALYSIS**</u>, or a <u>**KIDNEY TRANSPLANT**</u> is necessary to preserve life.

Dialysis

- Blood, taken from a vein runs into a **DIALYSIS MACHINE**, where it comes into close contact with a **SELECTIVELY PERMEABLE MEMBRANE**, which separates it from the **DIALYSIS FLUID**.
- **WASTE** diffuses from the **BLOOD** into the **DIALYSIS FLUID**. This must be done two or three times per week and takes about three hours per session.

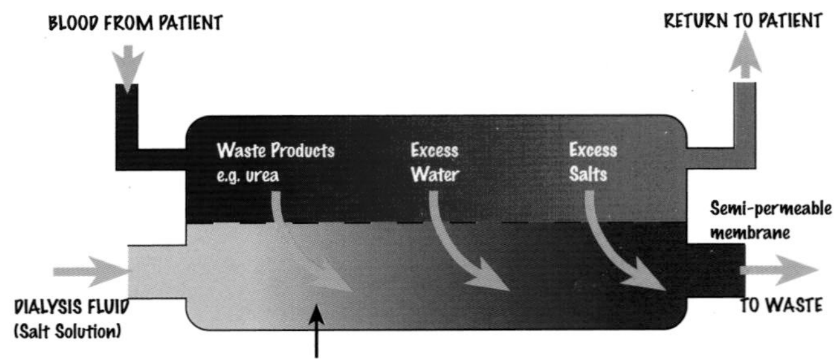

Kidney Transplant

- This involves taking a kidney from a suitably healthy donor and ...
- ... surgically attaching it to the recipient.
- The donor must be compatible in order to avoid tissue rejection.

	DIALYSIS	KIDNEY TRANSPLANT
ADVANTAGES	• No rejection can occur. • More readily available and can be used by patients waiting for a transplant.	• No need for regular dialysis - can lead less restricted life. • Nearly 80% success rate if tissue types match.
DISADVANTAGES	• Regular sessions in hospital or at home on dialysis machine (10 hours). • Diet has to be controlled - some foods can only be eaten when the person is connected to the dialysis machine.	• Rejection can occur where body's defence system "attacks" the kidney. • Anti-rejection drugs may need to be taken for the rest of the patients life.

HIGHER/SPECIAL TIER

Control Of Body Temperature

This is controlled by the NERVOUS SYSTEM in conjunction with the SKIN.

- The CORE TEMPERATURE of the body should be kept at around 37°C (best for enzymes!)
- MONITORING AND CONTROL is done by the THERMOREGULATORY CENTRE in the BRAIN ...
  ... which has receptors which are sensitive to the temperature of the blood flowing through it.
- There are also temperature receptors in the skin which provide information about skin temperature.

CORE BODY TEMPERATURE TOO HIGH

CORE BODY TEMPERATURE TOO LOW

THERMOREGULATORY CENTRE

DECREASING BODY TEMPERATURE

- BLOOD VESSELS IN SKIN DILATE (become wider) CAUSING GREATER HEAT LOSS as MORE heat is lost from the surface of the skin by RADIATION.
- SWEAT GLANDS RELEASE SWEAT WHICH EVAPORATES CAUSING COOLING.

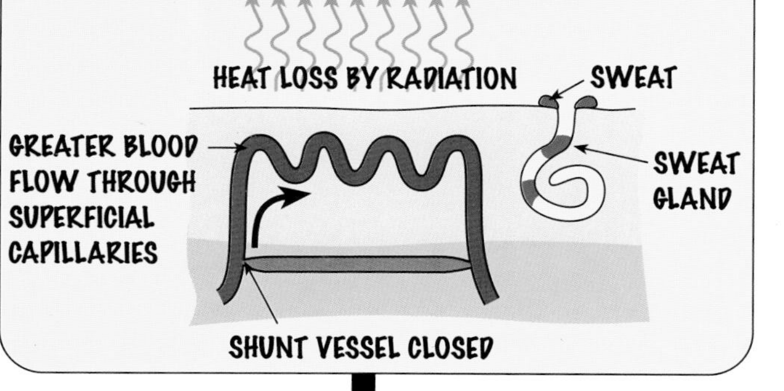

INCREASING BODY TEMPERATURE

- BLOOD VESSELS IN SKIN CONSTRICT (become narrower) REDUCING HEAT LOSS as LESS heat is lost from the surface of the skin by RADIATION.
- MUSCLES START TO 'SHIVER' CAUSING HEAT ENERGY TO BE RELEASED VIA RESPIRATION IN CELLS.

SWEATING STOPPED

REDUCED BLOOD FLOW THROUGH SUPERFICIAL CAPILLARIES

SWEAT GLAND

SHUNT VESSEL OPEN

CORE TEMPERATURE RETURNS TO NORMAL

DETECTED by the THERMOREGULATORY CENTRE

- REDUCED DILATION OF BLOOD VESSELS IN THE SKIN.
- SWEATING STOPS.

- REDUCED CONSTRICTION OF BLOOD VESSELS IN THE SKIN.
- SHIVERING STOPS.

- This final stage shows an important biological idea called NEGATIVE FEEDBACK.
- INFORMATION from the body is used to "switch off" a number of processes ...
- ... in order to maintain a CONSTANT INTERNAL ENVIRONMENT.

It's important to remember that the skin's other important role is as a water-proof, germ-proof layer which protects the delicate cells within it from drying out and infection.

Blood Sugar Levels

- Eating starchy, or sugary foods causes an increase in the amount of glucose in the blood.
- Normal cell activity removes some glucose from the blood but exercise removes a lot more.
- As glucose is the body's primary 'fuel' its level in the blood must be carefully controlled.
- The hormones INSULIN AND GLUCAGON released by the PANCREAS work together to ...
  ... CONTROL BLOOD SUGAR LEVELS.

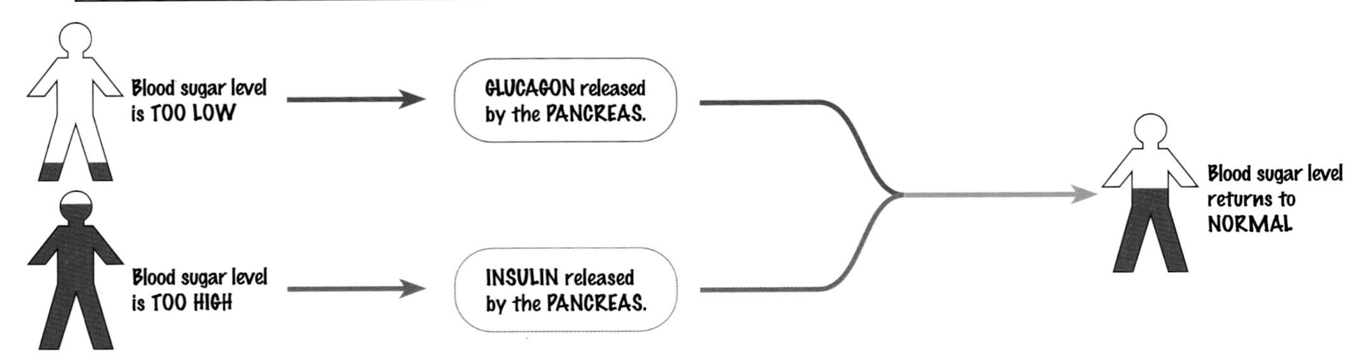

Diabetes

- DIABETES is a disease that is caused by ...
  ... the PANCREAS not releasing ENOUGH INSULIN.
  This can lead to a person's blood sugar level rising FATALLY HIGH.
- People who have diabetes can CONTROL THEIR BLOOD SUGAR LEVEL by ...
  ... carefully CONTROLLING THEIR DIET or by INJECTING INSULIN.

HIGHER/SPECIAL TIER

Control Of Blood Sugar

It is important to fully understand how BLOOD SUGAR LEVEL is controlled.

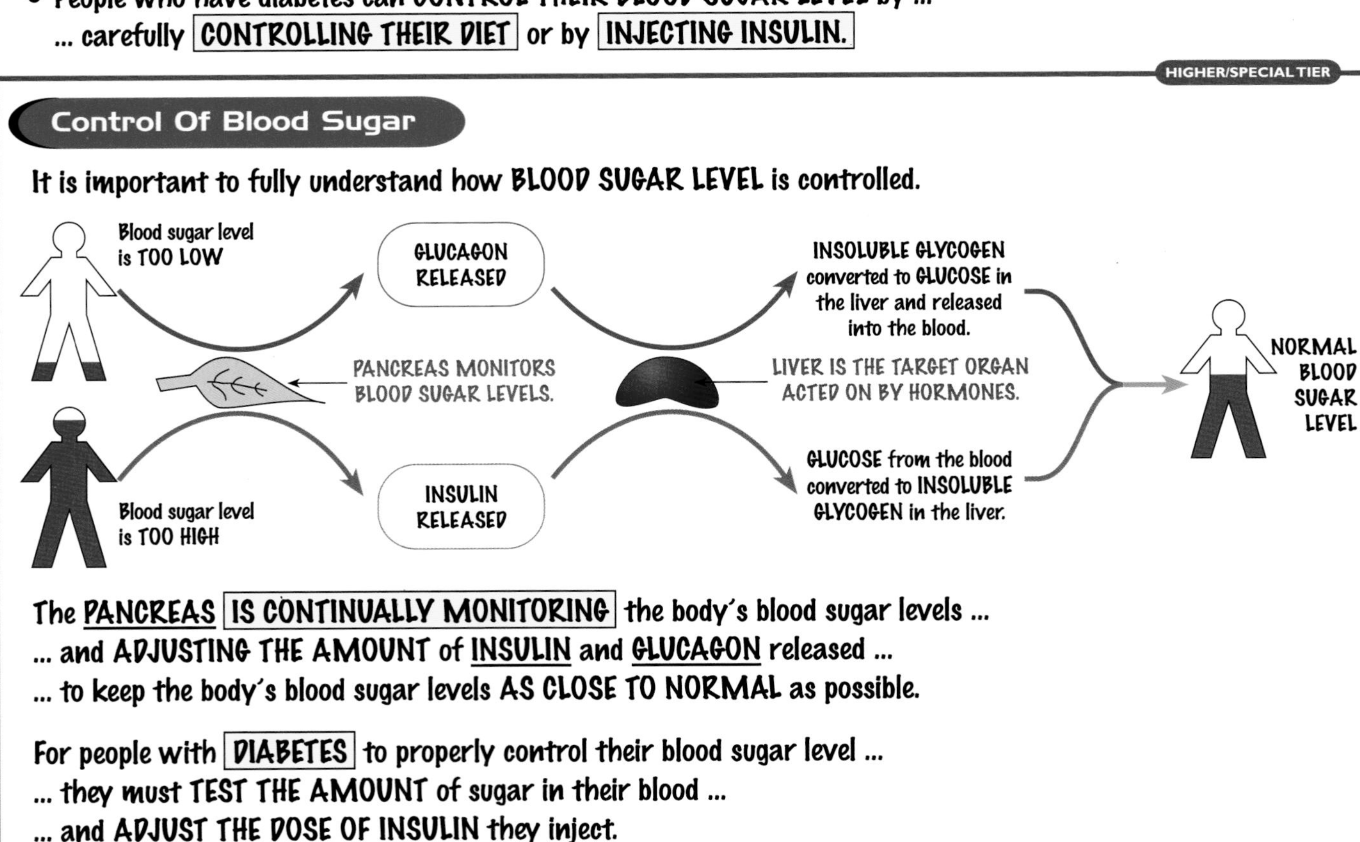

The PANCREAS IS CONTINUALLY MONITORING the body's blood sugar levels ...
... and ADJUSTING THE AMOUNT of INSULIN and GLUCAGON released ...
... to keep the body's blood sugar levels AS CLOSE TO NORMAL as possible.

For people with DIABETES to properly control their blood sugar level ...
... they must TEST THE AMOUNT of sugar in their blood ...
... and ADJUST THE DOSE OF INSULIN they inject.

Adrenaline

ADRENALINE is a hormone released to help the body cope with STRESSFUL SITUATIONS ...
... by INCREASING THE AMOUNT OF GLUCOSE in the blood and INCREASING a person's HEART RATE/PULSE RATE. It causes that feeling of nervousness before a special event.

Control Of Water And Ion Content

- Besides constantly removing UREA from the blood, the kidneys regulate the amount of water in the blood and the amount of various ions.

HIGHER/SPECIAL TIER

- Blood water level is controlled by the hormone A.D.H. which is produced in the pituitary.
- TOO MUCH WATER in the blood results in LESS A.D.H. being produced.

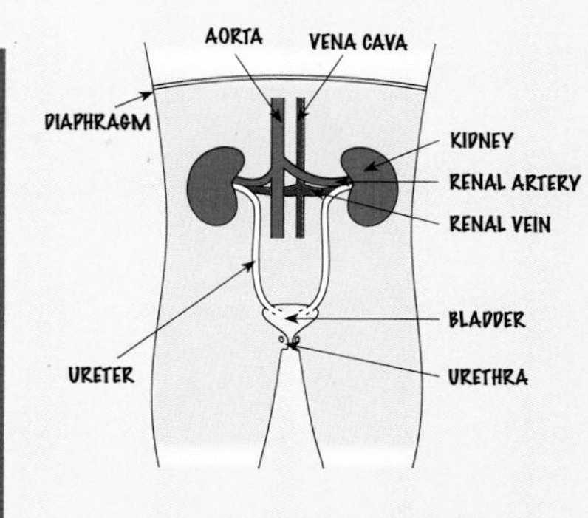

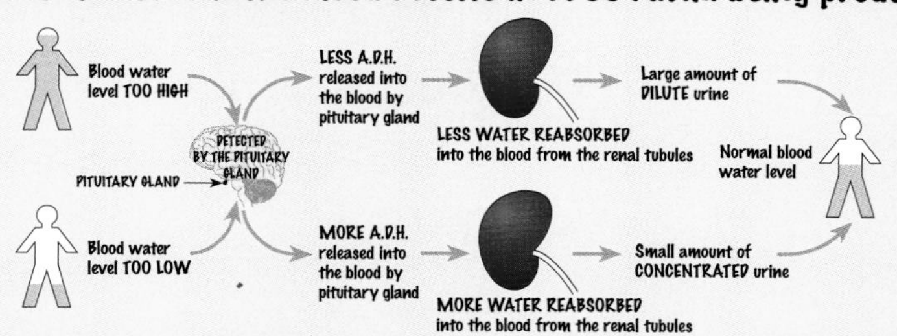

- The functional unit of the kidney is the NEPHRON, in which the following THREE processes occur:
  1. ULTRAFILTRATION.
  2. SELECTIVE REABSORPTION.
  3. RELEASE OF URINE.
- Kidney failure can be remedied by either ...
  ... a TRANSPLANT which is convenient though there are rejection problems ...
  ... or regular DIALYSIS which is restrictive and also not always available.

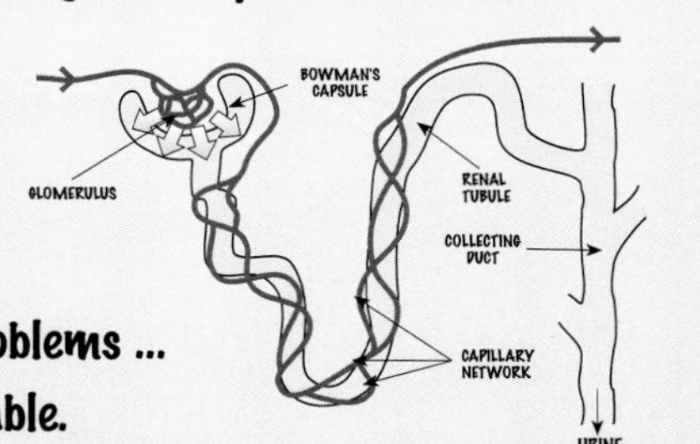

Control Of Blood Sugar

- Glucose (blood sugar) is the body's primary fuel and is monitored and controlled by the pancreas which secretes the hormones INSULIN and GLUCAGON.
- In DIABETES, insufficient INSULIN is produced and control of blood glucose is achieved by diet and/or injection of insulin.

HIGHER/SPECIAL TIER

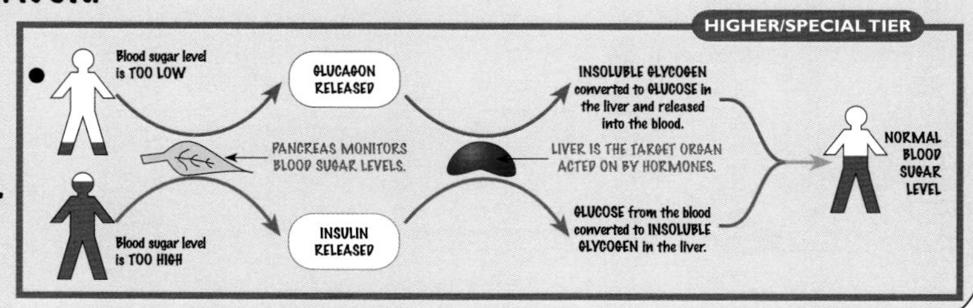

Thermoregulation

- Temperature is maintained at 37°C because enzymes work best at this temperature.
- Body temperature is decreased by SWEATING and DILATING SKIN CAPILLARIES.
- Body temperature is increased by SHIVERING and CONSTRICTING SKIN CAPILLARIES.

HIGHER/SPECIAL TIER

- The thermoregulatory centre in the brain monitors and controls body temperature.

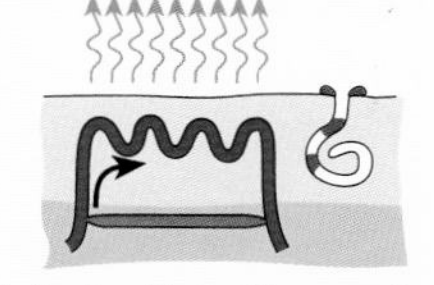
Reducing Body Temperature

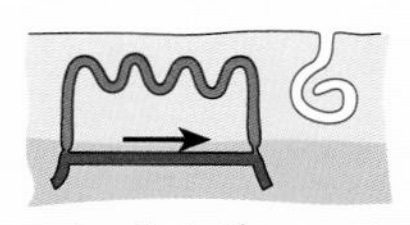
Increasing Body Temperature

Record the FIVE 'Control of water and ion content', THREE 'Control of blood sugar' and the FOUR 'Thermoregulation' facts onto your tape.
Now - READ, COVER, WRITE and CHECK the TWELVE facts.

STRUCTURE OF A FLOWERING PLANT

- Four main structural features.

1. FLOWER - contains the reproductive organs.
2. STEM - provides support and is a transport system for water, minerals and food.
3. LEAVES - photosynthesis occurs here.
4. ROOTS - anchor the plant and absorbs water.

PHOTOSYNTHESIS

- Process by which plants make their food, called glucose.
- Light, water, carbon dioxide and chlorophyll are needed.

$$\text{Carbon Dioxide} + \text{Water} \xrightarrow[\text{Light energy (sun)}]{\text{Chlorophyll}} \text{Glucose} + \text{Oxygen}$$

HIGHER/SPECIAL TIER

Plants convert glucose into ...

- STARCH
- CELLULOSE
- PROTEINS
- LIPIDS

FACTORS AFFECTING PHOTOSYNTHESIS

Rate of photosynthesis depends on ...

- Temperature
- Concentration of CO_2 (which is affected by the amount of water available)
- Light intensity

Rate of Photosynthesis / 0°C / 45°C TEMPERATURE
Rate of Photosynthesis / CONC^N OF CARBON DIOXIDE
Rate of Photosynthesis / LIGHT INTENSITY

Photosynthesis depends on all three factors as they all interact.

HIGHER/SPECIAL TIER

Photosynthesis is also affected by the amount of BLUE and RED light a plant absorbs.

Green Plants as Organisms

TRANSPIRATION AND WATER LOSS

- Transpiration is the loss of water through pores called stomata in leaves.
- Transpiration is needed for photosynthesis to take place.
- Continual flow of water from roots to leaves is the transpiration stream ... ... which is increased on a warm, dry and windy day (and vice versa).
- Size of stomata is controlled by guard cells.

TURGID GUARD CELLS → FLACCID GUARD CELLS

TRANSPIRATION AND SUPPORT

- If there is plenty of water available ... ... stomata are open allowing transpiration and plant cells are turgid.
- If there is not enough water available ... ... stomata are closed stopping transpiration and plant cells flaccid. The plant wilts.

HIGHER/SPECIAL TIER

- TURGOR plant cell is turgid.
- PLASMOLYSIS plant cell is flaccid.

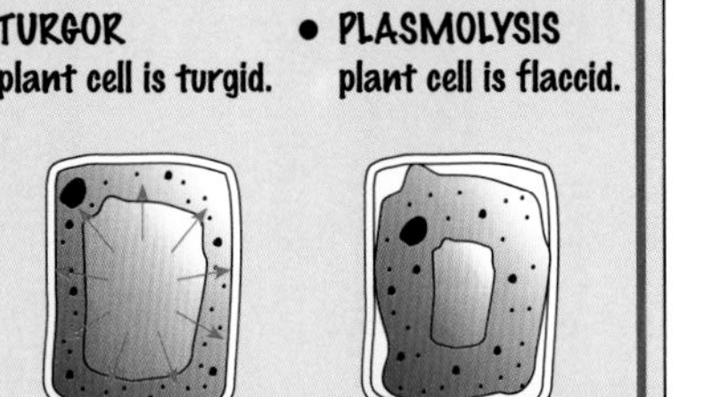

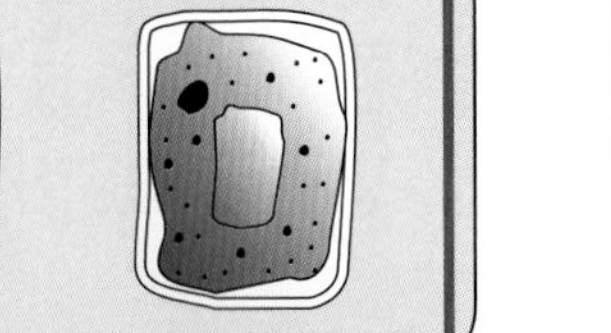

MINERAL REQUIREMENTS

- Minerals are needed to keep the plant healthy.
- Examples are nitrates, potassium, phosphates, magnesium and iron.
- Fertilisers are a source of minerals.

HIGHER/SPECIAL TIER

- Absence of minerals can result in poor growth and appearance.
- Minerals are taken up by the roots by active transport.

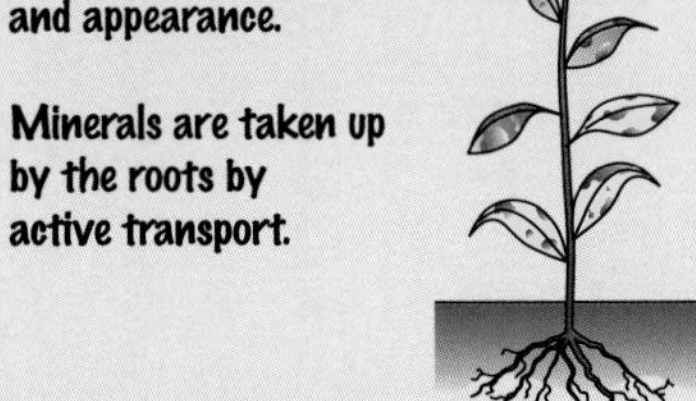

PLANT HORMONES

- Plant shoots grow ...
  1. Towards light.
  2. Upwards against gravity.
- Plant roots grow ...
  1. Towards moisture.
  2. Downwards in the direction of gravity.
- Hormones control these responses.
- Artificial hormones have many uses.

A flowering plant has many important STRUCTURAL FEATURES.

1. Flower

The flower contains the REPRODUCTIVE ORGANS of the plant which are required to make seeds.

2. Stem

The stem SUPPORTS the plant and provides a TRANSPORT SYSTEM.

- The stem contains tubes called **XYLEM TISSUE.** XYLEM transports WATER and MINERALS from the roots to the leaves (TRANSPIRATION).
- The stem also contains tubes called **PHLOEM TISSUE.** PHLOEM allows the movement of FOOD SUBSTANCES around the plant (TRANSLOCATION).
- The diagram below shows how Xylem and Phloem are arranged thin the stem.

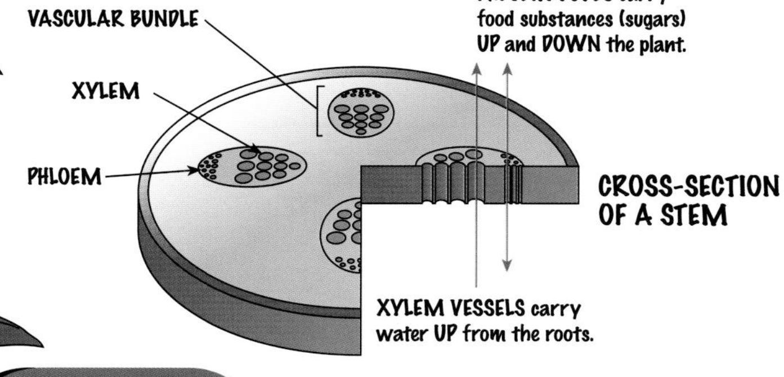

3. Leaves

Leaves are BROAD, THIN and FLAT ...
... to provide a LARGE SURFACE AREA to absorb sunlight.
The function of the leaf is PHOTOSYNTHESIS.

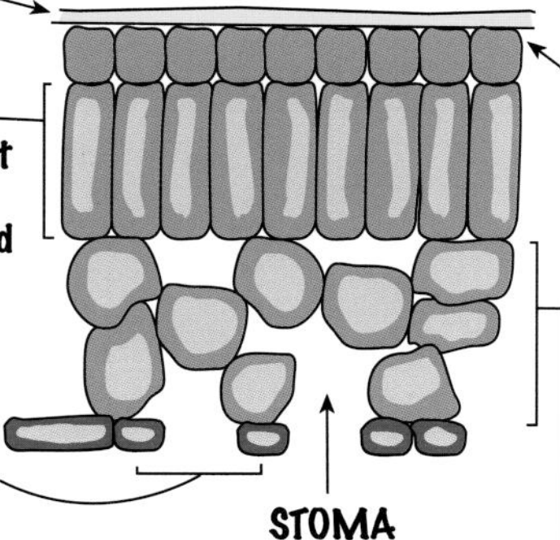

WAXY CUTICLE
(waterproof protection)

PALISADE CELLS
These cells contain the most chloroplasts (and therefore chlorophyll) and are situated near the upper surface for light absorption.

GUARD CELLS
Control the movement of gases through the stomata.

HIGHER/SPECIAL TIER

EPIDERMIS
The epidermis is transparent to allow light to pass through.

SPONGY LAYER
Contains many large air spaces which are connected to the stomata to allow carbon dioxide to diffuse through the open stomata into the air spaces and into photosynthesising cells.

4. Roots

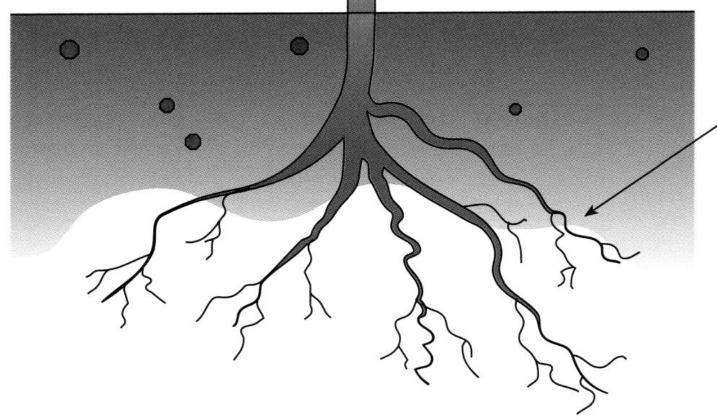

Roots ANCHOR the plants firmly in the ground and ABSORB WATER.
The root hair cells give an enormous surface area for absorption.

← ROOT HAIR

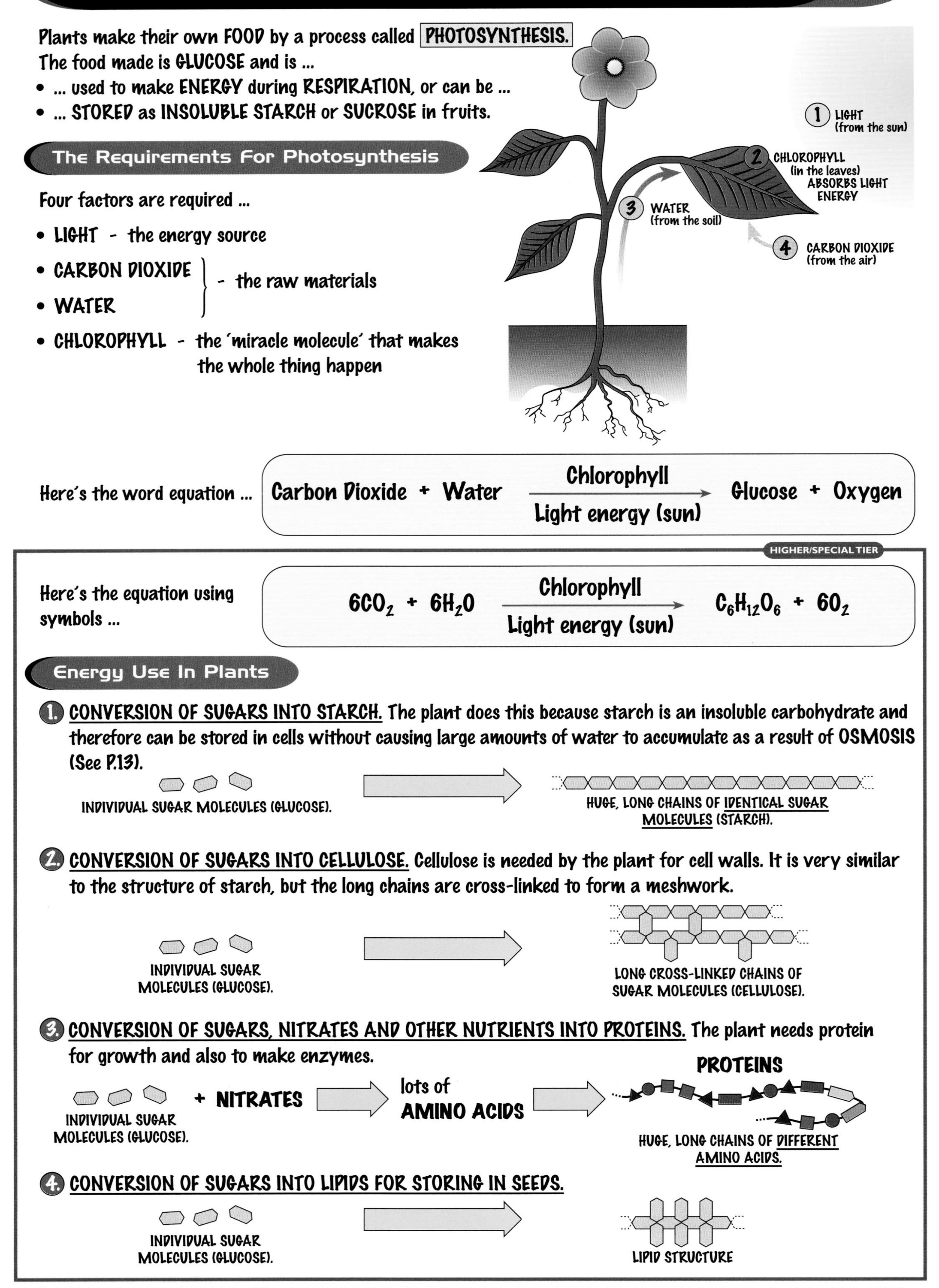

PHOTOSYNTHESIS

Plants make their own FOOD by a process called **PHOTOSYNTHESIS.**
The food made is GLUCOSE and is ...
- ... used to make ENERGY during RESPIRATION, or can be ...
- ... STORED as INSOLUBLE STARCH or SUCROSE in fruits.

The Requirements For Photosynthesis

Four factors are required ...
- LIGHT - the energy source
- CARBON DIOXIDE } - the raw materials
- WATER }
- CHLOROPHYLL - the 'miracle molecule' that makes the whole thing happen

Here's the word equation ...

$$\text{Carbon Dioxide} + \text{Water} \xrightarrow[\text{Light energy (sun)}]{\text{Chlorophyll}} \text{Glucose} + \text{Oxygen}$$

HIGHER/SPECIAL TIER

Here's the equation using symbols ...

$$6CO_2 + 6H_2O \xrightarrow[\text{Light energy (sun)}]{\text{Chlorophyll}} C_6H_{12}O_6 + 6O_2$$

Energy Use In Plants

1. **CONVERSION OF SUGARS INTO STARCH.** The plant does this because starch is an insoluble carbohydrate and therefore can be stored in cells without causing large amounts of water to accumulate as a result of OSMOSIS (See P.13).

2. **CONVERSION OF SUGARS INTO CELLULOSE.** Cellulose is needed by the plant for cell walls. It is very similar to the structure of starch, but the long chains are cross-linked to form a meshwork.

3. **CONVERSION OF SUGARS, NITRATES AND OTHER NUTRIENTS INTO PROTEINS.** The plant needs protein for growth and also to make enzymes.

4. **CONVERSION OF SUGARS INTO LIPIDS FOR STORING IN SEEDS.**

The factors that can LIMIT THE RATE OF PHOTOSYNTHESIS are ...

- TEMPERATURE
- CARBON DIOXIDE CONCENTRATION
- LIGHT INTENSITY

Temperature

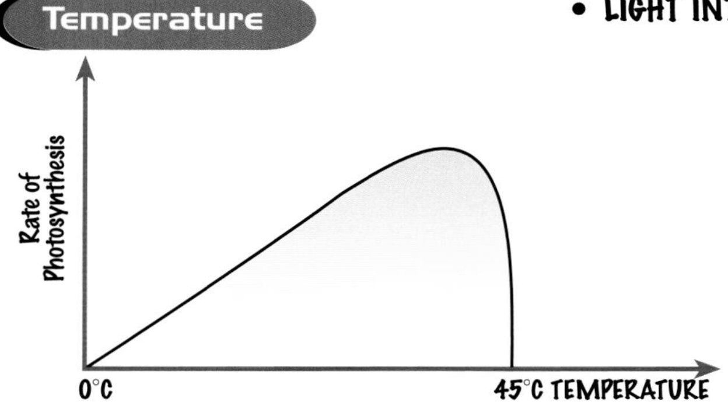

Photosynthesis is controlled by ENZYMES. Enzymes are destroyed at a temperature of around 45°C. This graph shows us that as the temperature increases so does the rate of photosynthesis up to the point where the enzymes are destroyed.

Carbon Dioxide Concentration

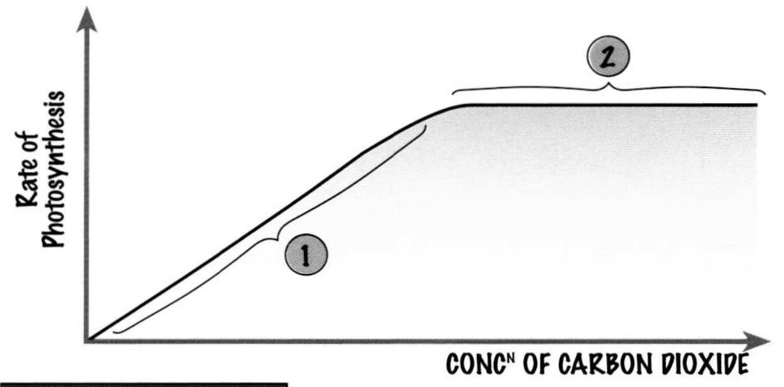

1. As the carbon dioxide concentration rises so does the rate of photosynthesis. This means carbon dioxide is limiting the rate of photosynthesis.
2. Rise in carbon dioxide now has no effect. Carbon dioxide is no longer the limiting factor. This means **SUNLIGHT** or **TEMPERATURE** must be the limiting factor.

LACK OF WATER

Water affects the plant indirectly, since lack of water causes the closure of **GUARD CELLS,** resulting in a REDUCTION in the amount of **CARBON DIOXIDE** that can be taken in by the leaf, and therefore a reduction in photosynthesis.

Light Intensity

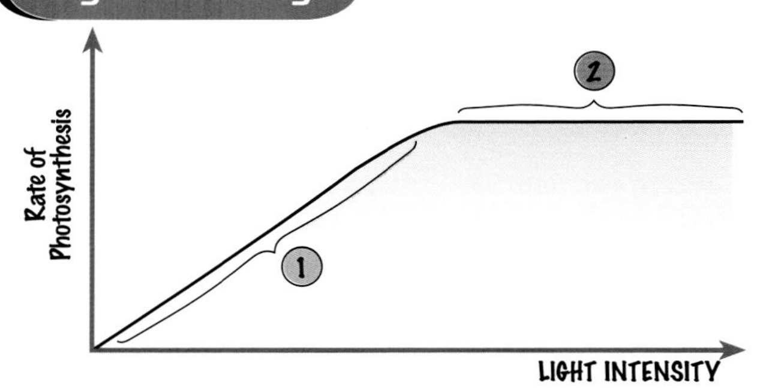

1. As the light intensity increases so does the rate of photosynthesis. This means light intensity is limiting the rate of photosynthesis.
2. Rise in light intensity now has no effect. Light intensity is no longer the limiting factor.
   This means **CARBON DIOXIDE** or **TEMPERATURE** must be the limiting factor.

In practice Temperature, Carbon dioxide concentration and Light intensity interact and any one of them at a particular time may be the factor that limits photosynthesis.

HIGHER/SPECIAL TIER

Wavelength of Light

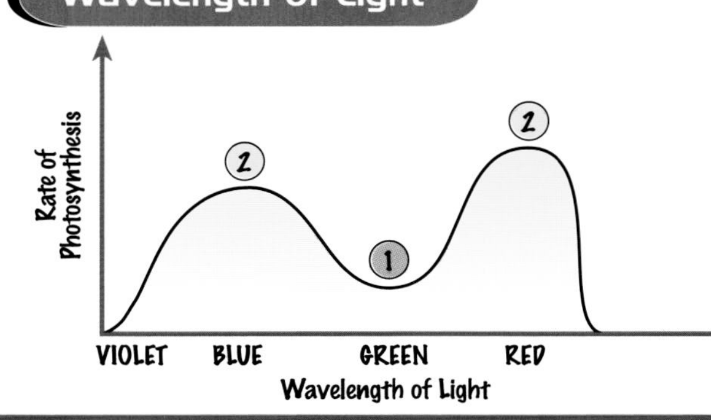

White light is made up of the whole spectrum of colours (different wavelengths).

1. Plants **REFLECT GREEN LIGHT** (and therefore look green).
2. They **ABSORB BLUE AND RED LIGHT.**
   This means that if the plant does not receive enough BLUE and RED light, photosynthesis will be affected.
3. In large greenhouses the amount of Blue and Red light can be artificially increased.

Transpiration

A plant loses water vapour through its leaves. This loss of water is called **TRANSPIRATION.**

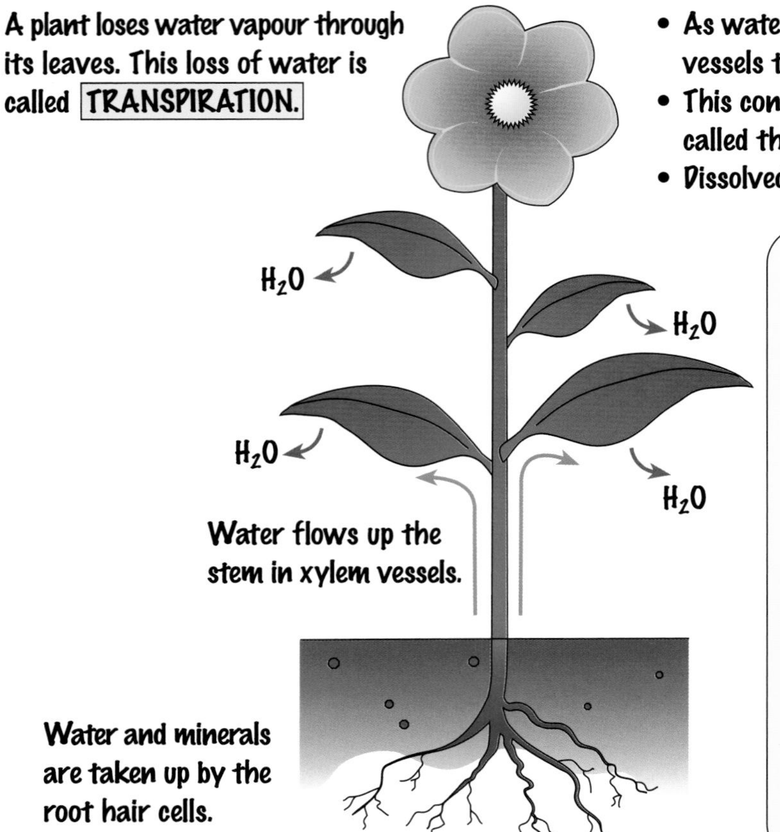

- As water transpires more water is 'pulled' up the xylem vessels to replace it.
- This continuous flow of water from roots to leaves is called the **TRANSPIRATION STREAM.**
- Dissolved in the water are some important MINERALS.

The TRANSPIRATION STREAM is ...

Fastest on:
- WARM/HOT
- DRY
- WINDY DAYS

This is because EVAPORATION is the driving force of transpiration and evaporation happens more quickly in these conditions.

Slowest on:
- COLD
- DULL
- DAMP DAYS

This is because evaporation is slower in these conditions

- TRANSPIRATION is IMPORTANT because it provides the plant with ...
  ... WATER for **PHOTOSYNTHESIS, SUPPORT and COOLING of the leaves.**
- It also provides ESSENTIAL MINERALS to **MAKE PROTEINS** to keep the plant HEALTHY ...
  ... and FUNCTIONING PROPERLY.

Controlling Water Loss

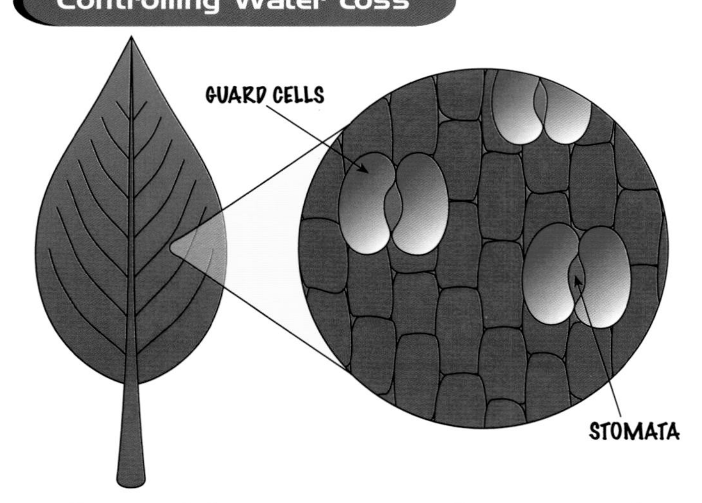

- A leaf has holes or PORES called STOMATA mainly on the UNDERSIDE OF THE LEAF.
- CARBON DIOXIDE and OXYGEN can DIFFUSE into and out of the leaf via the STOMATA.
- WATER VAPOUR also diffuses out of the leaf via the STOMATA.

WATER LOSS THROUGH TRANSPIRATION IS THE PRICE THE PLANT MUST PAY IN ORDER TO PHOTOSYNTHESISE.

- The size of the stomata is controlled by a pair of GUARD CELLS.
- If plants lose water faster than it is taken up by the roots ...
  ... the stomata can be closed to prevent wilting and eventual dehydration.

If the plant has lots of water then the stomata are fully open ...

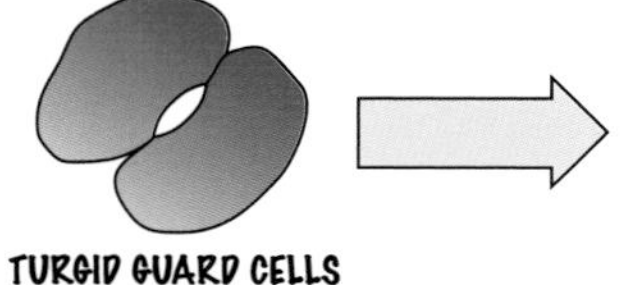

TURGID GUARD CELLS

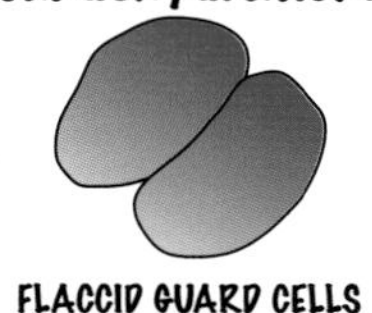

FLACCID GUARD CELLS

... when water isn't available, then the stomata are closed.

Maintaining Support

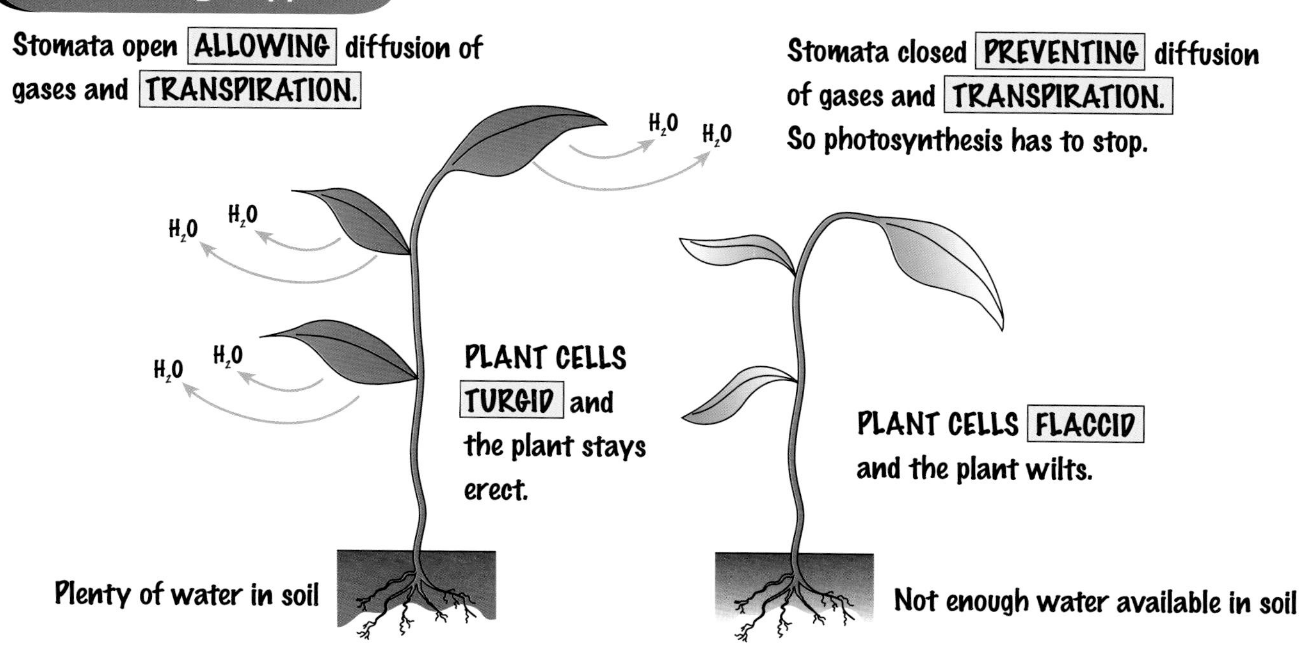

When the plant has plenty of water, the cell contents "swell up" and press against the cell wall. This increases the rigidity of the plant tissue and provides the main method of support in young, non-woody stems.

HIGHER/SPECIAL TIER

Turgor and Plasmolysis

TURGOR

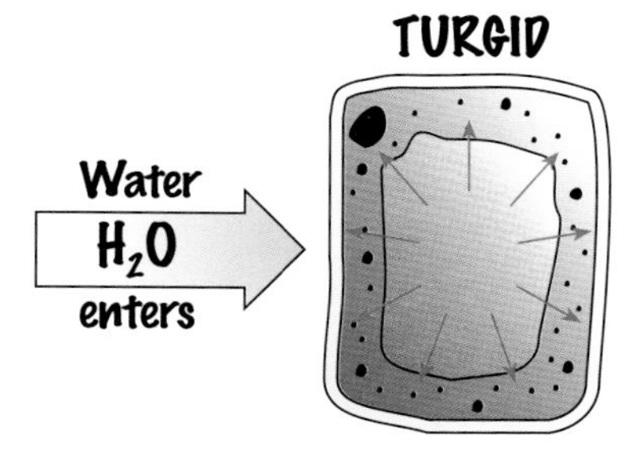

- If a cell is in a less concentrated solution, water passes in by OSMOSIS. (See P.13)
- Water flows through the cell wall and cell membrane into the cytoplasm and into the vacuole.
- The increased pressure of water in the vacuole presses the cytoplasm against the cell wall.
- When the cell can take no more water we say it is fully TURGID. It is this pressure which keeps the cells rigid and therefore provides support for the plant.

PLASMOLYSIS

- If a plant is in a more concentrated solution (not often in nature), water passes out of the cytoplasm through the cell membrane and cell wall and into the solution outside the cell.
- The pressure decreases and the cytoplasm pulls away from the cell wall.
- The cell is plasmolysed or FLACCID.

Other Factors Affecting Size Of Stomata

- If the guard cells receive light they can photosynthesise and make sugar (therefore increasing the concentration of the cell).
- WATER ENTERS by OSMOSIS and the GUARD CELLS become TURGID.

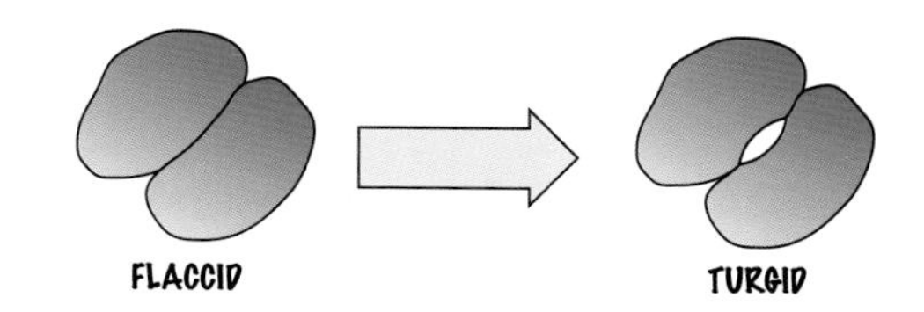

- Plants require ESSENTIAL MINERALS to MAKE PROTEINS in order ...
  ... to keep the plant HEALTHY and FUNCTIONING PROPERLY.
- Plants absorb these essential minerals as ions ...
  ... DISSOLVED IN WATER through their ROOT HAIRS.

Use Of Fertilisers

- Sometimes if the SOIL IS POOR or a piece of land is FARMED INTENSIVELY ...
  ... FERTILISERS are ADDED TO THE SOIL to make sure the essential minerals are present in large enough amounts.

Essential Minerals

The main minerals needed by a plant are:

- NITRATES for growth.
- POTASSIUM and PHOSPHATES to make enzymes, and ...
- MAGNESIUM and IRON to make chlorophyll.

HIGHER/SPECIAL TIER

NITRATES

- Needed to make proteins.
- If there's a shortage, it leads to ...
- ... STUNTED GROWTH and YELLOW OLDER LEAVES.

POTASSIUM

- Needed to help photosynthesis and make respiration ENZYMES.
- If there's a shortage, it leads to ...
- ... YELLOW LEAVES WITH DEAD SPOTS.

PHOSPHATES

- Needed in photosynthesis and respiration.
- If there's a shortage, it leads to ...
- ... POOR ROOT GROWTH and PURPLE YOUNGER LEAVES.

Active Transport

ESSENTIAL MINERALS are often taken up by roots AGAINST A CONCENTRATION GRADIENT ...
... BY ACTIVE TRANSPORT (see page 13).

Plant Responses

Plants are sensitive to: • **LIGHT** • **MOISTURE** • **GRAVITY**

- SHOOTS grow TOWARDS LIGHT (POSITIVE PHOTOTROPISM) and ...
  ... AGAINST THE FORCE OF GRAVITY (NEGATIVE GEOTROPISM).
- ROOTS grow TOWARDS MOISTURE and in the DIRECTION OF GRAVITY (POSITIVE GEOTROPISM).

These responses are controlled by HORMONES (often AUXINS) which coordinate and control growth.

Hormones are produced in the growing tips of shoots and roots but can then collect unevenly ...
... causing unequal growth rates in different parts of the plant.

Gravity

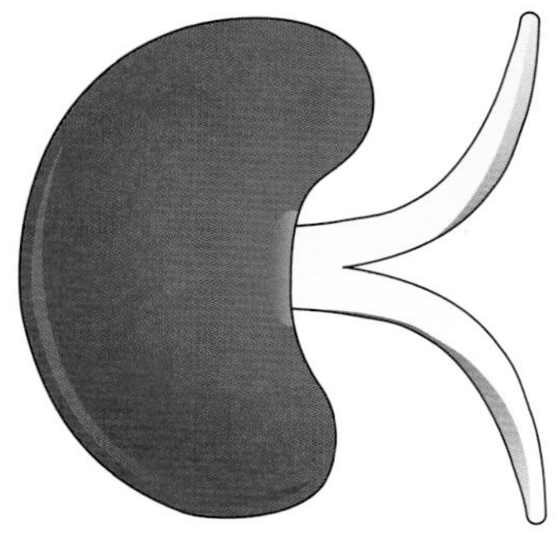
GERMINATING SEEDLING

In the Shoot ...
- ... HORMONE collects on the LOWER SIDE ...
- ... and STIMULATES THE GROWTH of the CELLS on this side.
- Therefore the SHOOT GROWS UPWARDS ...
- ... away from the force of gravity. This is NEGATIVE GEOTROPISM.

In the Root ...
- ... HORMONE also collects on the LOWER SIDE ...
- ... but SLOWS DOWN THE GROWTH of the CELLS on this side.
- Therefore the ROOT GROWS DOWNWARDS ...
- ... towards the force of gravity. This is POSITIVE GEOTROPISM.

HIGHER/SPECIAL TIER

The HORMONE (AUXIN) causes the CELLS TO ELONGATE and the SHOOT CURVES.

Light

- In shoots, LIGHT destroys HORMONES and causes them ...
  - ... to accumulate on the shaded part of the stem ...
    - ... which causes growth on that side ...
      - ... and the plant grows towards the sun.
        - This is POSITIVE PHOTOTROPISM.

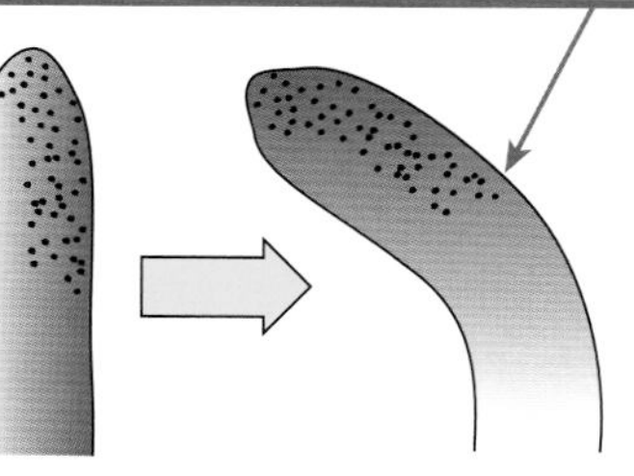

Artificial Use Of Hormones

Farmers USE HORMONES to INCREASE their YIELD and to ORGANISE RIPENING TIMES to suit their own convenience (It's quite unnatural really isn't it?).

- ROOTING COMPOUND - Consists of a hormone which encourages ...
  ... the GROWTH OF ROOTS ...
  ... in STEM CUTTINGS ...
  ... so lots of plants can be obtained from only one.
- RIPENING HORMONE - Causes plants to ripen at set time ...
  ... sometimes during transport.
  It is achieved by spraying.
- SELECTIVE WEEDKILLERS - Disrupt the normal growth patterns ...
  ... of their target plants ...
  ... leaving other plants untouched.

Green Plants As Organisms

- The reproductive organs of a plant are contained in the FLOWER.
- The STEM contains tubes called XYLEM TISSUE for the transport of water and minerals and PHLOEM TISSUE for the transport of food substances.
- LEAVES have a large surface area. Ideal for photosynthesis.
- ROOTS provide stability and absorb water.
- Photosynthesis is the process by which plants make their own food called GLUCOSE.

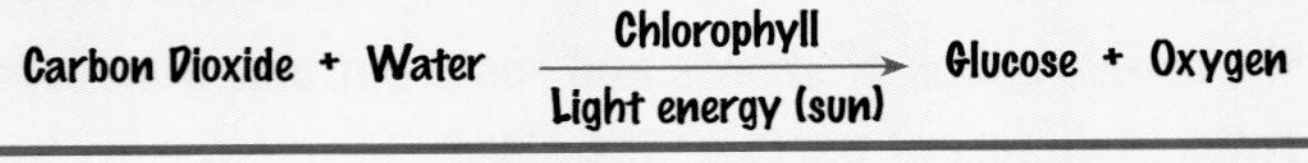

$$\text{Carbon Dioxide} + \text{Water} \xrightarrow[\text{Light energy (sun)}]{\text{Chlorophyll}} \text{Glucose} + \text{Oxygen}$$

HIGHER/SPECIAL TIER

$$6CO_2 + 6H_2O \xrightarrow[\text{Light energy (sun)}]{\text{Chlorophyll}} C_6H_{12}O_6 + 6O_2$$

- Plants convert sugars into i) starch for storage, ii) cellulose for making cell walls, iii) proteins for growth and enzymes and iv) lipids for storing in seeds.

- The rate of photosynthesis depends on the TEMPERATURE, CONCENTRATION OF CARBON DIOXIDE (which is also dependent on the amount of water available) and LIGHT INTENSITY.
- All three interact to affect the rate.

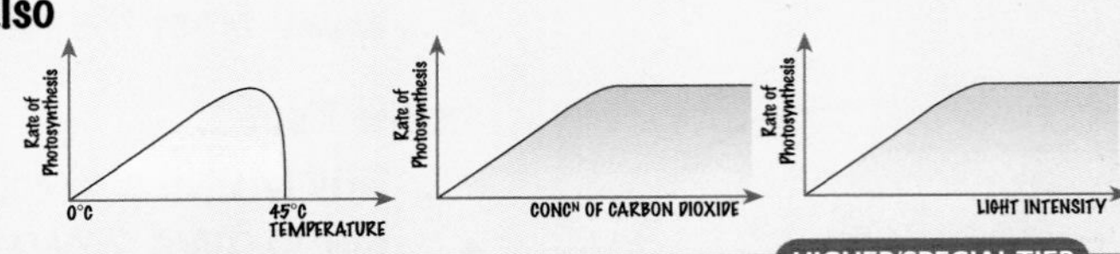

HIGHER/SPECIAL TIER

- Photosynthesis is also affected if a plant does not absorb enough blue and red light.

- Loss of water vapour through leaves is called TRANSPIRATION.
- The flow of water from root to leaf is called the TRANSPIRATION STREAM.
- Transpiration is vital to the plant as it provides water for photosynthesis, support and cooling of the leaves.
- Transpiration depends on the size of the STOMATA on the leaf which are controlled by GUARD CELLS.
- A plant is rigid if its stomata are open allowing transpiration to take place and vice versa.

HIGHER/SPECIAL TIER

- A plant cell is TURGID if water passes into it by osmosis.
- A plant cell is FLACCID if water passes out of it by osmosis.

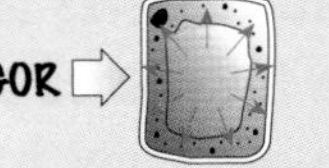

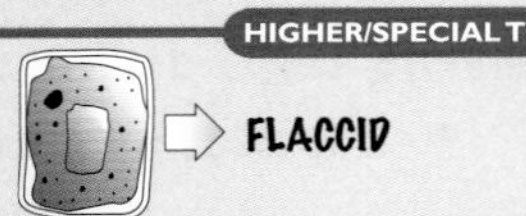

- Essential minerals are needed by a plant to make proteins which keep the plant healthy and working properly.
- Minerals dissolved in water are taken in by plants through root hairs.
- Fertilisers can be added to soil to provide essential minerals.
- Nitrates, potassium, phosphates, magnesium and iron are the main minerals needed by a plant.

HIGHER/SPECIAL TIER

- Shortage of nitrates leads to stunted growth and yellow older leaves.
- Shortage of potassium leads to yellow leaves with dead spots.
- Shortage of phosphates leads to poor root growth and purple younger leaves.

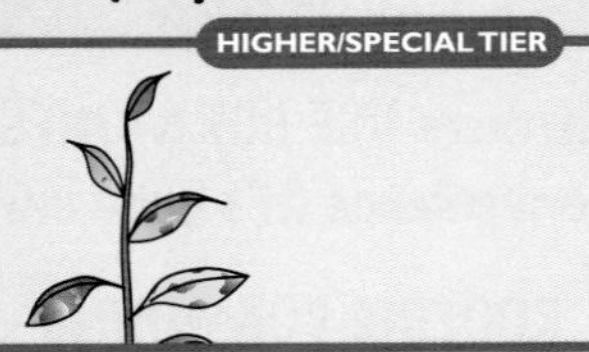

- Shoots are sensitive to light (POSITIVE PHOTOTROPISM) and gravity (NEGATIVE GEOTROPISM).
- Roots are sensitive to moisture and gravity (POSITIVE GEOTROPISM).
- The response of a shoot or root is controlled by hormones.
- ARTIFICIAL HORMONES can be used to increase the yield and organise the ripening time.

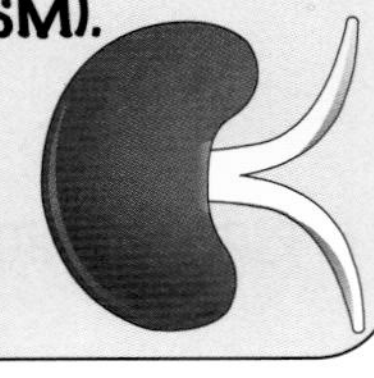

Record the TWENTY SEVEN 'Green Plants as Organisms' facts onto your tape.

Now - READ, COVER, WRITE and CHECK the TWENTY SEVEN facts.

TYPES OF VARIATION

- CONTINUOUS VARIATION
  Shows full range of intermediates e.g. height, weight, intelligence.
- DISCONTINUOUS VARIATION
  Shows no intermediates e.g. eye colour, blood group.

CAUSES OF VARIATION

- INHERITED FACTORS
  this is purely down to the genes you receive. e.g. eye colour, hair colour etc.
- ENVIRONMENTAL FACTORS
  This covers aspects of your upbringing such as quality of parents, school, life experiences etc.

THE NATURE OF THE GENE

- A gene is a section of D.N.A. which determines a particular inherited characteristic.
- Changes to the D.N.A. structure causes mutations which may be harmful, neutral or beneficial.

CELL DIVISION

- MITOSIS - Normal cell division which maintains the number of chromosomes.

- MEIOSIS - Reproductive cell division which halves the chromosome number.

Variation

Mechanism Of Inheritance

Artificial Inheritance

Monohybrid Inheritance

CLONING

- Clones are GENETICALLY IDENTICAL INDIVIDUALS.
- Taking cuttings, tissue culture, and embryo transplants all produce clones.
- Results in a reduction in the number of alleles in a population.

SELECTIVE BREEDING

- Selective breeding is responsible for many of the varieties of domestic livestock and fruit and vegetables on our farms.

ANCESTOR → CAULIFLOWER

- Like cloning, selective breeding results in a reduction in the number of alleles in a population.

INHERITANCE OF SEX AND SEX-LINKED DISORDERS

- The X and Y chromosomes are the sex chromosomes.
- XX = female, XY = male
- Haemophilia and colour blindness are sex linked disorders because the allele for them is carried on the X-chromosome.

WORK OF MENDEL

- Mendel was the founding father of genetics. He used pea plants.

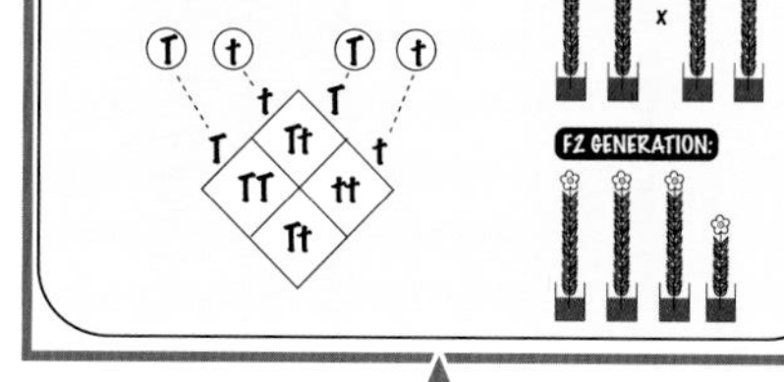

GENETIC ENGINEERING

- Genes are made to perform their 'task', but from inside a different organism.

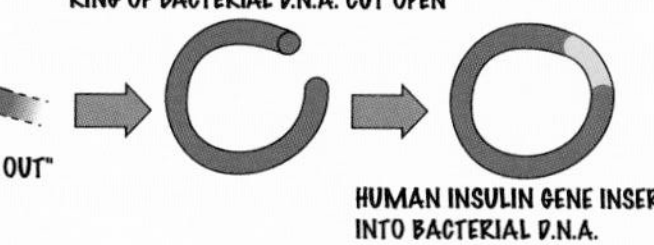
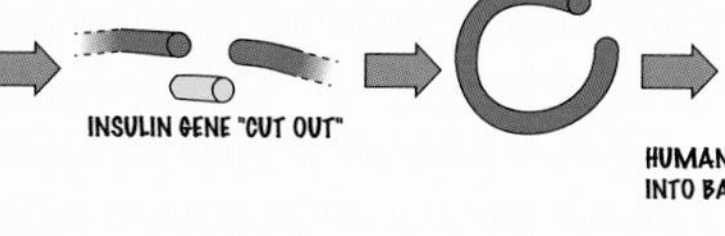

e.g. Commercial production of INSULIN.

INHERITED DISORDERS

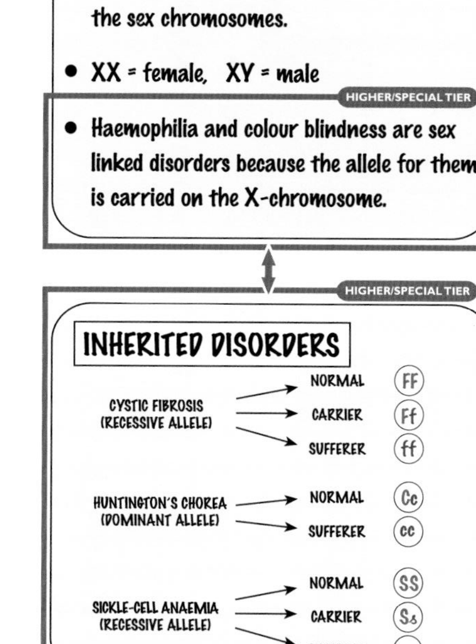
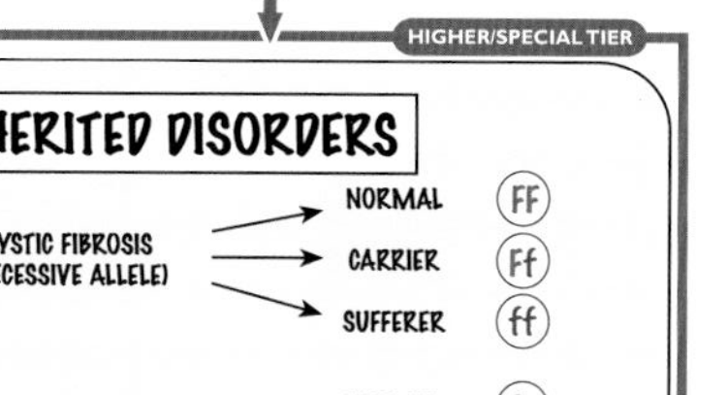
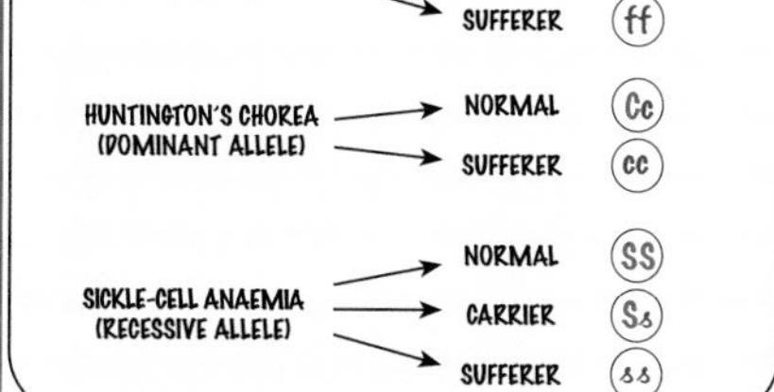
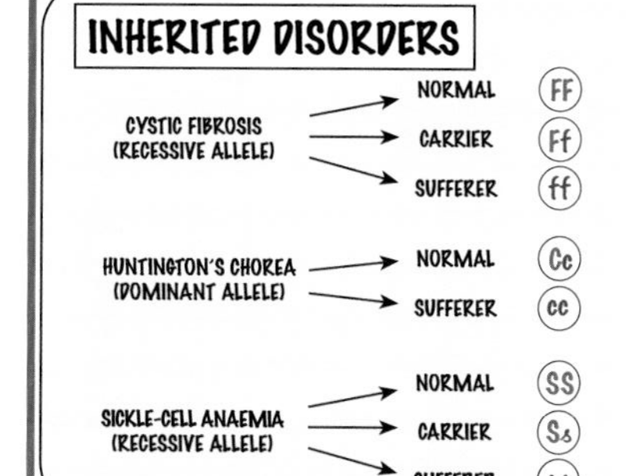
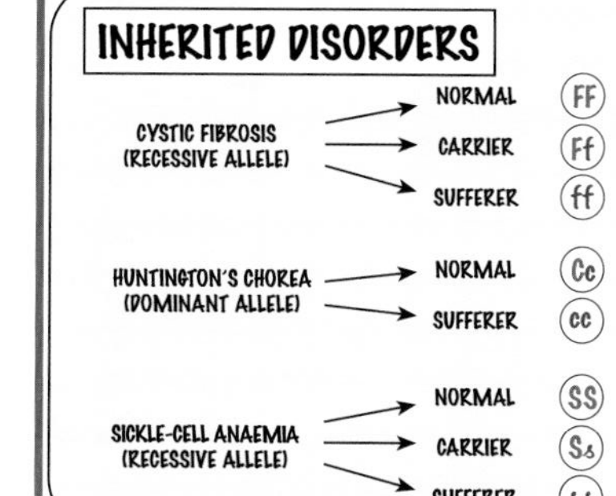

TERMINOLOGY OF INHERITANCE

PHENOTYPE		GENOTYPE	
TONGUE ROLLING	T	T	HOMOZYGOUS DOMINANT
BLUE EYES	b	B	HETEROZYGOUS
ATTACHED EAR LOBES	e	e	HOMOZYGOUS RECESSIVE

DIFFERENCES BETWEEN INDIVIDUALS of the **SAME SPECIES** is called **VARIATION.**

No two people are exactly the same ...

... even identical twins are different in some ways.

Types of Variation

- **CONTINUOUS VARIATION**

  Height is an example of continuous variation.
  Looking at the heights in an infant school year group ...
  ... there is a smooth change from very short pupils to the very tall pupils.
  We can show this in the following way ...

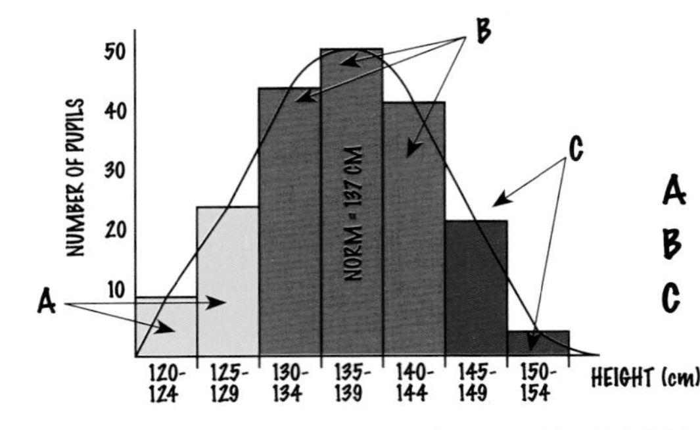

A = very short
B = most pupils are this height (the norm)
C = very tall

(This graph shows a **NORMAL DISTRIBUTION.**)

- **DISCONTINUOUS VARIATION**

  Tongue rolling is an example of discontinuous variation.
  You can either roll your tongue or you cannot ...
  ... there are **NO HALF MEASURES.**
  We can show this in a **BAR CHART.**

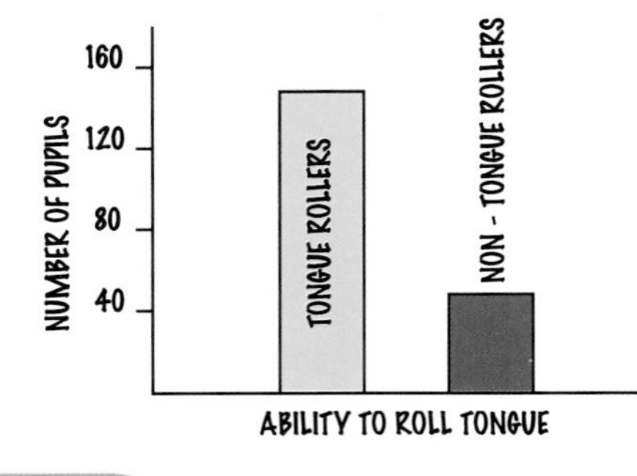

Other examples of discontinuous variation include eye colour, ear lobe type and blood groups.

Causes Of Variation

Variation may be due to ...

- ... **GENETIC CAUSES** because of the different genes they have inherited, or ...
- ... **ENVIRONMENTAL CAUSES** because of the conditions in which they have developed.

However, usually **VARIATION IS DUE TO A COMBINATION OF GENETIC AND ENVIRONMENTAL CAUSES**

An example of some environmental causes ...

An example of some genetic causes ...

The Genetic Information

This information is carried by **GENES** which are found on **CHROMOSOMES**.
Different genes control the development of different characteristics.
Many genes have different forms called **ALLELES** which may produce different characteristics i.e. genes for brown eyes and genes for blue eyes are **ALLELES**; in other words different forms of the same gene!

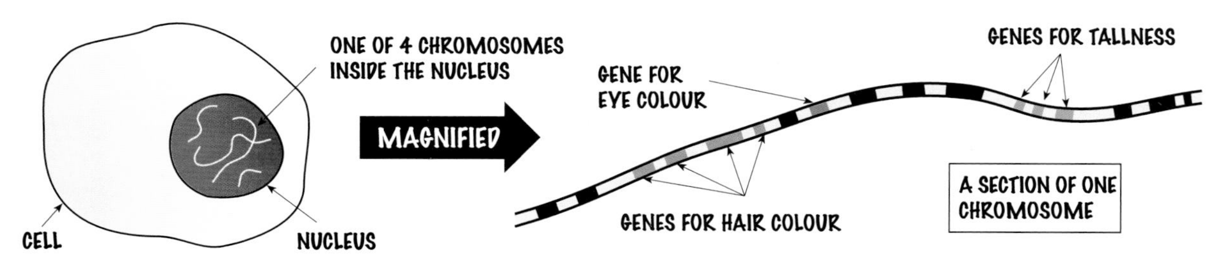

Chromosomes come in **PAIRS**, but different species have different numbers of pairs ...
e.g. Humans have 23 pairs which results in tremendous variation.

Mutations - Changes To The Genetic Information

New forms of genes and therefore **VARIATION** can arise from changes (**MUTATIONS**) in existing genes.
Mutations occur naturally, but their frequency is increased by ...

- EXPOSURE TO ULTRA-VIOLET LIGHT
- EXPOSURE TO X-RAYS
- EXPOSURE TO RADIOACTIVE SUBSTANCES
- EXPOSURE TO CERTAIN CHEMICALS

HIGHER/SPECIAL TIER

Inheritance v Environment

There has been lively debate for many years over the relative importance of genetic and environmental factors in determining human attributes. This is often referred to as the "Nature verses Nurture" argument.

	INHERITED FACTORS	ENVIRONMENTAL FACTORS
INTELLIGENCE	• The physical structure of the brain and nerve connections. • A person's natural ability in a subject??	• Quality of schooling. • Parental support. • Life experiences.
SPORTING ABILITY	• A person's natural physique/body structure. • A person's natural sporting ability and co-ordination.	• Good coaching and support. • Quality of facilities and the opportunity to practice.

Some people argue that **INHERITED FACTORS** are most important ...
... others consider **ENVIRONMENTAL FACTORS** are the key ...
... but other people think that **BOTH** play an equally important role.

The Genetic Information

- In normal cells chromosomes always exist in pairs.
- They consist of LONG, COILED MOLECULES called D.N.A.
- Genes are SECTIONS OF D.N.A. which DETERMINE INHERITED CHARACTERISTICS.
- This information is in the form of a CODE ...
- ... which controls the ORDER IN WHICH AMINO ACIDS ARE ASSEMBLED TO PRODUCE PROTEINS.

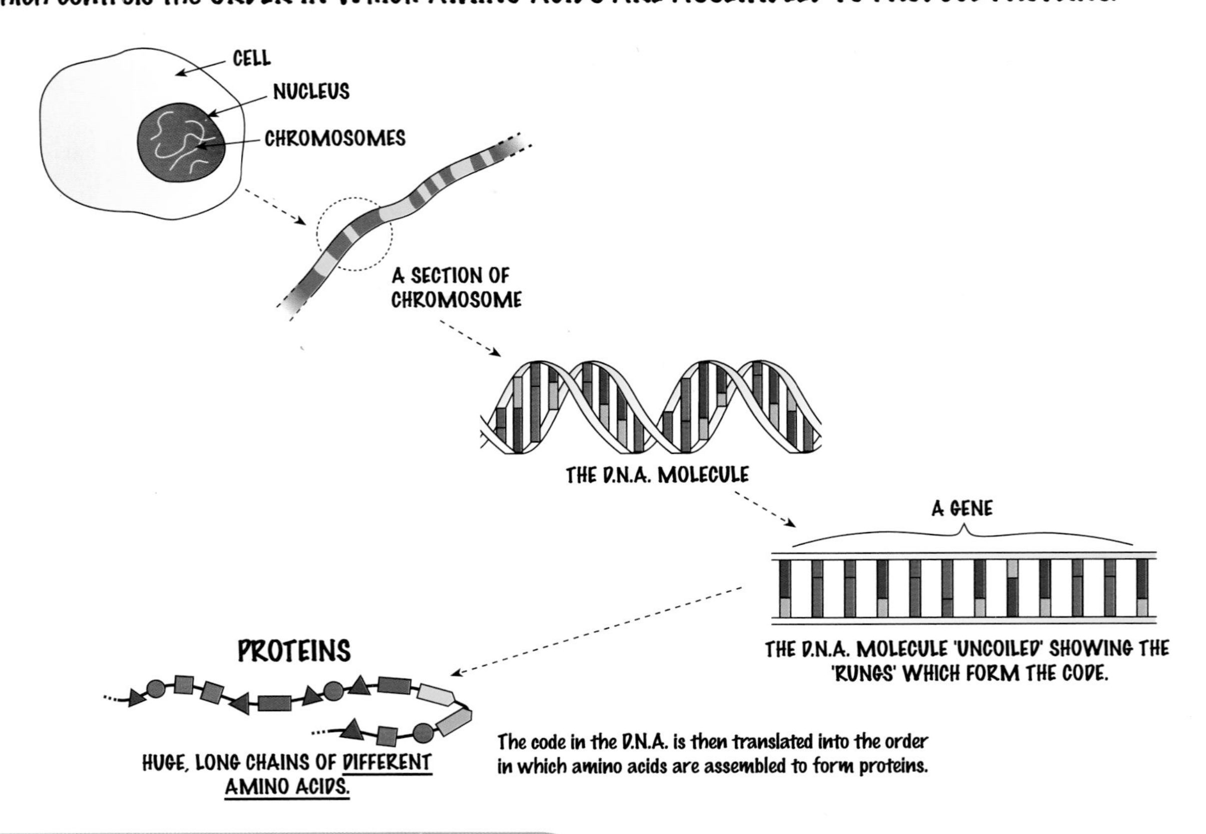

How Mutations Affect DNA Structure

Mutations are changes to the structure of the D.N.A. molecule which result in a new form of gene.
These changes can then be passed onto 'daughter' cells as a result of cell division.
In other words the organisation of part of the D.N.A. molecule is somehow disturbed resulting in ...
... the cell producing different sequences of amino acids and therefore different proteins!

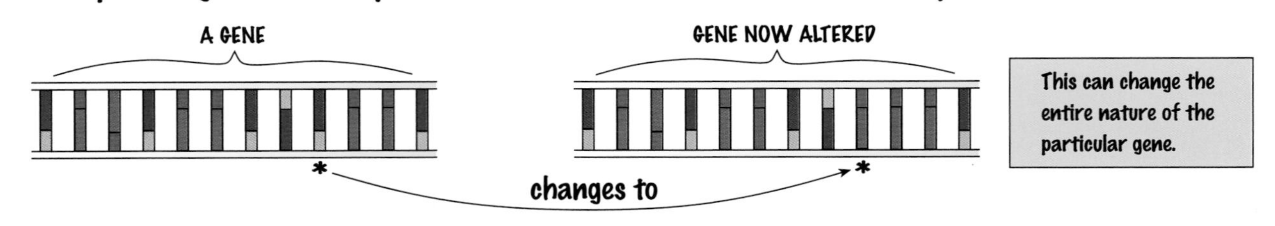

This can change the entire nature of the particular gene.

CAUSES	EFFECTS
• Mutations occur naturally but ...	• Most mutations are HARMFUL and in ...
• .... there is an increased risk of mutation if ...	• ... REPRODUCTIVE CELLS can cause DEATH or ABNORMALITY.
• ... individuals are exposed to MUTAGENIC AGENTS ...	• In BODY CELLS they may cause CANCER.
• ... e.g. IONISING RADIATION (Inc. U-V LIGHT, X-RAYS) ...	• Some mutations are NEUTRAL, and in RARE CASES ...
• ... RADIOACTIVE SUBSTANCES and CERTAIN CHEMICALS.	• ... may INCREASE THE SURVIVAL CHANCES OF AN ORGANISM, ...
• THE GREATER THE DOSE, THE GREATER THE RISK.	• ... and its OFFSPRING WHO INHERIT THE GENE.

There are TWO ways in which cells divide, either by **MITOSIS,** ... or **MEIOSIS.**

Mitosis

Takes place in **ASEXUAL** reproduction ... and produces **GENETICALLY IDENTICAL CLONES.**

The cells of offspring produced by asexual reproduction are produced by mitosis from the parental cells. Mitosis also produces all cells for GROWTH and REPAIR.

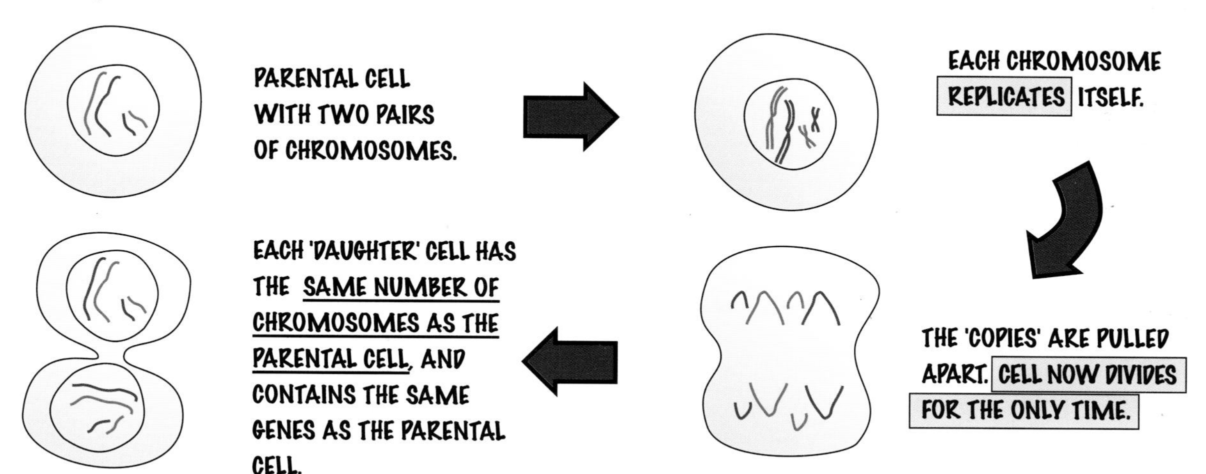

Meiosis

Takes place in **SEXUAL** reproduction ... and **PROMOTES VARIATION.**

This type of cell division occurs in the testes and ovaries and produces the gametes (eggs + sperm).

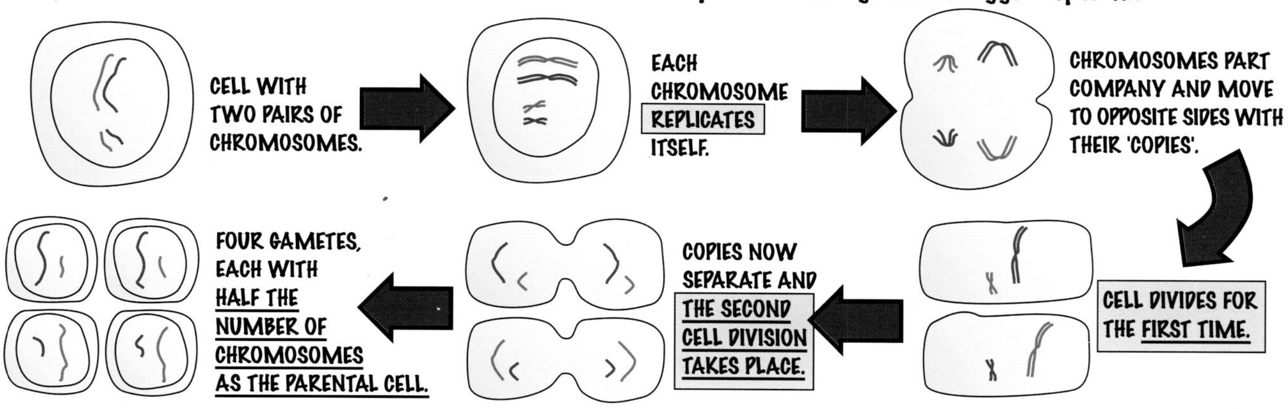

These GAMETES which have been produced in meiosis then FUSE randomly with gametes from another individual in order for a NEW INDIVIDUAL to be PRODUCED IN SEXUAL REPRODUCTION ...

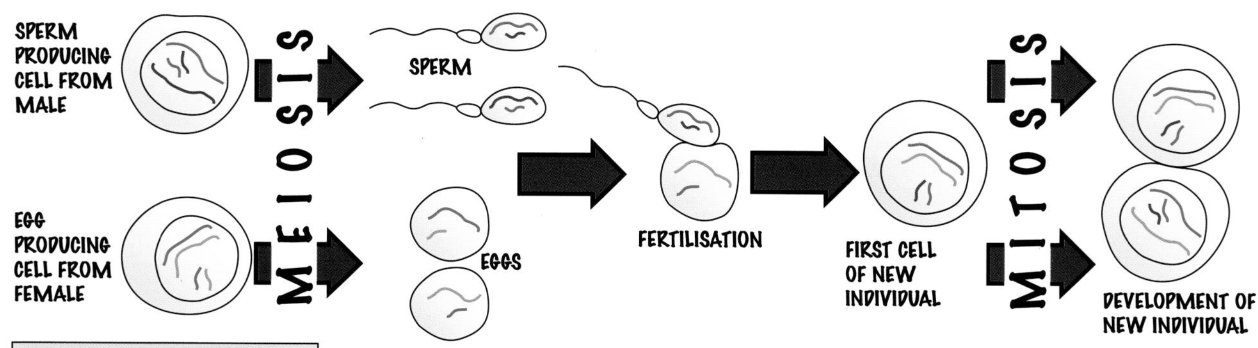

In **SEXUAL REPRODUCTION** ...

1. The GAMETES (eggs + sperm) are produced by MEIOSIS, WHICH 'SHUFFLES' THE GENES.
2. When gametes FUSE, ONE OF EACH PAIR OF GENES COMES FROM EACH PARENT.
3. The genes may be DIFFERENT ALLELES (see page P.66) and so produce DIFFERENT CHARACTERISTICS.

HIGHER/SPECIAL TIER

There are several long words associated with Genetics, but don't be put off. The more you use them, the more familiar they will become to you. Here they are ...

ALLELE This is an ALTERNATIVE FORM of a gene. So for instance if we were talking about genes for eye colour, we would say that there were two alleles for eye colour, Brown and Blue. Similarly the genes for being able/not able to roll your tongue are alleles.

DOMINANT This refers to an allele which controls the development of a characteristic when it is present on only one of the chromosomes in a pair.

RECESSIVE This refers to an allele which controls the development of a characteristic only if it is present on both of the chromosomes in a pair.

HOMOZYGOUS If both chromosomes in a pair contain the same allele of a gene then the individual is homozygous for that gene or condition.

HETEROZYGOUS If the chromosomes in a pair contain different alleles of a gene then the individual is heterozygous for that gene or condition.

GENOTYPE This refers to the particular pair of alleles representing a certain characteristic.
e.g. We can refer to a homozygous dominant (BB) a homozygous recessive (bb) or a heterozygous (Bb) genotype for eye colour.

PHENOTYPE This refers to the outward expression of a genotype e.g. BB and Bb above are two different genotypes but each produce a Brown-eyed phenotype. Only bb gives a blue eyed phenotype.

FOR EXAMPLE It's perhaps a little easier to understand if we look at a diagram of a ...
... pair of chromosomes and specifically at genes which code for ...
... Eye colour, tongue-rolling ability, and type of ear lobe.

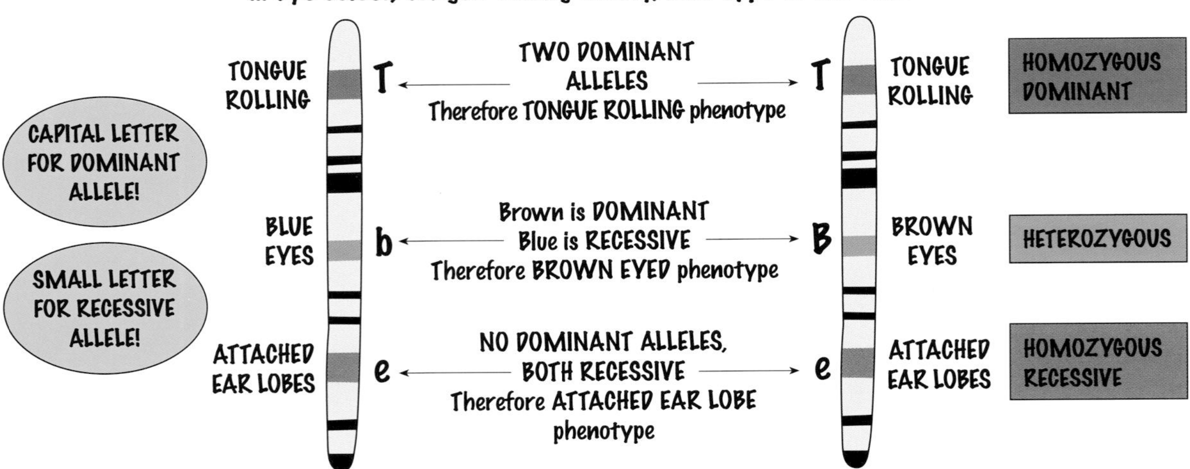

- DOMINANT ALLELES EXPRESS THEMSELVES IF PRESENT ONLY ONCE ...
  ... so an individual can be HOMOZYGOUS DOMINANT (BB) or HETEROZYGOUS (Bb) for brown eyes.
- RECESSIVE ALLELES EXPRESS THEMSELVES ONLY IF PRESENT TWICE ...
  ... so an individual can only be HOMOZYGOUS RECESSIVE (bb) for blue eyes.

So the possible combinations are ...

	HOMOZYGOUS DOMINANT	HETEROZYGOUS	HOMOZYGOUS RECESSIVE
TONGUE ROLLING	TT (can roll)	Tt (can roll)	tt (can't roll)
EYE COLOUR	BB (brown)	Bb (brown)	bb (blue)
EAR LOBES	EE (free lobes)	Ee (free lobes)	ee (attached lobes)

Gregor Mendel

- **GREGOR MENDEL** was born in Austria in 1822 ...
  ... his **WORK** on **PEA PLANTS** marks the **START OF MODERN GENETICS.**
- He investigated the **HEIGHT OF PEA PLANTS** ...
  ... which are either **TALL OR DWARF.**
- He started with **PURE-BREEDING** (Homozygous) Parent Plants and produced an **F1 GENERATION** ...
  ... which he allowed to **SELF-POLLINATE** and produce the **F2 GENERATION.**

We now call the inheritance of features controlled by **ONE PAIR OF ALLELES** **MONOHYBRID INHERITANCE.**

A Summary Of Mendel's Work

PARENTS:

'PURE BREEDING' TALL PLANT 'PURE BREEDING' DWARF PLANT

TALL x DWARF

TT x tt **PARENTAL GENOTYPE**

GAMETE GENOTYPES

T T t t

Tt Tt Tt Tt

F1 GENERATION:

F1 GENOTYPES

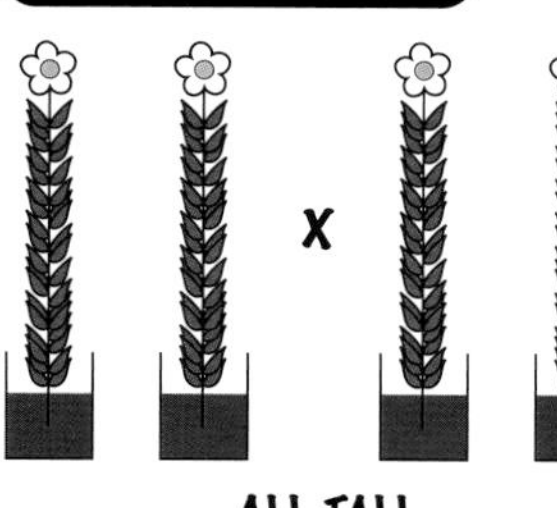

ALL TALL

F1 GAMETE GENOTYPES

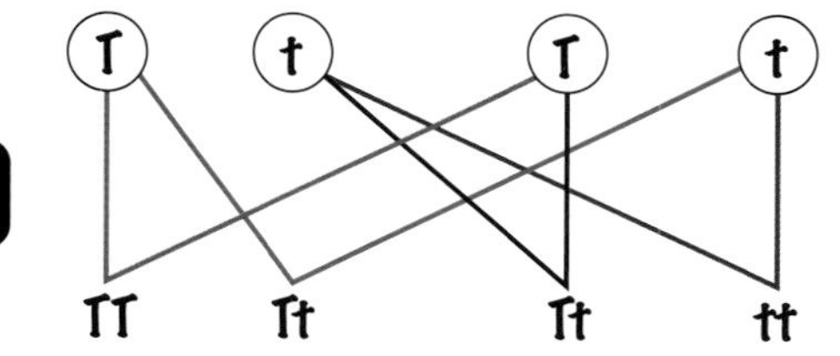

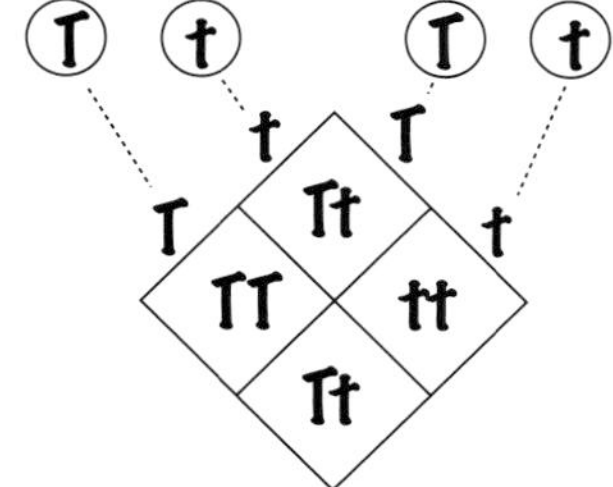

F2 GENERATION:

F2 GENOTYPES

(... a RATIO of 3 TALL to 1 DWARF)

TALL DWARF

- He called "dwarfness" a recessive characteristic and interpreted the genetic patterns responsible for his results.
- However, modern microscopes and techniques hadn't been invented, and no one knew about genes and chromosomes, so his work was not recognised until after his death.

Inheritance Of Sex - The Sex Chromosomes

- Humans have 23 pairs of CHROMOSOMES ...
- ... of which one pair are the SEX CHROMOSOMES.
- In females these are IDENTICAL and are called the X chromosomes.
- In males ONE IS MUCH SHORTER THAN THE OTHER and they're called the X and Y chromosomes. (Y being the shorter).

THE POSSIBLE PERMUTATIONS

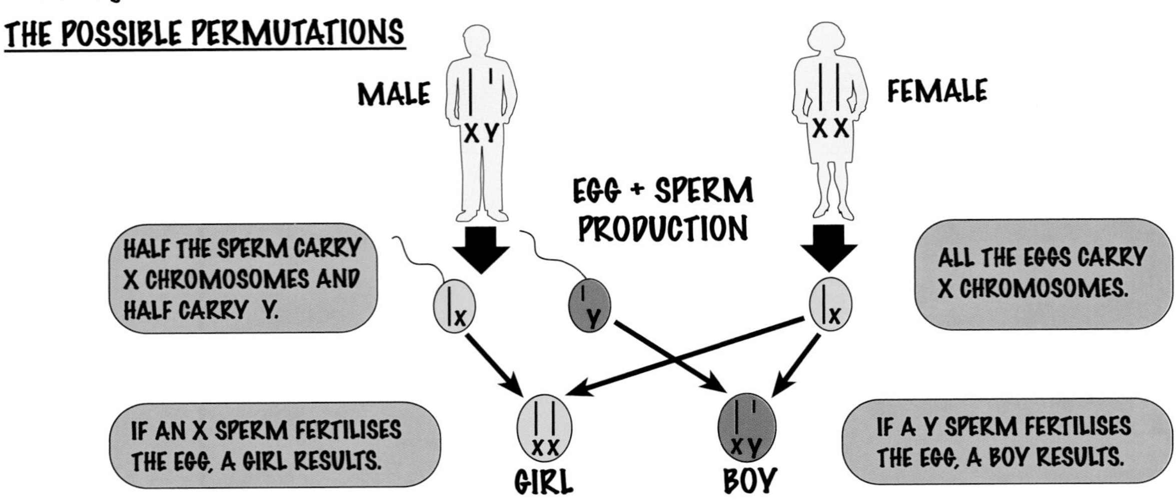

- Like all pairs of chromosomes, the SEX CHROMOSOMES SEPARATE DURING EGG + SPERM PRODUCTION ...
- ... (i.e. meiosis) resulting in just one in each sperm or egg. Haemophilia and colour blindness are disorders which are sex-linked.

HIGHER/SPECIAL TIER

Sex-linked Disorders

Some disorders, unfortunately are INHERITED. In such cases the 'laws of genetics' decide which offspring inherit the disease, which are 'carriers', and which are completely free of the responsible gene.
In SEX-LINKED CONDITIONS the issue is further complicated because the allele concerned is carried on the x chromosome. e.g. HAEMOPHILIA.

- Haemophilia is an inherited sex-linked condition in which the blood doesn't clot because of a missing chemical factor controlled by a single allele on the x chromosome.
- Men are usually most at risk but women can be carriers. Women are less likely to be sufferers since they have two x chromosomes and therefore have a chance to 'mask' the faulty gene.
- Colour blindness is inherited in exactly the same way.

POSSIBLE GENOTYPES:

X_BX_B	X_BX_b	X_bX_b	X_BY	X_bY
Normal female	Carrier female	Haemophiliac female, dies before birth	Normal male	Haemophiliac male

Normal female × Haemophiliac male

X_BX_B × X_bY

Gametes X_B X_B × X_b Y

X_BX_b	X_BY	X_BX_b	X_BY
Carrier female	Normal male	Carrier female	Normal male

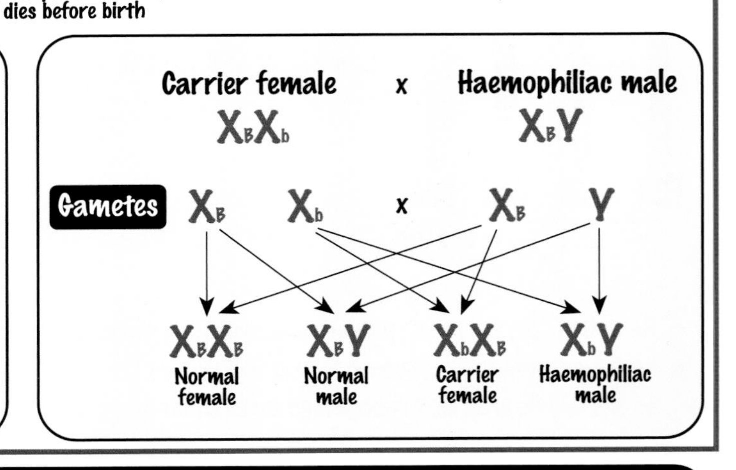

Inherited disorders are not only confined to the x chromosomes ...

Cystic Fibrosis - Caused By Recessive Alleles

- Cystic Fibrosis can be passed on by parents, neither of whom have the disease ...
- ... if each is carrying just one RECESSIVE allele for the condition.
- It is a disorder of cell membranes causing THICK and STICKY MUCUS ...
- ... especially in the LUNGS, GUT and PANCREAS, which leads to various complications.

HIGHER/SPECIAL TIER

PARENTS:- CARRIER MALE Ff — Ff CARRIER FEMALE

EGGS + SPERM:- F f F f

CHILDREN:- FF NORMAL, Ff CARRIER, Ff CARRIER, ff CYSTIC FIBROSIS

- This particular cross would result in a 1 in 4 chance of producing a sufferer.

Huntington's Chorea - Caused By A Dominant Allele

- Huntington's Chorea, a disorder of the nervous system, is passed on by one parent who has the disease ...
- ... and therefore has a DOMINANT allele for it.
- It produces TREMORS, and WRITHING and ultimately DEMENTIA (loss of sanity).

HIGHER/SPECIAL TIER

PARENTS:- HUNTINGTON'S CHOREA FEMALE Cc — cc NORMAL MALE

EGGS + SPERM:- C c c c

CHILDREN:- Cc HUNTINGTON'S, Cc HUNTINGTON'S, cc NORMAL, cc NORMAL

- Here there is a 1 in 2 chance of producing a sufferer.

Sickle-Cell Anaemia - Caused By A Recessive Allele

- Sickle-cell anaemia can be passed on by parents neither of whom has the disease ...
- ... if each is carrying just ONE RECESSIVE ALLELE for the condition.
- Sufferers produce abnormally shaped red blood cells (SICKLE-SHAPED!) ...
- ... and experience general weakness and ANAEMIA.

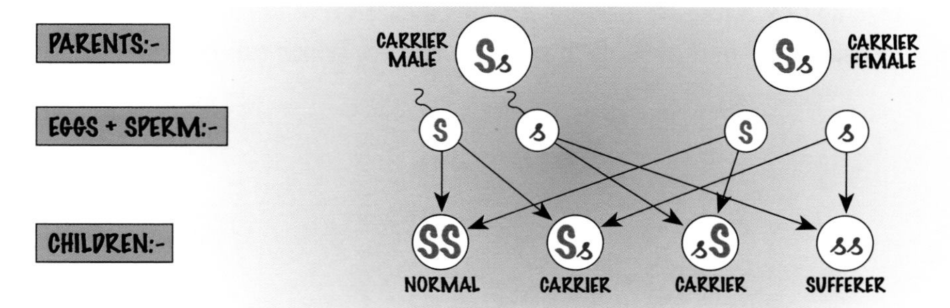

- The HETEROZYGOUS (Ss) INDIVIDUALS also show up to 50% sickling of cells ...
- ... but have an INCREASED RESISTANCE TO MALARIA which is an advantage ...
- ... in areas where MALARIA is prevalent.
- This advantage maintains the gene in the population.

Reproducing Plants Artificially

- Plants can reproduce **ASEXUALLY** i.e. without a partner and many do so naturally.
- All the offspring produced **ASEXUALLY** are **CLONES** ...
- ... i.e. they are **GENETICALLY IDENTICAL TO THE PARENT PLANT.**

TAKING CUTTINGS:

- When a gardener has a plant with all the **DESIRED CHARACTERISTICS** ...
- ... he may choose to produce lots of them by taking **STEM, LEAF** or **ROOT CUTTINGS** ...
- These should be grown in a **DAMP ATMOSPHERE** until **ROOTS DEVELOP.**

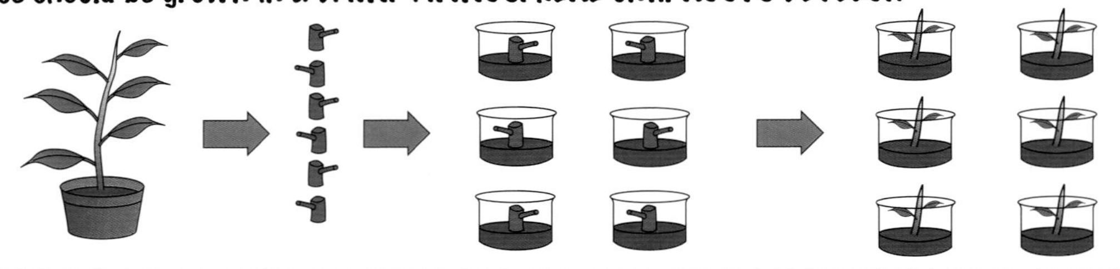

HIGHER/SPECIAL TIER

Cloning

CLONES are **GENETICALLY IDENTICAL INDIVIDUALS** e.g. identical twins. So if you've got an organism which is just ideal why not clone thousands of them? This is exactly what's happening in modern agriculture, and this is how ...

1. Taking cuttings ... This is dealt with above.
2. Tissue culture ...

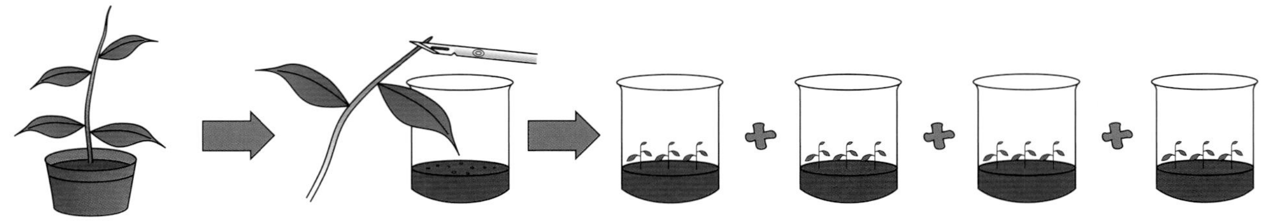

PARENT PLANT - with the characteristics that you want.

A few cells are scraped off into several beakers containing NUTRIENTS AND HORMONES.

A week or two later we've got lots and lots of genetically identical plantlets growing. And we can do the same to these ...

- This whole process must be **ASEPTIC** (carried out in the **ABSENCE OF HARMFUL BACTERIA**) ... ... otherwise the new plants will **ROT.**

3. Embryo transplants ... Instead of waiting for normal breeding cycles farmers can obtain many more offspring by using their best animals to produce embryos which can be inserted into 'mother' animals.

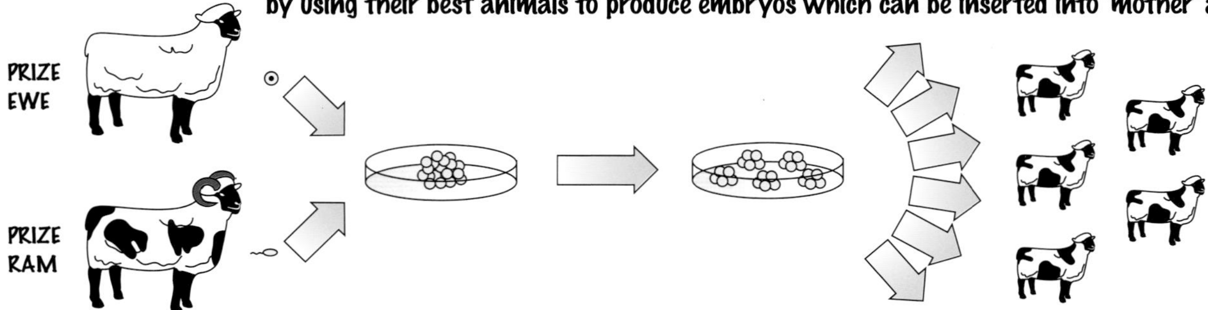

PARENTS with desired characteristics are mated.

Embryo is removed before the cells become specialised ...

... then split apart into several clumps.

These embryos are then implanted into the uteruses of sheep who will eventually give birth to clones.

Selective Breeding

NEW VARIETIES of organisms can be bred by taking advantage of VARIATION.

- Organisms with a DESIRED CHARACTERISTIC, are SELECTED and BRED WITH SIMILAR ORGANISMS ...
- ... resulting in offspring, some of which will have an EXAGGERATED VERSION OF THIS CHARACTERISTIC.
- These are then BRED AGAIN with SIMILAR INDIVIDUALS, and so on, UNTIL THE DESIRED RESULT IS ACHIEVED.
- Many of our domestic livestock, fruit and vegetables would be unrecognisable to someone who lived three hundred years ago.

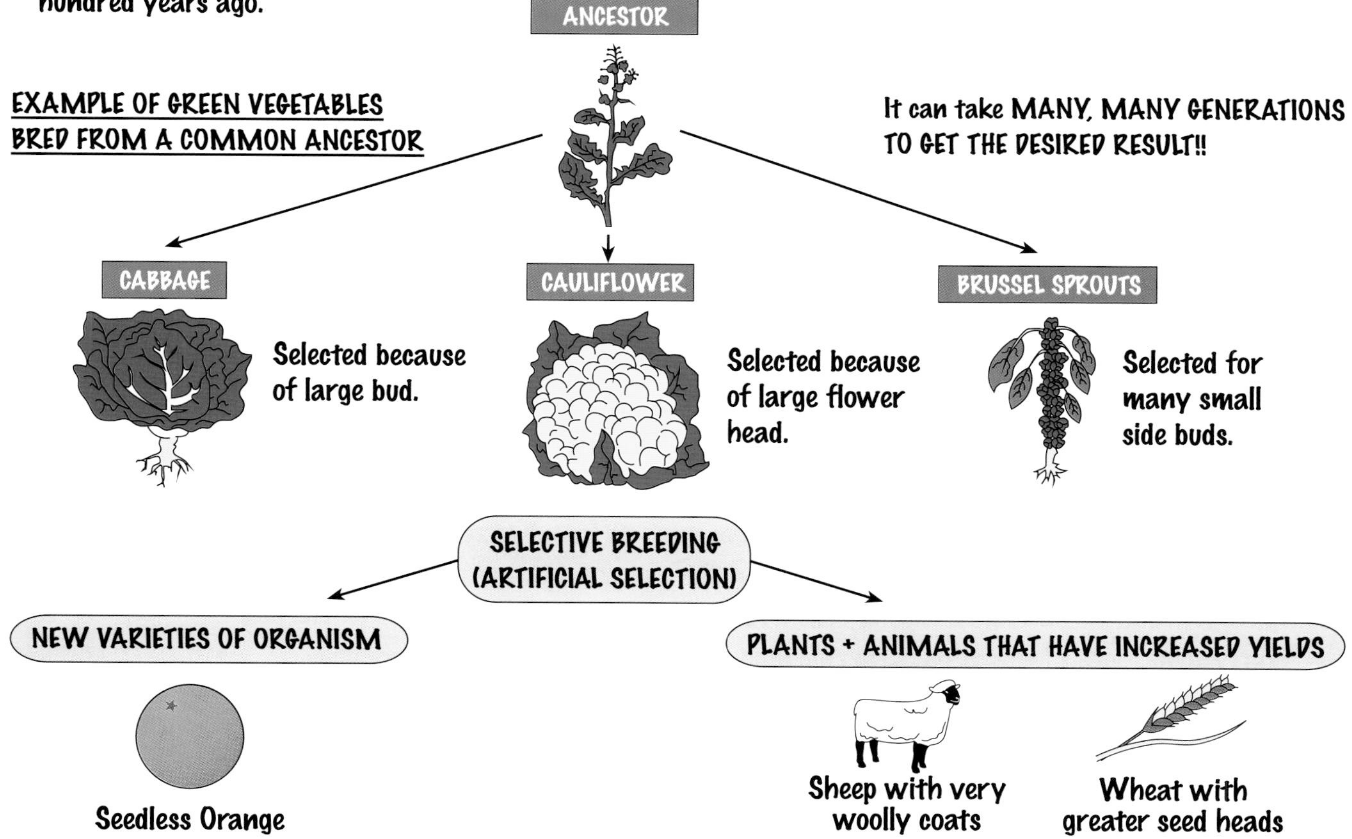

HIGHER/SPECIAL TIER

During SELECTIVE BREEDING it is important to have an EXTENDED BREEDING PROGRAMME ...
... to produce a GENETICALLY STABLE BREEDING POOL.

Advantages And Disadvantages Of Cloning And Selective Breeding

	ADVANTAGES	DISADVANTAGES
CLONING	• Allows LARGE NUMBERS of organisms with the DESIRED CHARACTERISTICS to be produced. • EFFICIENT PROCESS that can increase the economic performance of farmers and plant growers.	• Cloning results in a REDUCED NUMBER OF ALLELES in the population. • LOSS OF VARIATION which reduces the species ability to respond to environmental change.
SELECTIVE BREEDING	• Produces an organism with THE RIGHT CHARACTERISTICS for a particular function. • In farming and horticulture produces a MORE EFFICIENT and ECONOMICALLY VIABLE process.	• Intensive selection results in a REDUCED NUMBER OF ALLELES in the population. • LOSS OF VARIATION which reduces the species ability to respond to environmental change.

A Reminder About Genes

- Genes are sections of D.N.A. which code for a particular protein

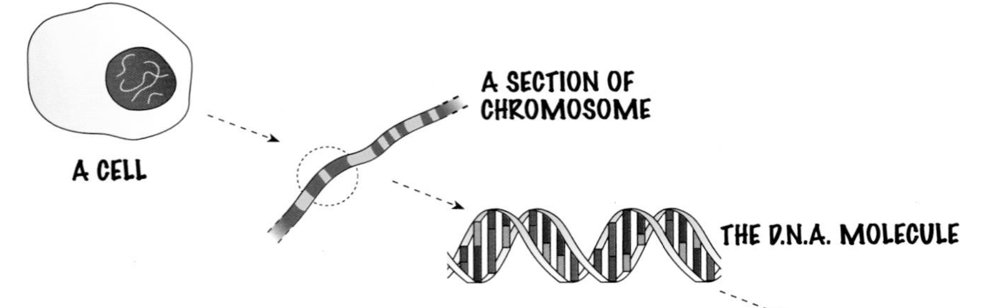

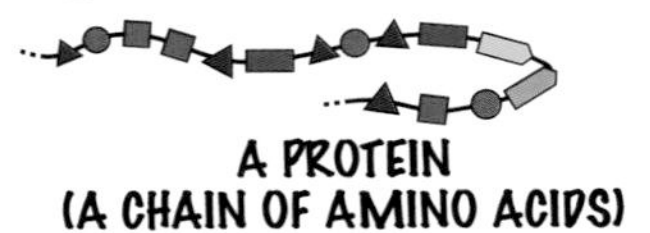

- Scientists now know which sections of D.N.A. make what ...
  ... (well they know quite a lot of it!!)
- This knowledge can be put to very good use!!

Genetic Engineering - The Process

- Basically genes can be 'cut out' of the D.N.A. of one organism using ENZYMES, ...
  ... and then spliced into the D.N.A. of a bacterium using different enzymes.
- The bacterium now has coded instructions to make a new substance and will pass these instructions on to its daughter cells which will pass them on to theirs etc. etc. etc.
- Pretty soon there's loads of bacteria churning out the new substance quite happily ...

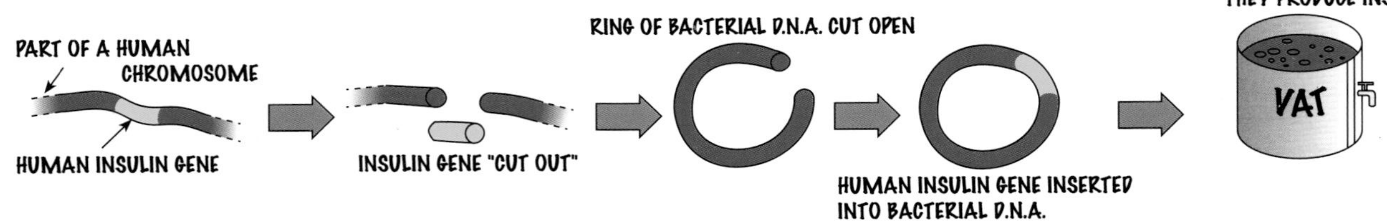

- When the above process has been completed the bacteria is CULTURED ON A LARGE SCALE ...
- ... and COMMERCIAL QUANTITIES OF INSULIN are then produced.

GENES CAN ALSO BE TRANSFERRED TO THE CELLS OF ANIMALS AND PLANTS AT AN EARLY STAGE IN THEIR DEVELOPMENT IN ORDER TO PRODUCE DESIRED CHARACTERISTICS!!

The Great Genetics Debate

- SCIENTISTS have made GREAT ADVANCES in their understanding of genes and ...

1. ... have IDENTIFIED GENES that control certain characteristics.
2. ... can determine whether a person's genes may lead to them having an INCREASED RISK of CONTRACTING A PARTICULAR ILLNESS e.g. breast cancer.
3. ... may soon be able to "REMOVE" FAULTY GENES and reduce genetic diseases.

- Some parts of society are CONCERNED that ...

1. ... unborn children will be GENETICALLY SCREENED and aborted if their genetic make-up is faulty.
2. ... parents may want to artificially DECIDE ON THE GENETIC MAKE-UP of their child.
3. ... some insurance companies may GENETICALLY SCREEN applicants and refuse to insure people who have an increased genetic risk of an illness or disease. This may prevent these people being able to drive or buy homes due to lack of insurance.

Variation

- Within the same species individuals will be different. This is VARIATION.
- There are two types of variation. 1. Continuous variation. 2. Discontinuous variation.

HIGHER/SPECIAL TIER

- Variation between individuals depends on genetic and environmental factors.

Mechanism Of Inheritance

- An individual has a particular characteristic due to genes. Genes are found on chromosomes.

HIGHER/SPECIAL TIER

- Genes are sections of D.N.A. if the structure of the D.N.A. molecule is changed, a new gene is formed. These mutations can be harmful, neutral or even beneficial.
- Cells can divide in two ways:
  1. Mitosis which takes place in ASEXUAL reproduction and normal cell division.
  2. Meiosis which takes place only in the testes and ovaries to produce gametes in sexual reproduction.
- The development of a new individual depends on mitosis and meiosis.

Monohybrid Inheritance

HIGHER/SPECIAL TIER

- Gregor Mendels' investigative work on pea plants is the start of modern genetics.

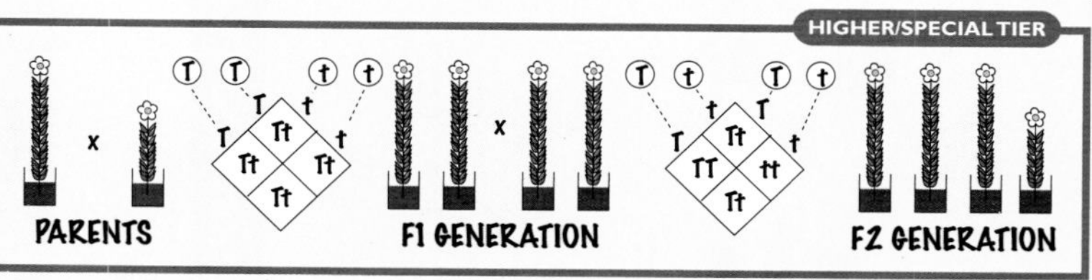

- The X and Y chromosomes are the sex chromosomes. XX = female, XY = male

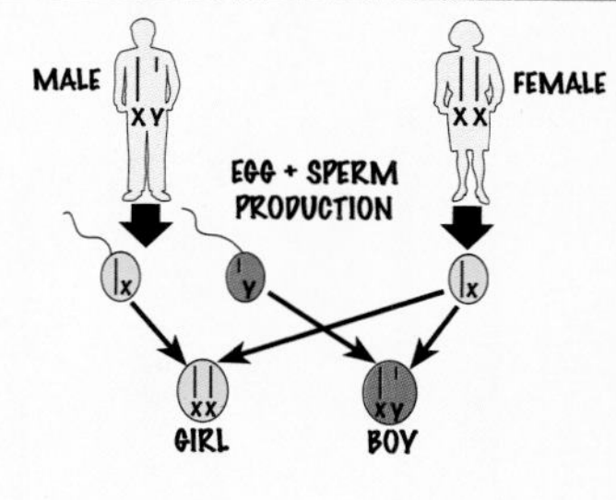

HIGHER/SPECIAL TIER

- Haemophilia and colour blindness are inherited sex linked disorders controlled by a single allele on the X chromosome.

- Cystic Fibrosis and Sickle-cell anaemia are caused by recessive allele while Huntington's Chorea is caused by a dominant allele.

Artificial Inheritance

- All offspring that produce ASEXUALLY produce CLONES. Taking cuttings is a simple way to reproduce clones of plants.

HIGHER/SPECIAL TIER

- Another method is TISSUE CULTURE while EMBRYO TRANSPLANTS can be used to produce many identical embryos which are then implanted in 'mother' animals.

- The continual breeding of organisms with desired characteristics has resulted in the formation of new varieties of organism. This is called SELECTIVE BREEDING.

HIGHER/SPECIAL TIER

- Cloning and selective breeding results in a reduced number of alleles in the population.
- There is great debate about the advantages and disadvantages of genetic engineering.

Record the THREE 'Variation' facts, FOUR 'Mechanism of Inheritance' facts, FOUR 'Monohybrid Inheritance' facts and FIVE 'Artificial Inheritance' facts onto your tape.

Now - READ, COVER, WRITE and CHECK the SIXTEEN facts.

ADAPTATIONS

- Animals and plants have **SPECIAL FEATURES** which make them well suited to their environment, and more likely to survive.

EXTINCTION

Four reasons for extinction ...

- Change in the environment.

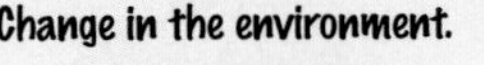

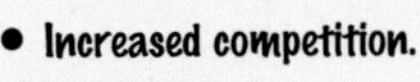
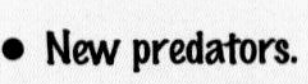
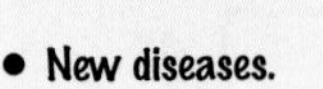

- Increased competition.
- New predators.
- New diseases.

FOSSIL FORMATION

Fossils are formed ...

- ... because of the absence of decay conditions due to ... **COLD, ACIDITY, or LACK OF OXYGEN.**
- ... because the hard parts of animals don't decay too quickly.
- ... because of petrification (turning to stone).

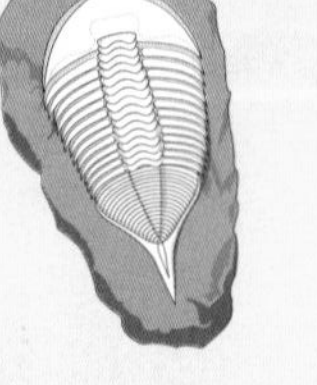
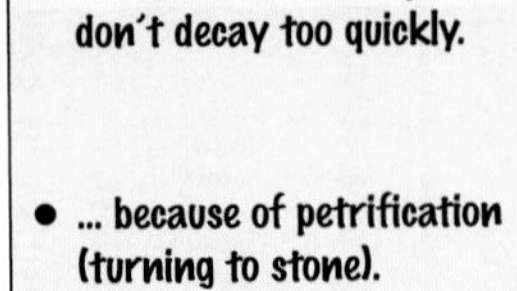

Adaptation, Extinction And Fossils

Evolution

THREE CLASSIC EXAMPLES

HIGHER/SPECIAL TIER

1. Development of long necks in giraffes.
2. The peppered moth.
3. Penicillin resistant bacteria.

EVOLUTION BY NATURAL SELECTION

... is based on 4 key points:-

1. There is **VARIATION** within populations.
2. There is **COMPETITION** for food, mates etc which tends to keep population sizes constant, by ensuring a "struggle for survival".
3. The **BEST ADAPTED** individuals will survive and breed producing offspring.
4. These survivors will therefore **PASS ON THEIR GENES** to their offspring resulting eventually in an 'improved" organism.

CONFLICTING THEORIES

HIGHER/SPECIAL TIER

- John-Baptiste Lamarck (1774 - 1829) suggested that use or mis-use brought about change i.e. giraffes got long necks by stretching for leaves.
- Charles Darwin (1809-1882) developed the theory of evolution by natural selection independently but at exactly the same time as Alfred Russel Wallace.

- **ADAPTATIONS** are **SPECIAL FEATURES OR BEHAVIOUR** which make an organism... ...**ESPECIALLY WELL SUITED TO ITS ENVIRONMENT.**
- **ADAPTATIONS** are part of the **EVOLUTIONARY PROCESS** (see p78) which 'shapes life' so that a habitat is populated by organisms which excel there. Adaptations increase an organism's chance of survival.

Examples Of How Organisms Are Adapted To Their Environment

- **SMALL SURFACE AREA/VOLUME RATIO** to **REDUCE HEAT LOSS.**
- **LARGE AMOUNT OF INSULATING FAT** beneath the skin.
- **WHITE COAT** so that it is **CAMOUFLAGED.**
- **LARGE FEET** to spread its weight on the ice.
- **POWERFUL SWIMMER** so that it can **CATCH ITS FOOD.**
- **HIBERNATES** in the worst weather.

- **LARGE SURFACE AREA/VOLUME RATIO** to **INCREASE HEAT LOSS.**
- **BODY FAT STORED IN HUMP** with almost none beneath the skin.
- **SANDY BROWN COAT** to **CAMOUFLAGE** it in the desert.
- **LOSES VERY LITTLE WATER** through sweating or in urine.
- **CAN DRINK UP TO 20 GALLONS OF WATER** in one go.

- **SMALL SURFACE AREA/VOLUME RATIO** to **REDUCE WATER LOSS.**
- **THICK, WAXY SURFACE** to **REDUCE WATER LOSS.**
- **STORES WATER** in spongy layer inside its stem.
- **SPINES PROTECT THE CACTI** from predators who would "steal" the **CACTI'S WATER STORE.**
- **STOMATA ONLY OPEN AT NIGHT** to **REDUCE THE AMOUNT OF WATER LOST** compared to day time.
- Some cacti have **SHALLOW SPREADING ROOTS** ...
  ... to **ABSORB SURFACE WATER** whilst others have ...
  ... **DEEP ROOTS** to tap into underground supplies of water.

- Fish are **STREAMLINED** in shape to allow them to **TRAVEL QUICKLY** through the water.
- They possess **GILLS** that can obtain **DISSOLVED OXYGEN FROM THE WATER.**
- **GILLS** have a **LARGE SURFACE AREA** which **INCREASE THE AREA** over which **OXYGEN CAN BE ABSORBED.**

ADAPTATION OR EXTINCTION

The **THEORY OF EVOLUTION** states...
...that all **LIVING THINGS** which **EXIST TODAY** and many more that are now **EXTINCT**...
...have **EVOLVED** from simple life forms, which first developed **3,000,000,000** (billion) years ago.

- **EVOLUTION** is the **SLOW, CONTINUAL CHANGE** of organisms over a **VERY LONG PERIOD**...
  ...to become **BETTER ADAPTED** to their environment.
- If the **ENVIRONMENT CHANGES, SPECIES MUST CHANGE** with it if they are **TO SURVIVE**.
- Species which **AREN'T ADAPTED** to their environment will become **EXTINCT**.
- **A SPECIES** is defined as a group of organisms which can freely interbreed to produce **FERTILE** offspring.

The Reasons For Extinction Of Species

1. **CHANGE IN THE ENVIRONMENT.** Imagine an organism which lives in an environment which is very cold. The organism may be well adapted to this environment by having say a thick furry coat. If however the environment warms up over a period of time, the organism wouldn't be as well adapted and would either **EVOLVE DIFFERENT ADAPTATIONS** for the new environment or become **EXTINCT.**

ONCE WELL ADAPTED

NOW POORLY ADAPTED

2. **INCREASED COMPETITION.** New or improved competitors may mean that the original organisms can no longer compete for **FOOD** or **HABITATS** and thus become extinct. This may happen to Britain's two native species of barnacle which are now being out competed by 'Elminius' the Australian barnacle which arrived in Britain on the hulls of ships during the Second World War. The Australian barnacle can withstand a greater range of temperature and has a faster rate of growth.

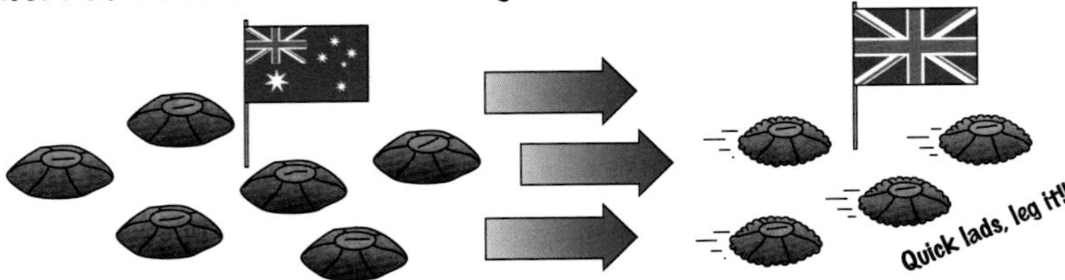

3. **NEW PREDATORS.** If extremely successful predators move in then a species may become extinct. The Dodo in Mauritius was a large, flightless, friendly bird but unfortunately it was driven to extinction by humans in the 17th Century.

4. **NEW DISEASES.** A new disease may sweep through a population, particularly if there is little variation within the population.

The Dinosaurs

DINOSAURS became **EXTINCT** about **65 MILLION YEARS AGO**...
...and **SCIENTISTS** have put forward **DIFFERENT THEORIES** to explain why they died out.

- The Earth's **CLIMATE GRADUALLY BECAME COOLER** and the dinosaurs' **FOOD SOURCE** died?
- The Earth was **HIT** by a **MASSIVE ASTEROID** and **LARGE CLOUDS OF DUST** formed a barrier that stopped the sun's rays warming the Earth?
- A **DEADLY VIRUS** infected and wiped out the dinosaurs?

Whatever happened, the one thing we do know is that the **DINOSAURS** were **UNABLE TO ADAPT.**

The Fossil Record

FOSSILS are the **'REMAINS'** of **PLANTS OR ANIMALS** from many years ago...
...which are **FOUND IN ROCK.**

The **FOSSIL RECORD** is **INCOMPLETE** because...

1. ...some **BODY PARTS** may **NOT BE FOSSILISED**
2. ...some fossils have **NOT YET BEEN DISCOVERED**
3. ...**FOSSILISATION RARELY OCCURS** because **MICROBES DECAY** the organic material that makes up living things.

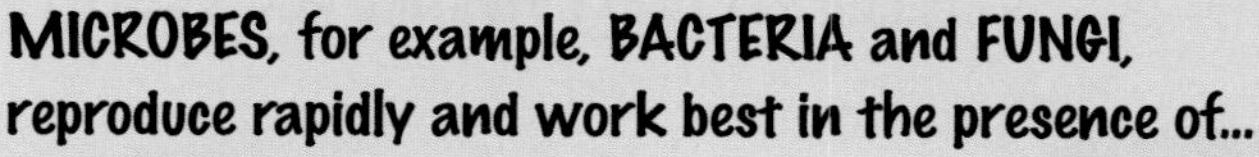

MICROBES, for example, **BACTERIA** and **FUNGI**,
reproduce rapidly and work best in the presence of...
- ...**OXYGEN**
- ...**MOISTURE**
- ...**A SUITABLE TEMPERATURE AND pH**

In the **ABSENCE** of these **CONDITIONS**, **DECAY WILL NOT HAPPEN**

How Fossils Are Formed

1. DUE TO THE ABSENCE OF DECAY CONDITIONS

EXAMPLES

A Woolly mammoths preserved in Arctic perma-frost.
... Here it's **TOO COLD** for the decay microbes.

WOOLLY MAMMOTH

B Woolly rhinoceros preserved in tar pits.
... **NO OXYGEN** or **MOISTURE**.

TRINIDADIAN TAR PIT

C Ancient humans preserved in peat bogs.
... **TOO ACIDIC** for the microbes.

A very wrinkly but fully preserved arm!

D Fossilised tree resin (Amber) preserves trapped insects.
... **NO OXYGEN** or **MOISTURE**.

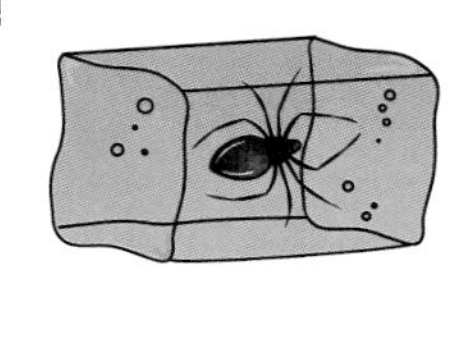

2. FROM THE 'HARD' PARTS OF ANIMALS.

The hard parts don't decay too quickly and so allow time for sediments to cover them and minerals to impregnate them. Things like bones, shells, teeth, and beaks and claws to a lesser extent can also be impregnated by minerals and preserved (See 'petrification').

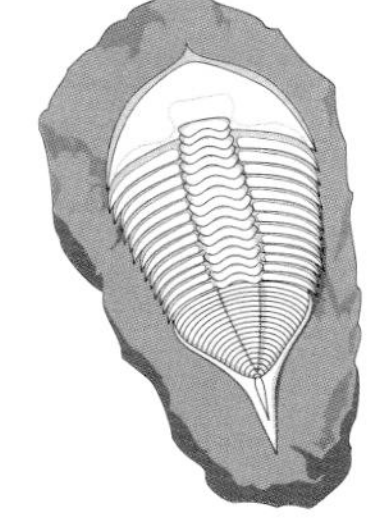

3. BY PETRIFICATION. This means literally 'turning to stone', and this is exactly what happens.
There are two ways ...

A The space left by a decaying organism is filled by minerals in the form of sediment.
This forms a cast of the original organism.

B Water rich in mineral salts in solution may get into the tissues before they decay.
This literally petrifies the organism. A petrified forest in Arizona is 170 million years old.

Fossil Evidence For Evolution

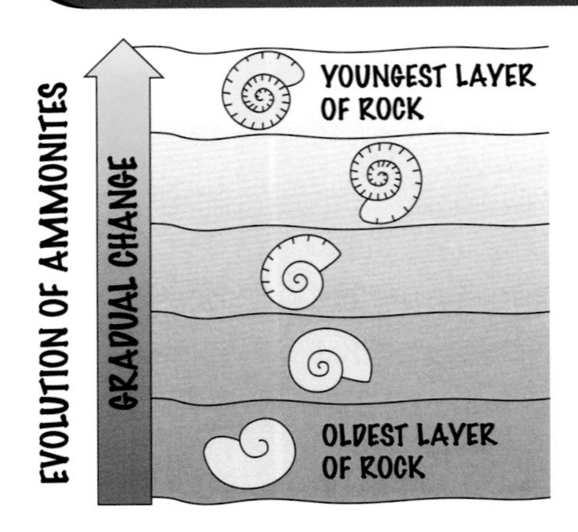

- If we look at exposed rock strata, ...
- ... it is possible to follow the GRADUAL CHANGES which have taken place in an organism over time.
- Even though the fossil record is incomplete, these gradual changes confirm that ...
- ... SPECIES HAVE CHANGED OVER LONG PERIODS OF TIME ...
- ... providing STRONG EVIDENCE FOR EVOLUTION.

Evolution By Natural Selection

Evolution is the change in a population over a large number of generations ...
... that may result in the formation of a new species; which are better adapted to their environment.

There are 4 key points to remember:-

1. Individuals within a population show VARIATION (i.e. differences due to their genes).
2. There is COMPETITION between individuals for food and mates etc., and also predation and disease. This keeps population sizes constant in spite of the production of many offspring, i.e. there is a "struggle for survival", and many individuals die.
3. Individuals which are BEST ADAPTED to the environment are more likely to survive, breed successfully and produce offspring. This is termed 'SURVIVAL OF THE FITTEST'.
4. These 'survivors' will therefore PASS ON THEIR GENES to these offspring resulting in an improved organism being evolved through NATURAL SELECTION.

VARIATION and COMPETITION ensure BEST ADAPTED organisms PASS ON THEIR GENES

AN EXAMPLE

VARIATION
- The LENGTH of a Giraffe's neck is controlled by its GENES.
- Some Giraffes have LONGER NECKS than others.

COMPETITION
- The Giraffes COMPETE for FOOD i.e. leaves on a tree

BEST ADAPTED
- THE Giraffes with the LONGER NECKS are best adapted.
- They will find MORE FOOD, LIVE LONGER and BREED MORE OFTEN.

PASS ON THEIR GENES
- The GENE FOR A LONGER NECK IS PASSED ONTO the Giraffe's many OFFSPRING.

HIGHER/SPECIAL TIER

The Peppered Moth

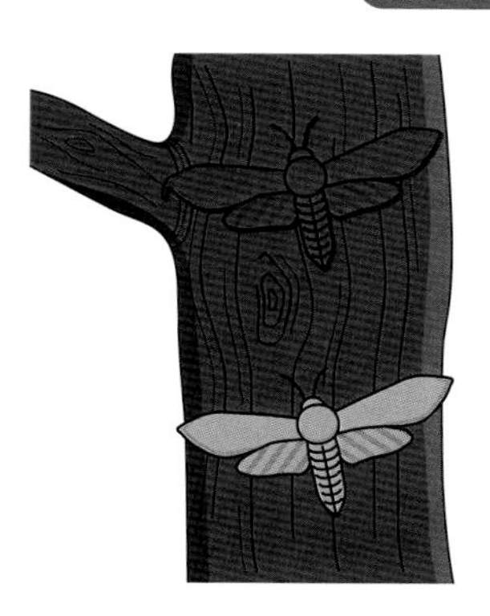

The Peppered Moth is a PALE COLOUR and...
...was ADAPTED TO ITS ENVIRONMENT
The moth was CAMOUFLAGED against silver birch trees and the BIRDS THAT ATE the moth found it DIFFICULT to see them.

During the INDUSTRIAL REVOLUTION the air became more POLLUTED - and the silver birch trees started to get very sooty.

VARIATION
- Following the INDUSTRIAL REVOLUTION a new variety of DARK-COLOURED MOTH appeared.
- The dark colour was probably due to a GENETIC MUTATION.

COMPETITION
- The WELL CAMOUFLAGED DARK COLOURED MOTH was eaten LESS OFTEN than the PALE COLOURED MOTH.

BEST ADAPTED
- The DARK COLOURED MOTH SURVIVED LONGER and was able to BREED MORE OFTEN.

PASS ON THEIR GENES
- The DARK COLOURED MOTHS PASSED ON THEIR GENES MORE OFTEN and the DARK COLOURED Peppered Moth are found in areas where the air is polluted.

Penicillin-Resistant Bacteria

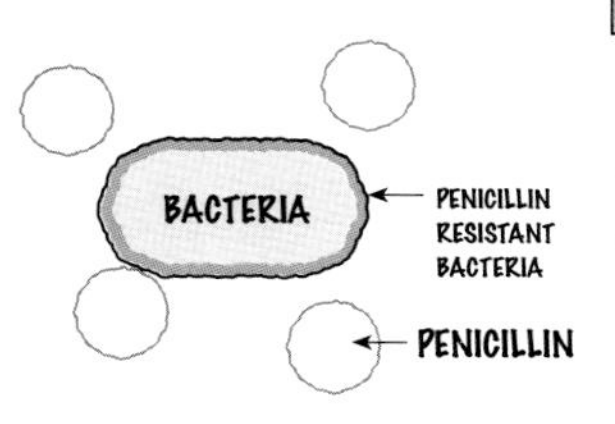

VARIATION
Bacteria MUTATED. Some were resistant to the ANTIBIOTIC PENICILLIN others were not.

COMPETITION
The non-resistant bacteria were more likely to be killed by the penicillin.

BEST ADAPTED
The PENICILLIN-RESISTANT bacteria survived and reproduced more often.

PASS ON THEIR GENES
More bacteria are becoming resistant to penicillin. This is a major health issue.

Conflicting Theories Of Evolution

JOHN - BAPTISTE LAMARCK (1774-1829) was the first SCIENTIST to try to explain the "VARIETY OF LIFE".
- He suggested that an ORGANISM CHANGED to become MORE ADAPTED to its environment.
- For example, a GIRAFFE'S LONG NECK was caused by it STRETCHING TO REACH LEAVES. The longer neck was passed onto its offspring.

CHARLES DARWIN (1809-1882) thought that 'SURVIVAL OF THE FITTEST" explained EVOLUTION.
- VARIATION existed within species.
- If the variation was BENEFICIAL to the SPECIES it would COMPETE FOR RESOURCES MORE EFFECTIVELY.
- The BEST ADAPTED individuals would SURVIVE LONGER and BREED MORE OFTEN.
- The new BENEFICIAL ADAPTATION will be PASSED ON to their OFFSPRING.
- DARWIN'S IDEAS are the ones that the STUDY OF EVOLUTION are based on.

Adaptation, Extinction And Fossils

- Adaptations are special features or behaviour which make an organism especially well-suited to its environment.
- All animals and plants have adaptations which increase their chance of survival.
- Species which aren't adapted to their environment will compete less successfully and may eventually become EXTINCT.
- Similarly, if the environment changes, a species must adapt to the change to be successful.
- The four main reasons for extinction of species are:-

... LIFE IN A VERY COLD CLIMATE - THE POLAR BEAR

... LIFE IN A VERY HOT CLIMATE - THE CAMEL

... LIFE IN A VERY HOT CLIMATE - A CACTUS

... LIFE IN AN AQUATIC (WATERY) ENVIRONMENT - THE FISH

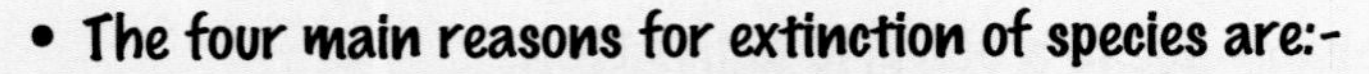

- Fossils are the "remains" of organisms which have been preserved. This demands particular circumstances i.e. the absence of decay conditions and so the fossil record is far from complete.

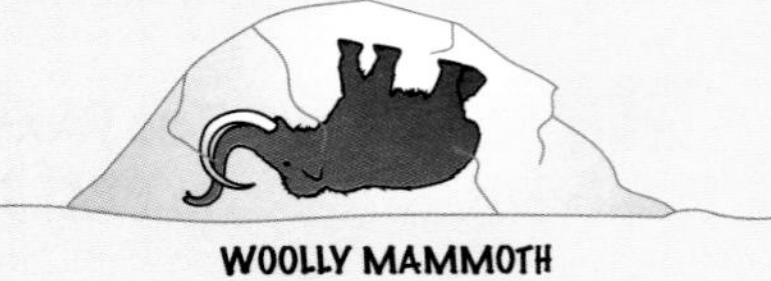
WOOLLY MAMMOTH

- Fossils are usually formed from the hard parts of organisms and petrification may occur.

Evolution

- Evolution is the change in a population over a large number of generations that may result in the formation of a new species.
- The fossil record provides strong evidence for evolution as it shows gradual changes in organisms over long periods of time.

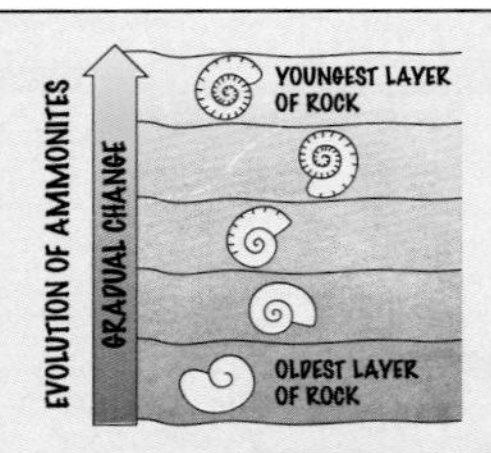

HIGHER/SPECIAL TIER

- Evolution by natural selection was first suggested by Charles Darwin and Alfred Russel Wallace.
- The four key points are:-
  1. There is VARIATION within populations.
  2. There is COMPETITION between individuals within the population.
  3. Individuals which are BEST ADAPTED to their environment are more likely to survive and breed successfully.
  4. These "survivors" will therefore PASS ON THEIR GENES to their offspring who in turn will go through the same process resulting eventually in the evolution of a new organism.

HIGHER/SPECIAL TIER

- Three classic examples are: Long necks in giraffes.
  Peppered Moth.
  Penicillin resistant bacteria.

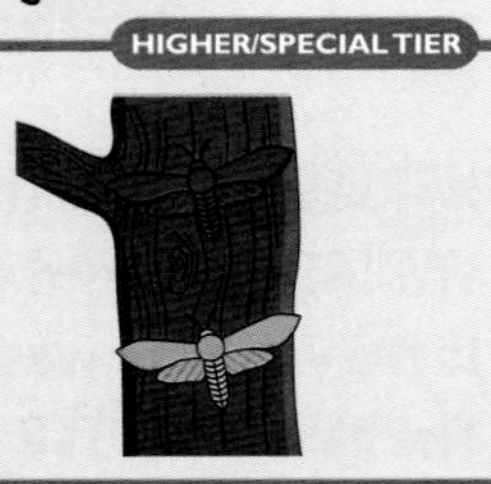

Record the SEVEN 'Adaptation, Extinction and Fossils' facts, and FIVE 'Evolution' facts onto your tape.

Now - READ, COVER, WRITE and CHECK the TWELVE facts.

NITROGEN CYCLE

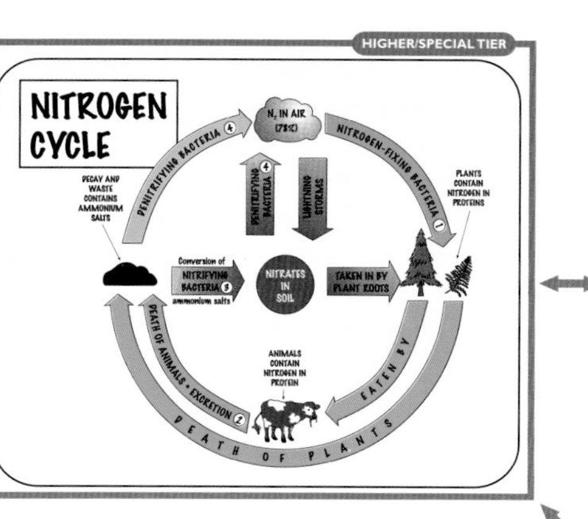

PYRAMIDS OF NUMBERS/BIOMASS

- N.B. remember those that don't work!

SAMPLING METHODS

1. POOTERS
2. SWEEPNETS
3. PITFALL TRAPS
4. QUADRATS

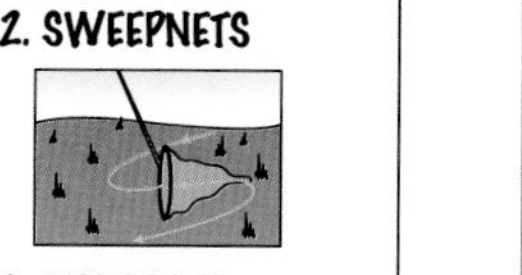
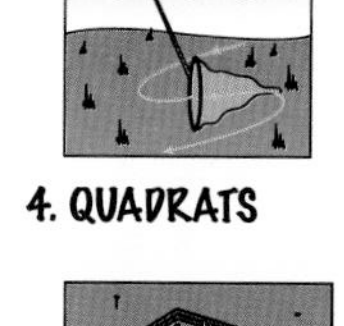
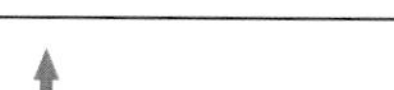
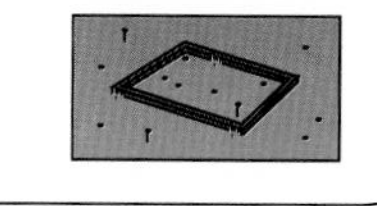
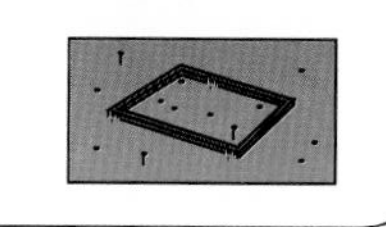

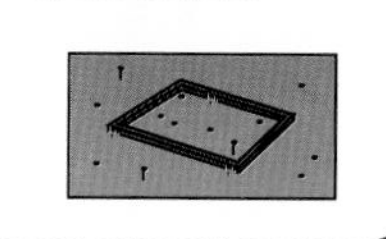
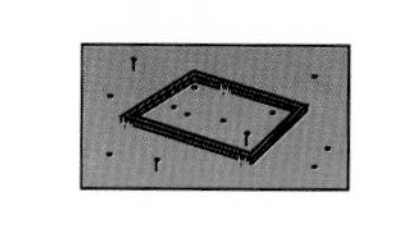

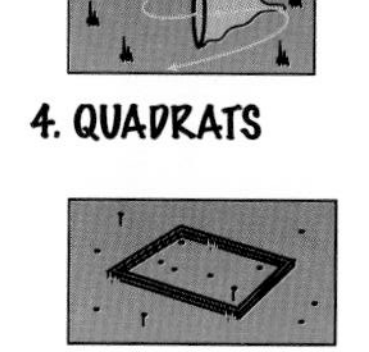
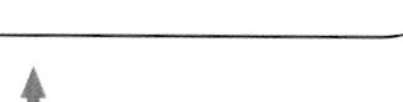

OZONE LAYER AND GREENHOUSE EFFECT

- Ozone screens out harmful U-V light. The ozone layer is getting thinner due to CFC's.
- Increased amounts of carbon dioxide and methane are causing global warming.

CARBON CYCLE

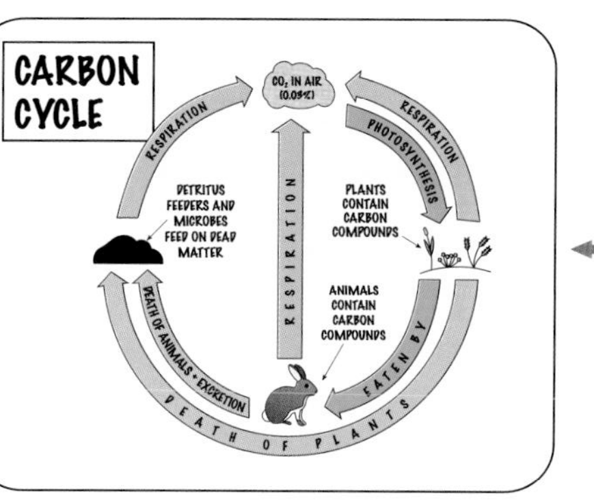
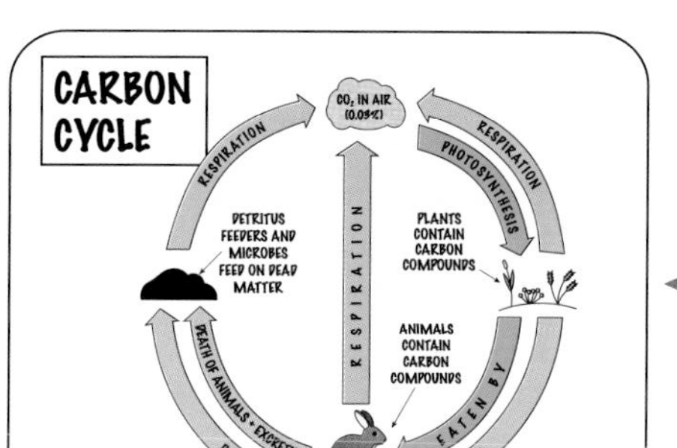

FOOD CHAINS AND FOOD WEBS

FACTORS AFFECTING POPULATION SIZE

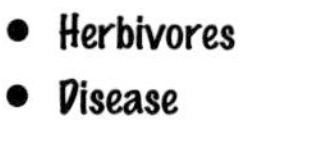
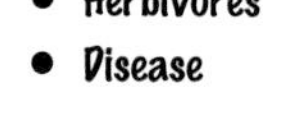
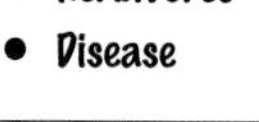

ANIMALS	PLANTS
• Competition	• Light
• Disease	• Water
• Predators	• Minerals
• Migration	• Space
	• Herbivores
	• Disease

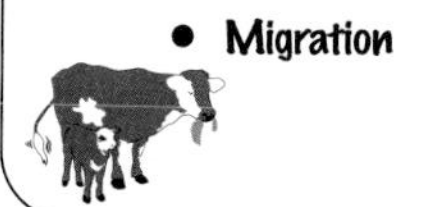

EFFECTS OF POPULATION GROWTH

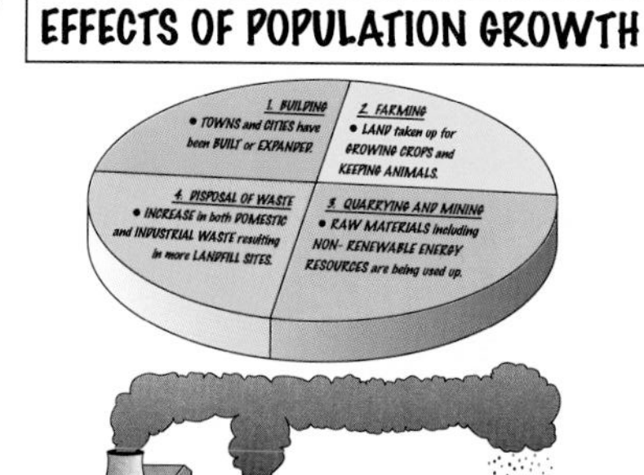

Ecology

Managing The Environment

ENERGY LOSS AND FOOD PRODUCTION

- Energy is lost at each trophic level in a foodchain ...

- ... and about 10% of the energy is passed on to the next level.

FOOD PRODUCTION MANAGEMENT

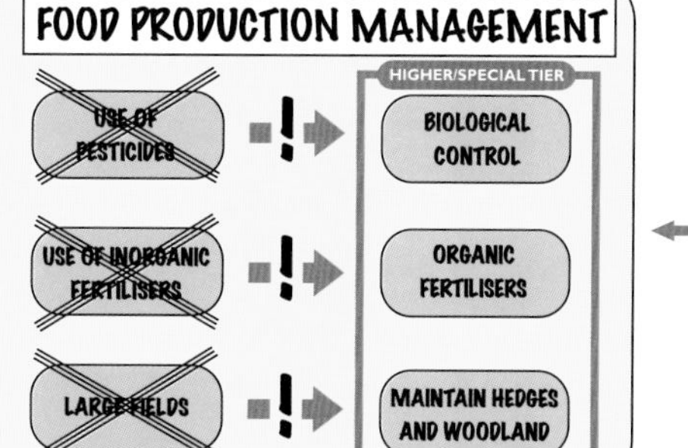
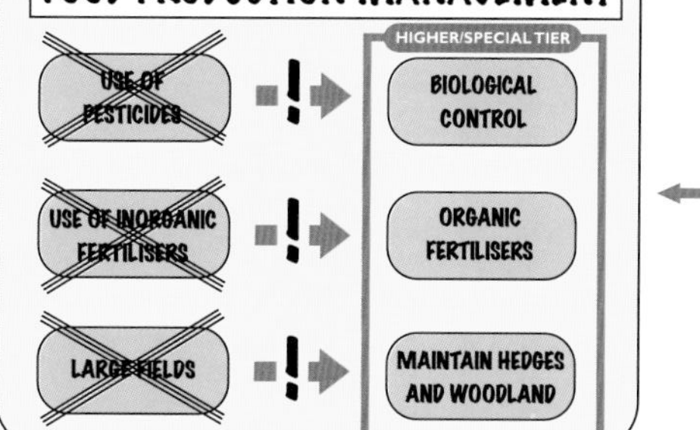

ACCUMULATION OF PESTICIDE/EUTROPHICATION

- Pesticide increases in concentration along the foodchain.
- INORGANIC FERTILISERS
  GROWTH
  DEATH
  MICROBES
  OXYGEN
  SUFFOCATION

EUTROPHICATION

MANAGED ECOSYSTEMS

- North Sea fish stocks.
- Salmon Farming.
- Commercial greenhouses.

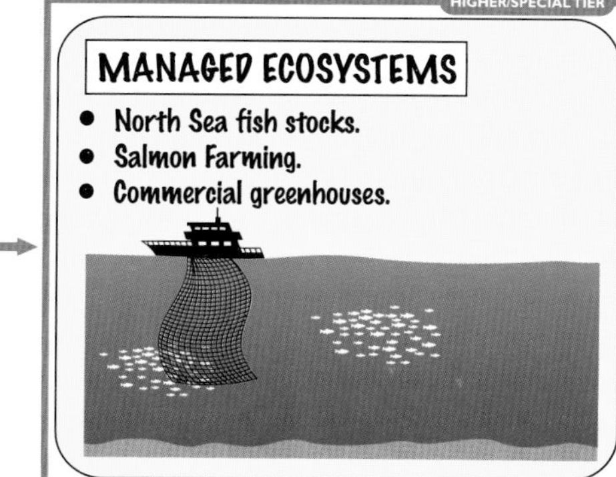

Two Important Definitions

- A population is the total number of individuals of the SAME SPECIES ...
  ... which live in a certain area e.g. the number of field mice in a meadow.
- A community is all the organisms in a particular area ...
  ... i.e. many populations of plants and animals.

Sampling Methods

The size and distribution of a population can be measured by employing one or more of the following techniques ...

1. USING POOTERS

This is a simple technique in which insects are gathered up easily without harming them. You have to be systematic about your sampling in order to get representative results and it's difficult to get ideas of numbers. However you do get to find out what species are actually present.

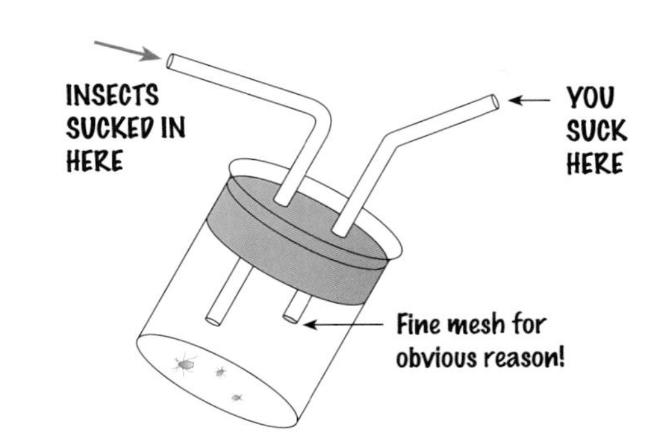

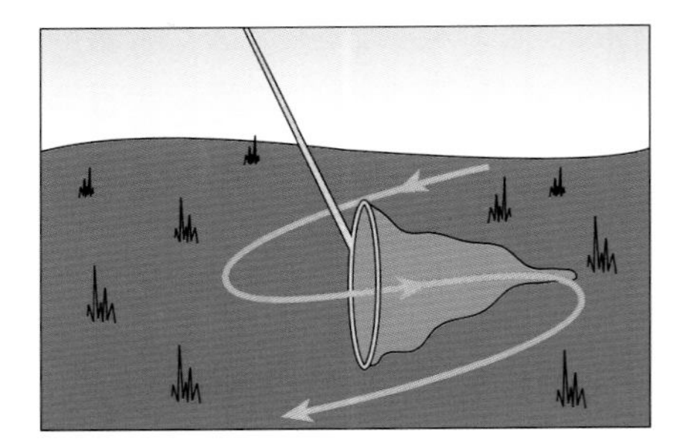

2. USING SWEEPNETS

These are employed in long grass or even moderately dense woodland where there are lots of shrubs. Again, it's difficult to get truly representative samples particularly in terms of the relative numbers of organisms.

3. USING PITFALL TRAPS

These are set into the ground and used to catch beetles etc. Sometimes a mixture of ethanol and water is placed in the bottom of the trap to kill the samples but we personally can't see a good reason for this. Far better to just let them go.

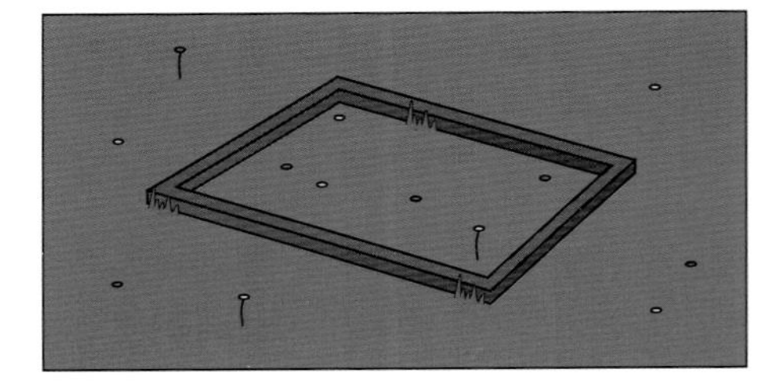

4. USING QUADRATS

These are used for estimating plant populations. They will provide excellent results as long as the quadrats are thrown randomly. A system must be worked out beforehand and stuck to rigidly.

HIGHER/SPECIAL TIER

When SAMPLING, CARE MUST BE TAKEN TO:

1. ... Take a BIG ENOUGH SAMPLE to make the results a GOOD ESTIMATE.
   The LARGER THE SAMPLE then the MORE ACCURATE the results.

2. ... SAMPLE RANDOMLY.
   The MORE RANDOM THE SAMPLE the more likely it is to be REPRESENTATIVE OF THE POPULATION.

What Affects The Size Of A Population ?

The SIZE OF ANY POPULATION of plants or animals ...
... will CHANGE WITH TIME.
This is due to many factors:

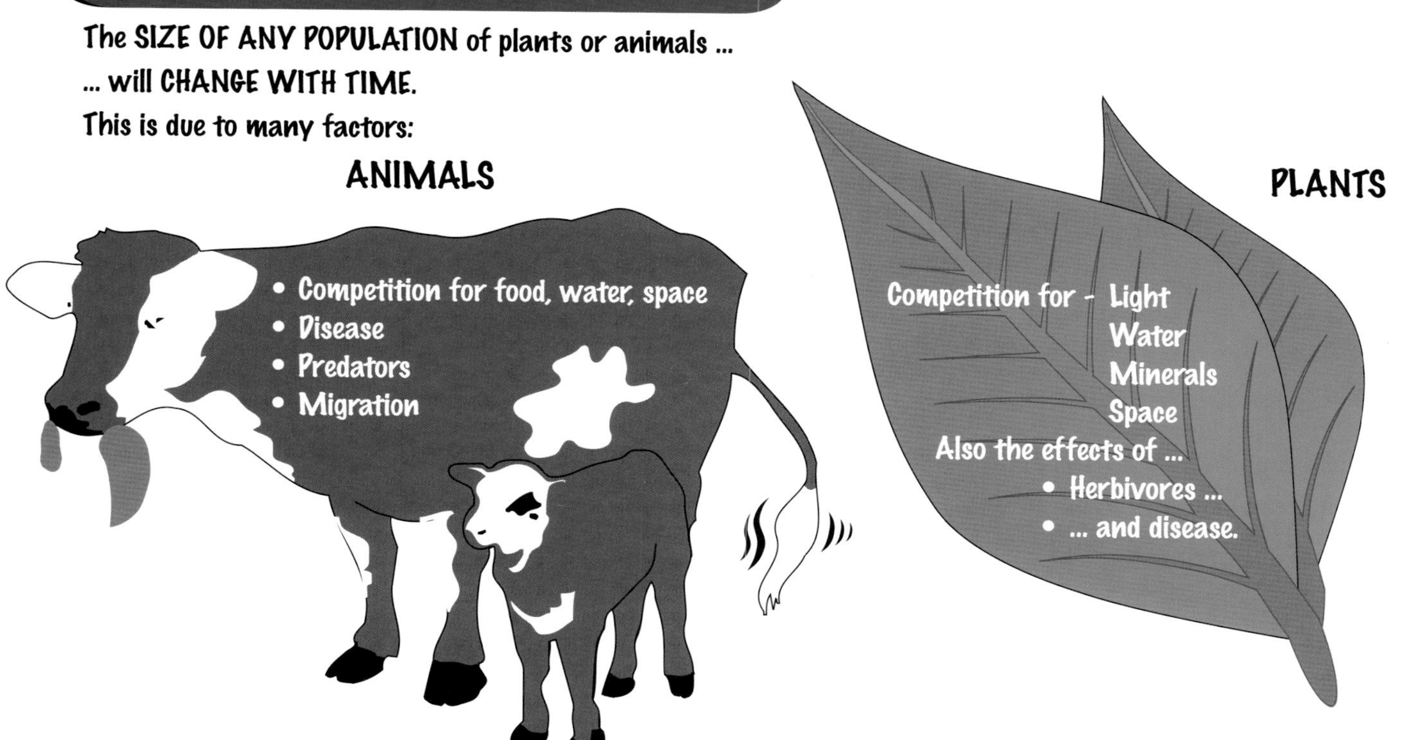

If plants and animals cannot compete for essential resources they may die.

Predator Prey Cycles

- PREDATORS are ANIMALS that KILL and EAT OTHER ANIMALS while ...
- ... the ANIMALS that are EATEN are called the PREY.
- Within a NATURAL ENVIRONMENT there is a DELICATE BALANCE ...
- ... between the POPULATION of the PREDATOR and its PREY.

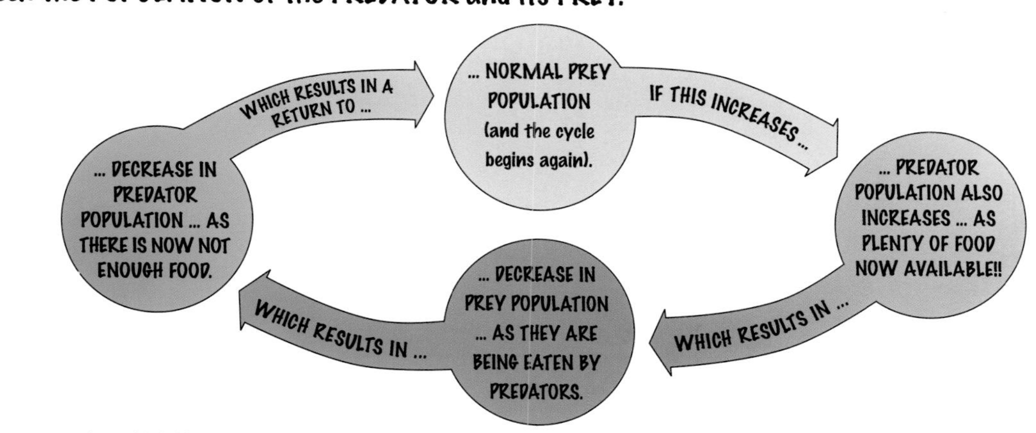

A classic example - LYNX AND HARES CYCLE

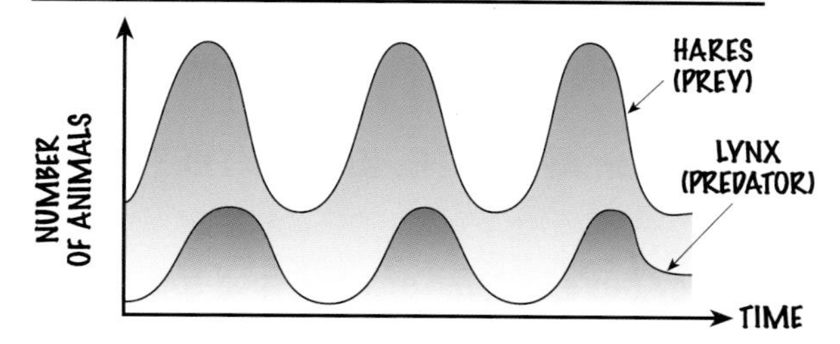

- Over a period of time the POPULATION of ...
- ... LYNX and HARES does a FULL CYCLE.
- There are always more ...
- ... HARES than LYNX while ...
- ... the POPULATION PEAK for the LYNX always comes ...
- ... AFTER the POPULATION PEAK for the HARES.

N.B. THE ABOVE GRAPH WOULD BE VERY SIMILAR FOR ANY PREDATOR AND PREY POPULATION CYCLE.

Food Chains

These show which organism is eating which other organism. They also show the transfer of energy and materials from organism to organism.

- Radiation from THE SUN is the SOURCE OF THIS ENERGY and is CAPTURED BY GREEN PLANTS in PHOTOSYNTHESIS.
- GREEN PLANTS only CAPTURE A SMALL PART OF THIS ENERGY and store it in STARCH MOLECULES.

LETTUCE → SLUGS → MISTLE THRUSHES → HAWKS

All food chains start with a green plant called the PRODUCER.

The SLUG is a HERBIVORE (plant eater) and the PRIMARY CONSUMER.

The MISTLE THRUSH is a CARNIVORE (meat eater) and the SECONDARY CONSUMER.

The HAWK is the TOP CARNIVORE and the TERTIARY CONSUMER.

The ARROWS show THE FLOW OF ENERGY and BIOMASS along the foodchain

Food Webs

Food chains are often INTERCONNECTED to form food webs.
In practice these can be very complicated because many animals have varied diets.

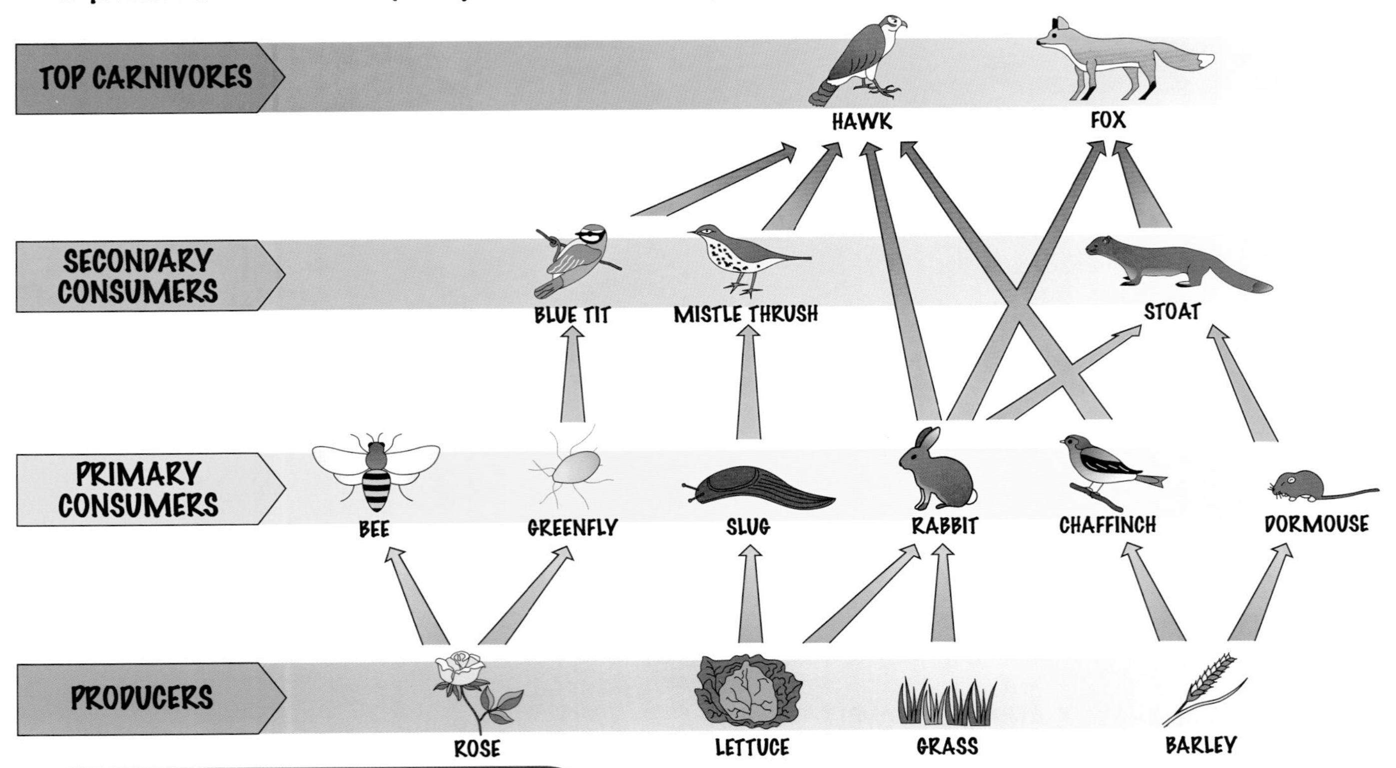

Interdependence Of Organisms

An INCREASE or DECREASE in the NUMBER OF PLANTS or ANIMALS can AFFECT THE REST OF THE FOOD WEB.
For example, if the RABBITS were KILLED OFF by a disease ...

- ... the NUMBER OF STOATS would DECREASE SLIGHTLY because they have lost one of their food sources.
- ... the NUMBER OF DORMICE may DECREASE as more become eaten by the stoats.
- ... the NUMBER OF LETTUCE and GRASS PLANTS will INCREASE as there are fewer rabbits eating them

Pyramids Of Numbers

The **NUMBER OF ORGANISMS** at each stage (trophic level) of a food chain can be shown as a **PYRAMID OF NUMBERS.** Take the following food chain ...

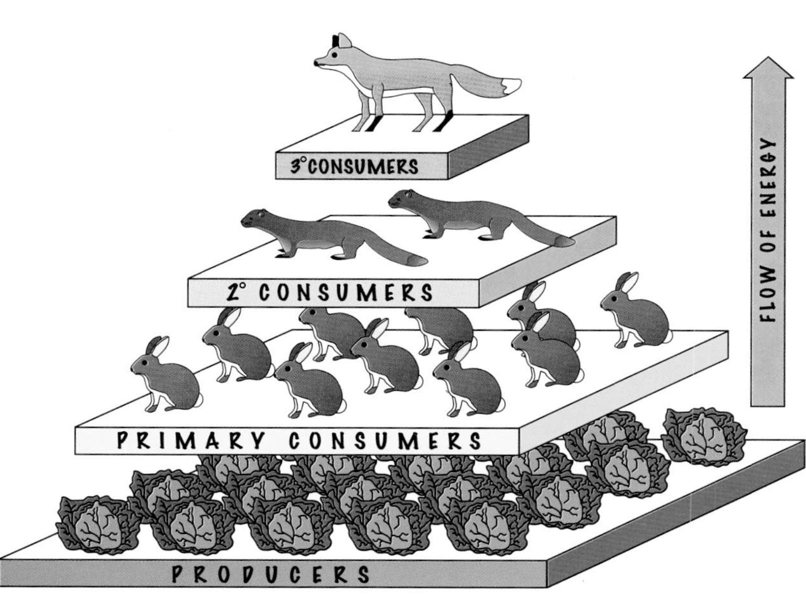

- As we go from one trophic level to the next ... ... the number of organisms decreases quite dramatically.
- The PRODUCER is always at the BASE of the pyramid.
- Lots of lettuces feed fewer rabbits which feed even fewer stoats which feed just one fox!
- For simplicity, pyramids of numbers usually look like this ...

FOX
STOATS
RABBITS
LETTUCES

Food Chains That Don't Form Pyramids Of Numbers!

- Because pyramids of numbers don't take into account the SIZE OF THE ORGANISMS, ... it is possible to end up with some odd looking "pyramids". Look at the following example.

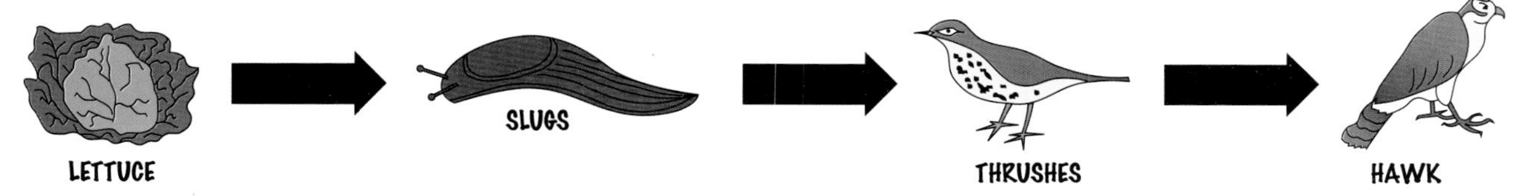

- Because LOTS OF SLUGS FEED ON ONE LETTUCE, the base of the pyramid is smaller than the next stage!!
- This happens because the lettuce is a large organism compared to the slug.
- This situation also happens when trees start off food chains.

HAWK
THRUSHES
SLUGS
LETTUCE

Pyramids Of Biomass

- These pyramids deal with the mass of living material (biomass) at each stage of the chain.
- Because this TAKES INTO ACCOUNT THE MASS OF THE ORGANISMS at each trophic level, these pyramids are ALWAYS PYRAMID-SHAPED.

Because of this, the food chain above would give us ...

HAWK
THRUSHES
SLUGS
LETTUCES

- If enough information is given, ... the pyramid of biomass can be drawn to scale.

HIGHER/SPECIAL TIER

Transfer Of Energy And Biomass

- Biomass and energy are lost at every stage of a food chain because ...
- ... materials and energy are lost in an organism's faeces (waste), and ...
- ... energy is 'lost' as movement energy and 'waste' heat energy originally provided by respiration.
- This last statement is particularly true of warm blooded animals (birds and mammals).

THE FOX, INCREDIBLY, GETS THE LAST TINY BIT OF ENERGY LEFT AFTER ALL THE OTHERS HAVE HAD A SHARE.

THE FOX GETS THE BIOMASS THAT REMAINS TO BE PASSED ON AFTER ALL THIS!

THE STOATS RUN AROUND, MATE, EXCRETE, KEEP WARM etc. AND GENERALLY PASS ON 1/10th OF ALL THE ENERGY THEY GOT FROM THE RABBITS.

THE STOATS LOSE QUITE A BIT OF BIOMASS IN DROPPINGS AND URINE

THE RABBITS, RUN AROUND, MATE, EXCRETE, KEEP WARM etc. AND PASS ON 1/10th OF ALL THE ENERGY THEY GOT FROM THE LETTUCE.

THE RABBITS LOSE QUITE A LOT OF BIOMASS IN THEIR DROPPINGS AND SOME IN URINE.

THE SUN IS THE ENERGY SOURCE FOR ALL ORGANISMS, BUT ONLY A FRACTION OF THE SUN'S ENERGY IS ACTUALLY CAPTURED IN PHOTOSYNTHESIS.

A LOT OF THE BIOMASS REMAINS IN THE GROUND AS THE ROOT SYSTEM.

Improving The Efficiency Of Food Production

So, since the loss of ENERGY and BIOMASS is due mainly to ...

... it follows that we can improve the efficiency of food production by ...

❶ Reducing the number of stages in the food chain.

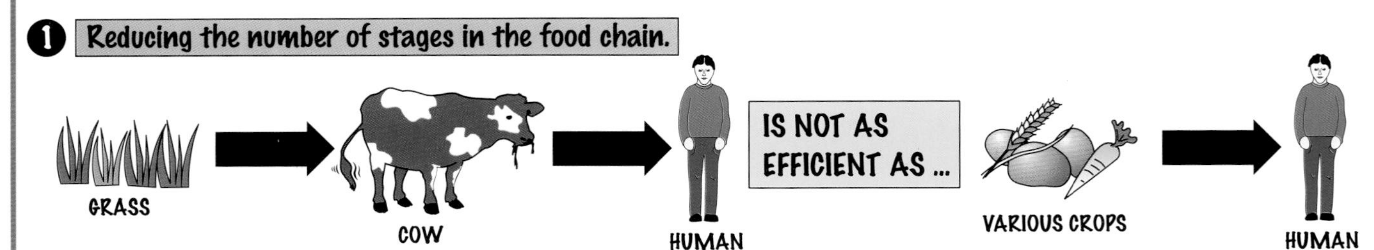

Far more people can be fed by growing crops rather than using land for grazing.

❷ Limiting an animals movement, and controlling its temperature.

More of the food eaten by the animal is converted into biomass ...
... because less energy is 'lost' through heat and movement.

Many people feel that this way of rearing animals is unacceptable.

Food production involves the management of ecosystems to improve the efficiency of energy transfer from the sun to human food. Such management imposes a duty of care for the environment, in order to avoid the destruction of ecosystems ...

Damaging Ecosystems

Methods of food production which have damaged ecosystems include:-

PESTICIDES

- Widespread use of **PESTICIDES** leading to ...
- ... WHOLESALE, INDISCRIMINATE, DESTRUCTION OF INSECTS, causing ...
- ... BREAKS IN THE FOOD CHAIN ...
- ... ACCUMULATION OF PESTICIDES IN ORGANISMS HIGHER UP THE FOOD CHAIN ...
- ... and REDUCTION IN THE NUMBER OF POLLINATING INSECTS.

INORGANIC FERTILISERS

- Widespread use of **INORGANIC FERTILISER** leading to ...
- ... large amounts being washed off the land into water courses.
- This LEACHING EFFECT results in EUTROPHICATION of STREAMS and LAKES, (see next page)
- ... resulting in REDUCED OXYGEN CONTENT of the water, ...
- ... and the DEATH OF LARGE NUMBERS OF AQUATIC ORGANISMS.

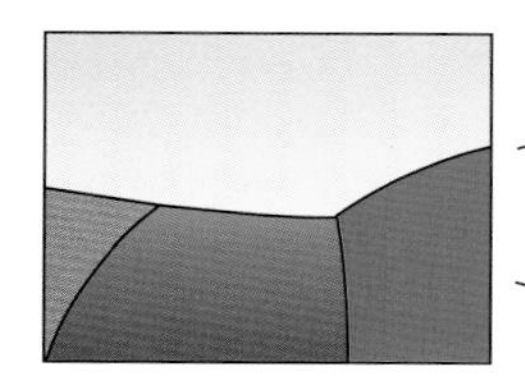

LARGE FIELDS

- Widespread use of **ENORMOUS FIELDS** ...
- ... results in the REMOVAL OF MILES OF NATURAL HABITAT e.g. HEDGES.
- The loss of the hedges REMOVES THE NATURAL WINDBREAKS, ...
- ... causing TOPSOIL TO BE GRADUALLY BLOWN OFF THE LAND.

Managing Ecosystems

It is possible to have efficient food production and maintain a balanced ecosystem. In addition to the 'solutions' below, hard decisions have to be made taking into account ...
... • HISTORICAL, ... • POLITICAL, ... • ECONOMIC, SOCIAL, and ENVIRONMENTAL ISSUES.

HIGHER/SPECIAL TIER

BIOLOGICAL CONTROL

- Using a NATURAL ENEMY of the pest ...
- ... to CONTROL PEST NUMBERS.
- e.g. GUPPY FISH eat MOSQUITO LARVAE.

ORGANIC FERTILISERS

- GREEN MANURE (ploughed-in legumes) ...
- ... and BROWN MANURE (animal dung) ...
- ... is NOT WASHED OUT OF THE SOIL VERY EASILY.

MAINTAIN HEDGES AND WOODLAND

- TO PROVIDE NATURAL WINDBREAKS.
- ENCOURAGE REFORESTATION ...
- ... TO MAINTAIN HABITATS.

Accumulation Of Pesticides

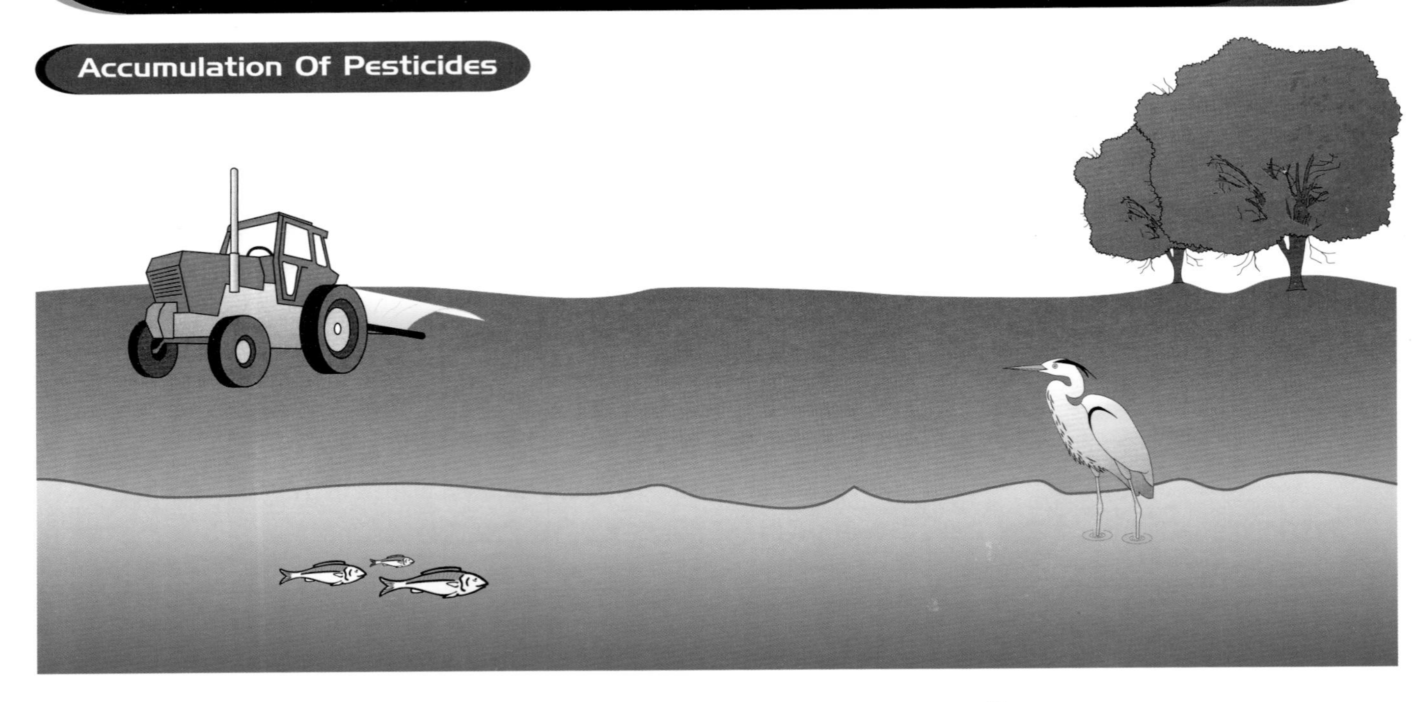

1 Pesticide flows into the river and is **ABSORBED BY ALGAE** (tiny plants).	2 Small fish eat the algae.	3 Birds feed on the small fish.
1 If each tiny plant absorbs 2 units of pesticide.	2 A small fish eats five plants. $5 \times 2 = 10$ units of pesticide	3 Each bird eats four fish. $4 \times 10 = 40$ units of pesticide

The PESTICIDE INCREASES IN CONCENTRATION ALONG THE FOOD CHAIN.

So while the pesticide may not damage the algae, or even the small fish ...
... its accumulation as it moves up through different trophic levels could easily kill the bird.

HIGHER/SPECIAL TIER

Eutrophication

This is the process whereby stretches of water can become stagnant very quickly due to a sequence of events started by carelessness in the overuse of fertiliser.
There are 6 stages:-

1. **INORGANIC FERTILISERS** ... used by farmers may be washed into lakes and rivers.
2. **GROWTH** ... of water plants caused by this fertiliser, happens rapidly.
3. **DEATH** ... of some of these plants due to lack of light from overcrowding.
4. **MICROBES** ... which feed on dead organisms now increase massively in number.
5. **OXYGEN** ... is used up quickly by this huge number of microbes (as they respire)
6. **SUFFOCATION** ... of fishes and other aquatic animals due to lack of oxygen in the water.

- Untreated sewage can have the same effect.

HIGHER/SPECIAL TIER

The second half of the twentieth century has seen a substantial increase in the degree to which humans artificially control or manage various ecosystems.

North Sea Fish Stocks

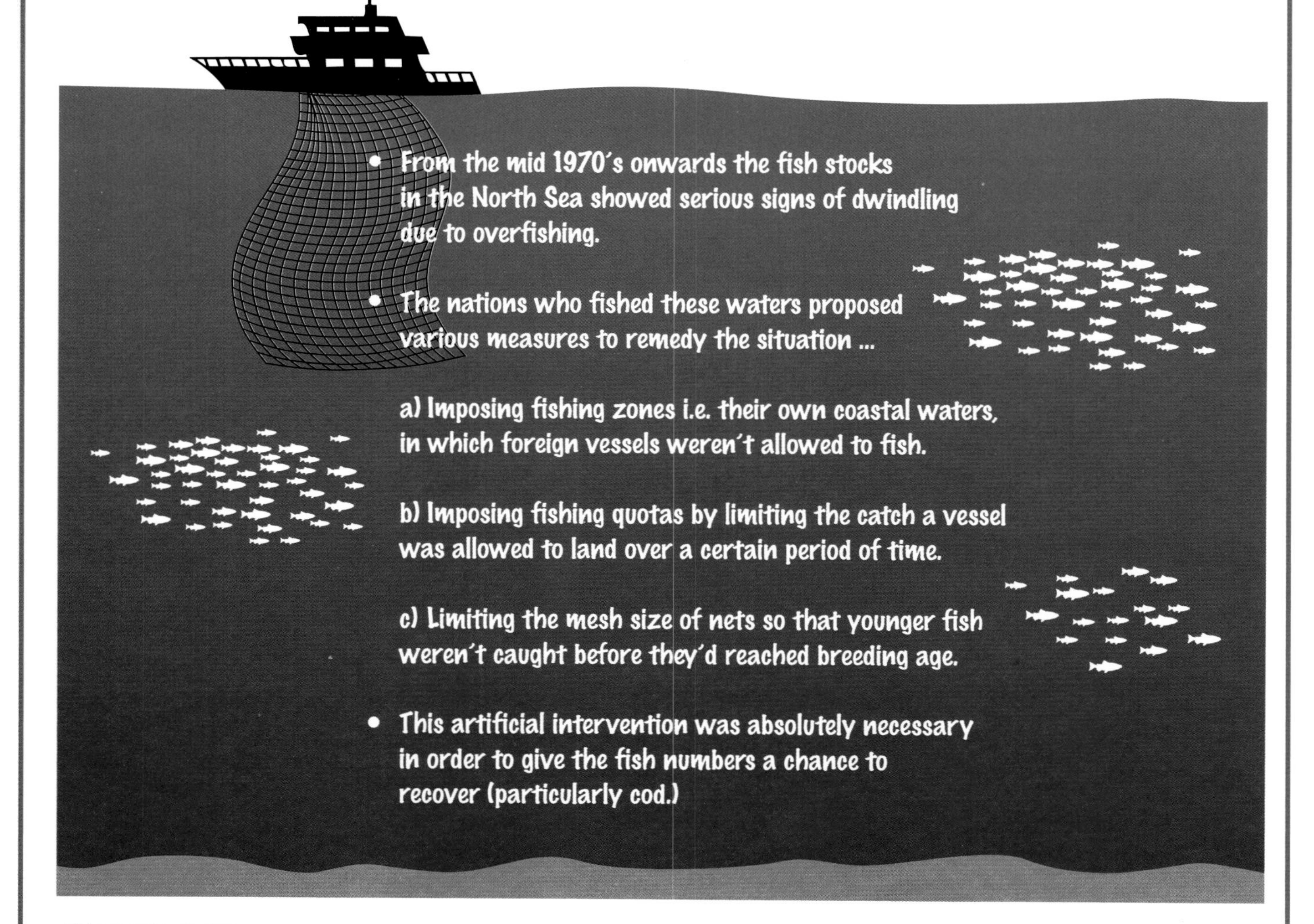

Fish Farms

- Salmon is now often 'farmed' in open sea-lochs in Scotland.
- The fish are protected from predators by wire mesh cages which also serve to limit their movement thus encouraging faster growth rate.
- Their feeding is closely regulated to ensure they have exactly the right amount in order to avoid eutrophication problems (see p. 88) which could be caused by waste food.
- The young salmon are hatched in the laboratory and are looked after carefully until they are ready to go to sea.

Greenhouse Horticulture

- Commercial growers are increasingly using vast greenhouses to cultivate crops.
- Advantages include the ability to control:-
  TEMPERATURE, LIGHT INTENSITY, CARBON DIOXIDE LEVEL, PESTS, NUTRIENTS, and WATER.

Recycling The Materials Of Life

- Living things remove materials from the environment for growth and other processes, ...
- ... but when these organisms excrete waste or die, these materials are returned to the environment.
- The key to all this are the **MICROBES** ...
  ... which break down the **WASTE** and ...
  ... the **DEAD BODIES** so that they can ...
  ... be absorbed and used by plants ...
  ... for **GROWTH**.

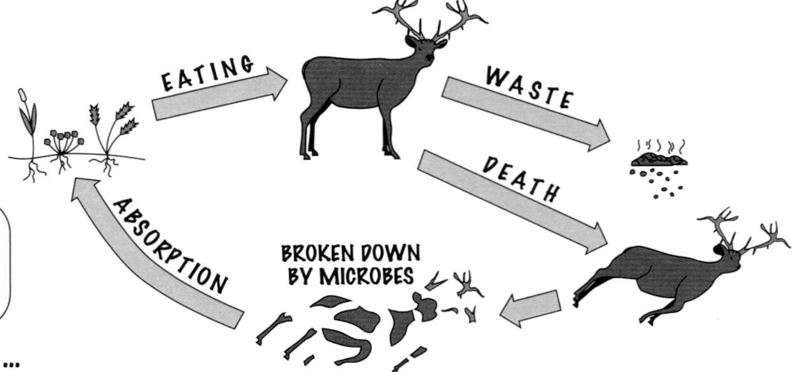

MICROBES digest materials faster in ...
... **WARM, MOIST CONDITIONS** where ...
... there is plenty of **OXYGEN**.

Humans also quite deliberately use **MICROBES** ...

1. AT SEWAGE WORKS ...	2. IN COMPOST HEAPS ...
• ... to break down **HUMAN WASTE**.	• ... to break down **PLANT MATERIAL WASTE**.

The Carbon Cycle

In a stable community, the processes which remove materials ...
... are balanced by processes which return materials. A sort of constant recycling.
The constant recycling of carbon is called the Carbon Cycle.

CO_2 IN AIR (0.03%)

RESPIRATION
RESPIRATION
PHOTOSYNTHESIS
RESPIRATION
DETRITUS FEEDERS AND MICROBES FEED ON DEAD MATTER
PLANTS CONTAIN CARBON COMPOUNDS
ANIMALS CONTAIN CARBON COMPOUNDS
DEATH OF ANIMALS + EXCRETION
EATEN BY
DEATH OF PLANTS

- As the detritus feeders and microbes feed on the dead plants and animals they **RESPIRE** releasing carbon dioxide into the atmosphere.
- When plants and animals **DIE**, other animals and microbes feed on their bodies causing them to breakdown.
- Carbon dioxide is removed from the atmosphere by green plants for **PHOTOSYNTHESIS**.
- Some of the Carbon Dioxide is returned to the atmosphere by green plants during **RESPIRATION**.
- The carbon obtained by photosynthesis is used to make **CARBOHYDRATES, FATS & PROTEINS** in plants ...
- ... and when the plants are eaten some of this carbon becomes **CARBOHYDRATES, FATS AND PROTEINS** in animals.
- Animals **RESPIRE** releasing Carbon Dioxide into the atmosphere.

The 3 main processes of the cycle ...

1. PHOTOSYNTHESIS 2. RESPIRATION 3. TRANSFER OF CARBON

HIGHER/SPECIAL TIER

The THREE main process by which **CARBON DIOXIDE** is **REMOVED FROM THE ATMOSPHERE:-**
- **PHOTOSYNTHESIS** - absorbed by plants and used to make carbohydrates, fats and proteins.
- **DISSOLVED IN THE SEA** - the huge surface area provided by the sea absorbs large amounts of carbon dioxide.
- **LOCKED IN CARBONATE ROCKS** - carbonate rocks are formed from the skeletons of shelled sea creatures.

HIGHER/SPECIAL TIER

The Nitrogen Cycle

This is the RECYCLING OF NITROGEN COMPOUNDS.
As for the carbon cycle AIR, PLANTS, ANIMALS and DECAY PRODUCTS are involved.

- NITROGEN IS A VITAL ELEMENT WHICH IS USED IN THE PRODUCTION OF PROTEINS.

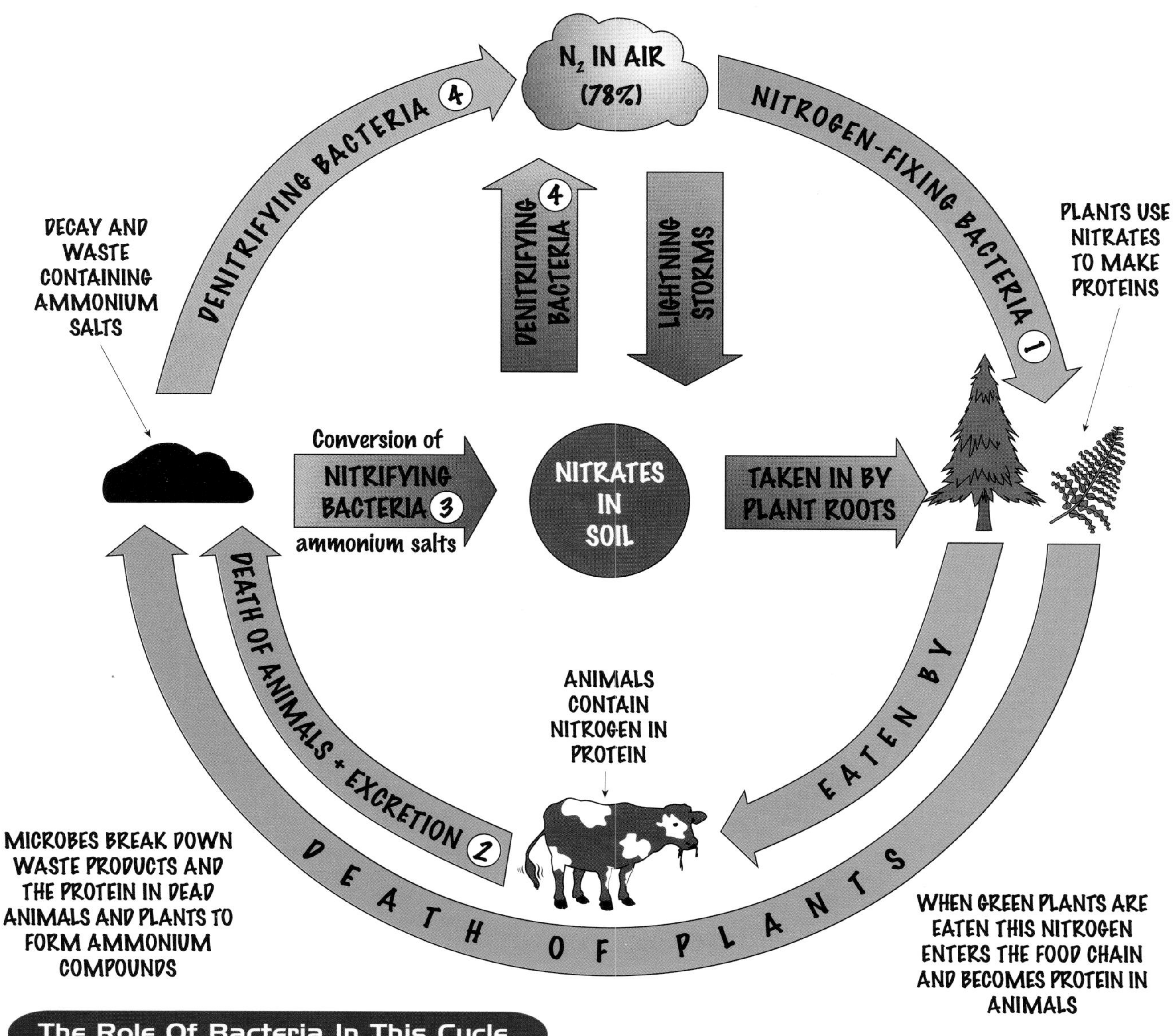

The Role Of Bacteria In This Cycle

1. NITROGEN - FIXING BACTERIA ...
- ATMOSPHERIC NITROGEN ⇨ NITRATES IN SOIL.
- Some live free in the soil, while some ...
- ... are associated with the root systems of certain plants.

2. PUTREFYING BACTERIA ...
- UREA (from urine) ⇨ AMMONIUM COMPOUNDS.

3. NITRIFYING BACTERIA ...
- AMMONIUM COMPOUNDS ⇨ NITRATES IN SOIL.

4. DENITRIFYING BACTERIA ...
- NITRATES ⇨ ATMOSPHERIC NITROGEN ...
- AMMONIUM COMPOUNDS ⇨ ATMOSPHERIC NITROGEN.

The Population 'Explosion' - The Effect On Plants And Animals

For centuries the world **POPULATION** has been **INCREASING**. With increased numbers of humans the **LAND** which was once **OCCUPIED BY A VARIETY OF PLANTS AND ANIMALS** may no longer be **SUITABLE** or **AVAILABLE**.

The reasons are:

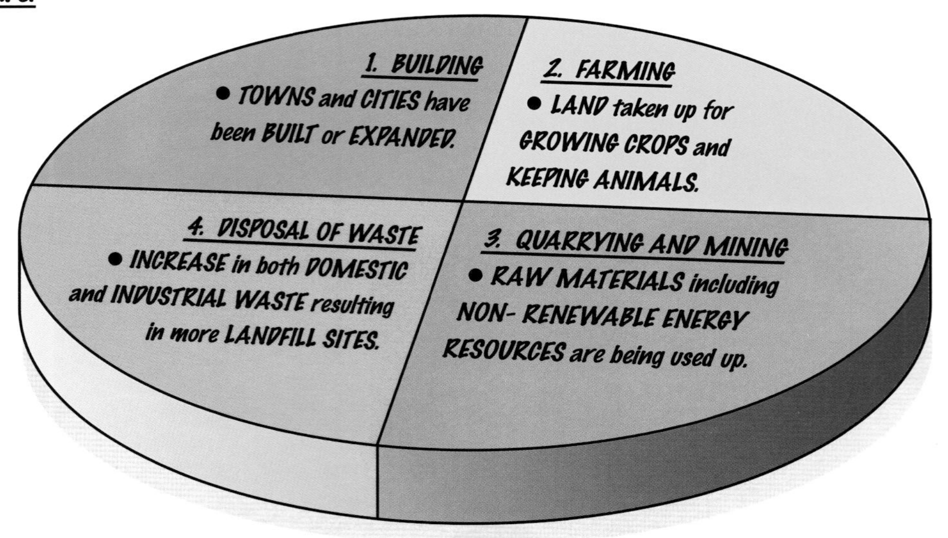

Air Pollution

When fossil fuels are burned **CARBON DIOXIDE** is released into the atmosphere. **SULPHUR DIOXIDE** and **NITROGEN OXIDES** are also released from ...

... **INDUSTRY**, **POWER STATIONS** and **MOTOR VEHICLE EXHAUSTS**.

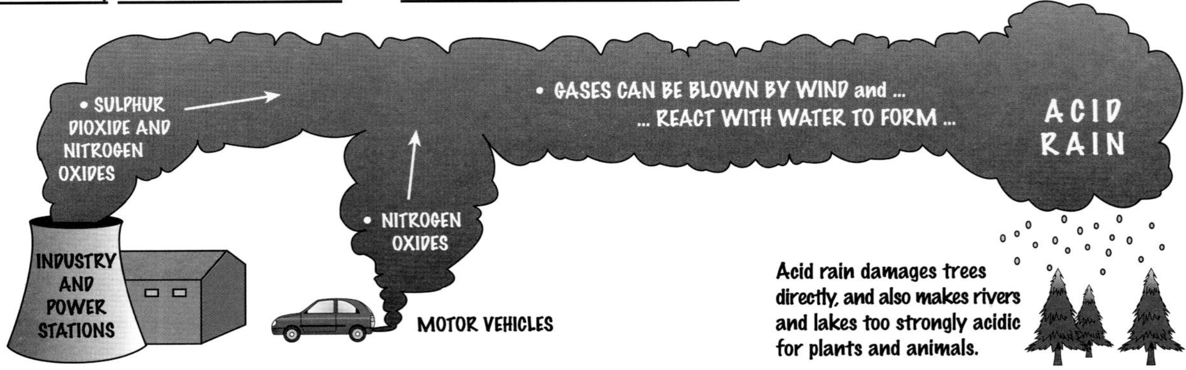

NAME OF WASTE GAS	EFFECT ON PLANTS AND ANIMALS
SULPHUR DIOXIDE	● The gases themselves can HARM PLANTS AND ANIMALS ...
NITROGEN OXIDES (Nitrogen oxide and nitrogen dioxide)	● ... but the main problem is the formation of ACID RAIN.

Pollution Free Fuel

BIOGAS is produced when **BACTERIA DECOMPOSE PLANT OR ANIMAL WASTE**.
BIOGAS is mostly **METHANE** ...
... and can be burnt to provide energy to **RUN MACHINERY** and **HEAT BUILDINGS**.

BIOFUEL is produced by the **FERMENTATION** of **SUGAR CANE** ...
... which produces **ALCOHOL**.
The **ALCOHOL** is used as a **PETROL SUBSTITUTE** in lorries, cars and buses in **BRAZIL**.

HIGHER/SPECIAL TIER

The Ozone Layer

- **OZONE** is a gas found naturally HIGH UP in the EARTH'S ATMOSPHERE ...
  ... which prevents TOO MANY HARMFUL ultraviolet (UV) rays REACHING THE EARTH.
- Recently SCIENTISTS have noticed that the OZONE LAYER is BECOMING THINNER ...
  ... and more people are SUFFERING FROM SKIN CANCER.
- Many people blame the use of CFC'S (chlorofluorocarbons) ...
  ... in factories, fridges and aerosol cans for this CHANGE IN THE OZONE LAYER.

Deforestation

- DEFORESTATION involves the LARGE SCALE CUTTING DOWN OF TREES.
  There are FEWER TREES using carbon dioxide in PHOTOSYNTHESIS and CARBON DIOXIDE LEVELS INCREASE.
  The TREES ARE BURNT which means MORE CARBON DIOXIDE is released.
- DEFORESTATION can also lead to ...
  ... SOIL EROSION that leads to less fertile land for growing crops, ...
  ... and the DESTROYING OF HABITATS.

The Greenhouse Effect And Global Warming

- The **SUN'S RAYS** pass through the earth's Atmosphere and are ABSORBED.
  The WARMER EARTH'S SURFACE RERADIATES the HEAT to WARM UP THE ATMOSPHERE.
  THE RERADIATED HEAT eventually moves into OUTER SPACE.
- OVER RECENT YEARS an increase in the amount of carbon dioxide and methane in the atmosphere has REDUCED THE AMOUNT OF HEAT MOVING INTO OUTER SPACE.

- CARBON DIOXIDE and METHANE are GREENHOUSE GASES.

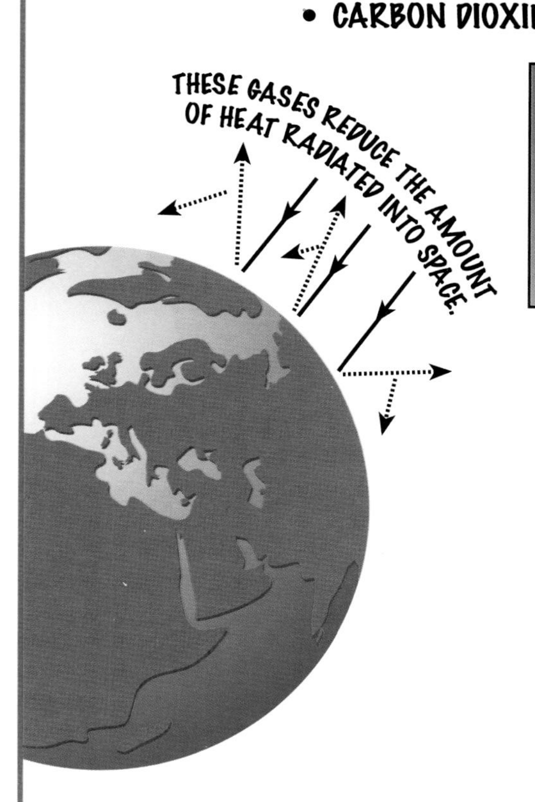

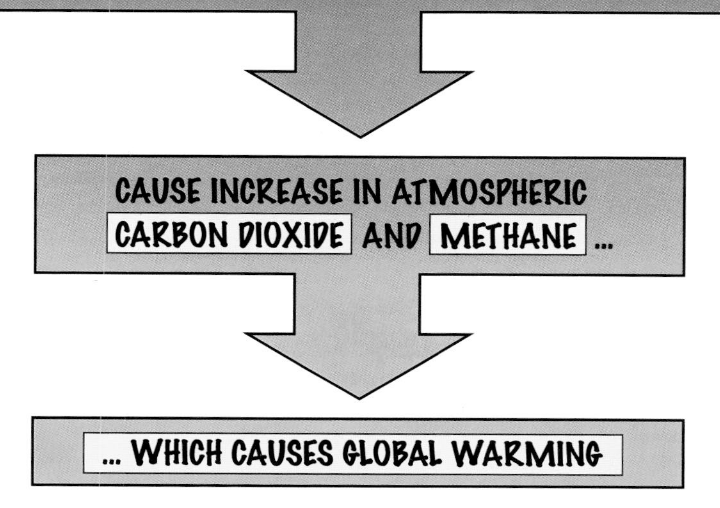

- Only a few degrees Celsius rise in temperature may lead to ...
  - ... CLIMATE CHANGES, and a RISE IN SEA LEVEL.

Ecology

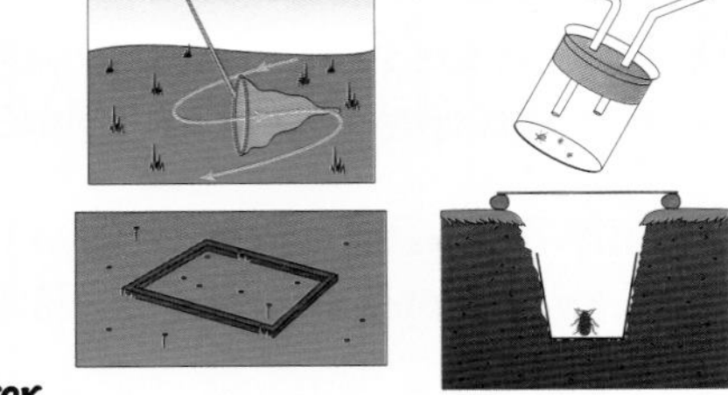

- Population size can be sampled using:
  a) POOTERS b) SWEEPNETS c) PITFALL TRAPS d) QUADRATS

HIGHER/SPECIAL TIER
- The sample taken should be as large as possible ...
  ... and as random as possible, for good results.

- Factors affecting population size include competition for food, water, space, light and minerals. Also the effects of disease, predators (or herbivores) and migration.

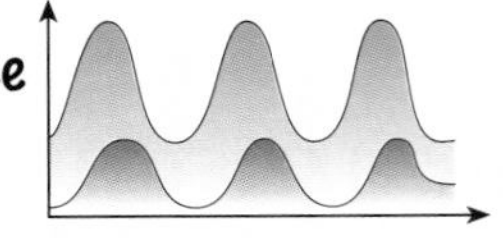

- In a natural environment there is often a delicate balance between the population of a predator and its prey.

- Food chains can be linked together to form food webs in which arrows show the direction of flow of energy and biomass.
- Pyramids of numbers/biomass reflect the proportion of energy and biomass being passed from one trophic level to another in a particular food chain. Pyramids of biomass are more meaningful.
- The Carbon cycle and the Nitrogen cycle recycle these two elements so that they are constantly being incorporated into living things and before being released again into the general environment.

HIGHER/SPECIAL TIER
- Huge increases in population have had a serious impact on the environment. In particular, the deterioration of the ozone layer which filters out harmful U-V light and the increase in the greenhouse effect which causes global warming.

Managing The Environment

HIGHER/SPECIAL TIER
- Biomass and energy are lost at every stage of a food chain because materials and energy are lost in an organism's faeces and energy is lost as movement energy and waste heat energy.
- From this it follows that short food chains are more efficient for food production.
- Agricultural ecosystems can be managed to increase food production without damaging the environment by:
  a) Using biological controls instead of pesticides, b) Using organic fertilisers,
  c) Maintaining hedges and woodland.
- Other examples of managed ecosystems include North Sea fish stocks, salmon farming and greenhouse horticulture.

- Pesticides can become more concentrated as they pass along the food chain resulting in the death of organisms near the top of the chain.

HIGHER/SPECIAL TIER
- Eutrophication can make bodies of water stagnant due to rapid growth of plant life caused by excess fertiliser. The death of these plants and the action of microbes on them reduces the oxygen content of the water.

Record the EIGHT 'Ecology', and the SIX 'Managing the environment' facts onto your tape.
Now - READ, COVER, WRITE and CHECK the FOURTEEN facts.